Transformations

Leadership
for
Brain-Compatible
Learning

Contributing Editor,

Jane Rasp McGeehan

Books for Educators, Inc.
We do the research for you!
Kent, Washington

Transformations
Leadership for Brain-Compatible Learning

© 1998 Susan J. Kovalik
Printed in the United States of America

ISBN 1-878631-40-3

Contributing Editor: Jane McGeehan
Copy Editor: Kathleen Wolgemuth
Cover Design: Kristina Roe
Layout and Design: Kristina Roe

Books for Educators, Inc.
17051 SE 272nd Street, Suite 18
Kent, Washington 98042
www.books4educ.com

We dedicate this book to
the master teachers—
leaders all.

Contents

Introduction

Bold change. It is exciting to discuss, difficult and challenging to undertake, and exhausting in the best of circumstances. There must be compelling reasons to invite the accompanying ambiguity and chaos into our lives as professional educators and community leaders. Anyone who has lived in or near schools during the last ten years knows that there is already plenty of ambiguity and chaos present, even if one is simply nurturing the status quo. Who wants even more?

Schools have been particularly resistant to sustained change. Innovations spark enthusiasm and hope then fizzle, leaving little evidence that they ever existed. Yet, contained in what we are now learning about the biology of human learning are those compelling reasons to undertake dramatic new ways of doing business in our schools. In light of this emerging body of knowledge, the authors of this book believe that there is a window of opportunity presenting itself to educators and concerned citizens. Technology, changing families, increasingly diverse communities, different expectations of employees, more jobs and careers requiring a higher level of technical proficiency, the global economy, demands of citizens in a democracy, a more urgent appreciation of the need for each of us to become lifelong learners, and an initial understanding of the incredibly complex, integrated bodymind learning system of humans are just a few of the factors combining to make dramatic change in our schools not only a viable option, but an absolutely urgent need. Effective leaders will provide the necessary catalyst and ensure the environment of support essential for the creation of the brain-compatible schools envisioned by the authors.

These leaders will be both formal and informal. If you are a new school administrator, this book is for you. If you are a seasoned veteran in school administration, this book is for you. If you aspire to become a school administrator, this book is for you. While this book is written with school administrators in mind, it is clear that change of the magnitude discussed here will only happen if there are effective leaders among all segments of the community being served. If you are a teacher leader, this book is for you. If you are a community leader active in supporting the urgent push for schools that really work, this book is for you. Leadership in schools is all new today whether you have been involved for two or for twenty years. It is not enough to tinker around the edges of the traditions we have called school. If you are the leader who seeks to be at the forefront of informed, reasoned change, read on!

Transformations is your field guide for creating schools and school districts grounded in recent brain research findings. It is designed to accompany *ITI: The Model* by Susan Kovalik (Kovalik and Olsen 1994). Do not expect a compilation of research and theory. Other books exist to meet such needs. Rather, this book is written by teachers and administrators who have actually been part of creating brain-compatible schools, classrooms, and districts inspired by Kovalik's Integrated Thematic Instruction (ITI) model. The authors share their successes and failures openly so that you may have the benefit of their experiences to inform your decisions.

Overarching questions are addressed from the various points of view of the authors. These include:

- What does it mean to create a brain-compatible school or school district?

- What behaviors must the school leadership demonstrate to facilitate the creation of the brain-compatible learning environment?

- What specific support does staff need during the implementation process?

- How can educators guard against fatigue, disillusionment, and abandonment of change efforts?

- What behaviors and habits on the part of leaders sustain bold change beyond the initial excitement about an innovation?

These and related questions provide the focus for selecting and sharing experiences of the authors. The Contents gives a preview of the main topics and supporting details within each chapter. Many readers will find it unnecessary to review the elements of the ITI model presented early in the book, and will prefer to skip ahead to specific topics. The authors wrote chapters that can stand alone with the hope that the flexibility that affords the reader makes the book practical and useful. If it comes off the shelf regularly, we will have achieved our goal. Once the reading stops, the real work of school change begins.

Appendix Material

Items included in the appendix sections are of a practical nature to add to the reader's understanding and provide tools to assist in leading others through exciting, transforming changes in schools and school districts.

Acknowledgements

It is only through a concerted team effort that any book comes into being. I wish to acknowledge the authors for their insights and commitment, Kathleen Wolgemuth for her thoughtful, caring, and instructive suggestions and general enthusiasm for the project, Joseph McGeehan for encouragement and gentle prodding when needed, and the incredibly talented staff at Books For Educators who demonstrated patience and perseverance. Finally, I gratefully acknowledge the wisdom and inspiration I gained from dialogue with and learning from Susan Kovalik and Karen Olsen, whose advice has been invaluable at every step of the project.

Jane Rasp McGeehan
March, 1998

I

What Is Brain-Compatible and Why Is It Important?

by Jane Rasp McGeehan

Introduction

As I enter a second grade classroom serving a high proportion of Hispanic and Title I students, I am drawn by the uplifting strains of Vivaldi. I glance about the inviting space and see purposeful displays of the year-long theme and key points currently under study. As part of the in-depth study of the farm, students are learning about corn, a product that is essential to the local economy. A wide variety of resources is present in the classroom to support this study: topical books, textbooks, literature, real corn and corn stalks, models and posters of the corn plant, and maps showing where corn is grown. The classroom is free of clutter and is thoughtfully decorated in soft blues and greens with the occasional accent of yellow corn here and there. The institutional school windows are softened by decorative curtains across the top in the same color scheme. There are clearly defined areas for student computer use, for research, for independent and cooperative student work, and for large group instruction. Lamps and plants enhance the healthful setting for young learners.

The teacher sits on a white, wicker rocking chair, her students gathered around as she reads aloud from a story, "Raccoon and Ripe Corn." Questions and discussion follow that relate the story to the key point about corn that was introduced earlier that day. Discussion is lively, and students clearly feel free to share their thoughts and ideas with the group. The teacher labels behavior that matches prior expectations with statements such as, "Thank you, Karen, for being responsible and an active listener." The students return to their desks arranged in tables to facilitate cooperation, and retrieve their three-ring binders to prepare to complete the daily oral language activity. They get to work without delay copying and correcting sentences that contain additional information about corn. Punctuation and capitalization are the focus for the corrections, providing the teacher with a meaningful opportunity to reinforce these previously taught skills. I see that each student is creating a booklet about corn to reflect new learning. Some of the information relates to a trip to the farm that occurred earlier in the unit of study.

I am reluctant to leave this calm, exciting, and productive community of learners, because even as an adult I am strongly drawn to their work and shared adventures as learners.

You have just glimpsed a classroom with curriculum and teaching strategies befitting Hart's term "brain-compatible" (Hart 1983). The eight brain-compatible elements identified by Susan Kovalik (Kovalik and Olsen 1994) as part of the ITI model combine to characterize the school and classroom that is designed to work with rather than hinder the brain in the learning process. This chapter provides a brief description of these eight elements and of key aspects of brain research that underlie them.

The Researcher and Practitioner Gap

There is a gap, perhaps even a chasm, separating most researchers from the practitioners in the field of education. Action based on a foundation of solid research makes sense and is right because it bases educational decisions on what is known to be effective for learning. Too often in the recent past practitioners have been either unaware of meaningful research that should have informed their practice, or were unable to weave seemingly unrelated pieces of information into a viable whole. Hence, tradition and intuition formed a large part of the basis for decisions and subsequent actions in schools and classrooms.

Education is now poised to move beyond tradition and intuition.

Technology and Brain Research

Enter the brain research findings. Powerful technologies have given scientists their first-ever glimpse into the workings of normal, healthy human brains. Prior to such advances as the PET scan (positive emission tomography) and functional MRI (magnetic resonance imaging in real time), those who sought to understand the human brain had to rely largely on the study of unfortunate individuals who had been injured or who required brain surgery. Now the findings of neuroscientists, cognitive psychologists, biologists, and others are also based on what is happening in the brains of healthy individuals.

Given the researcher to practitioner gap, it is easy to imagine that research conducted outside the field of education would seldom affect daily habits of teachers in classrooms. Fortunately, several deeply committed and insightful educators made it their mission to relate the relevant brain research findings to teachers and administrators through widely read journal articles and books. Foremost among them are Leslie Hart, Susan Kovalik, Renate and Geoffrey Caine, Howard Gardner, Joseph LeDoux, Candace Pert, Robert Sylwester, and Ronald Kotulak. Their books and presentations have captured the attention of practitioners in such life-changing ways that they are altering dramatically the ways in which schools do business. The reader is urged to consult the list of references for these writers at the end of the book and seek out the works cited.

Brain Basics Summarized

Out of the continually emerging richness of the brain research findings, six important concepts influenced Susan Kovalik as she created her model for achieving brain-compatible learning:

- Emotions are the gatekeeper to performance
- Intelligence is a function of experience
- Humans in all cultures use multiple intelligences to solve problems and to create products
- The brain's search for meaning is a search for meaningful patterns
- Learning is the acquisition of useful mental programs
- Personality—one's basic temperament—affects learning.

1. Emotions As Gatekeeper

Robert Sylwester states the situation clearly in his book, *A Celebration of Neurons*. "We know emotion is very important to the educative process because it drives attention, which drives learning and memory" (Sylwester 1995, 72). All sensory data entering the brain are screened by brain structures designed to detect imminent danger. Joseph LeDoux explains that such possible threats to safety or even survival are detected unconsciously (LeDoux 1996). A brain triggered by its amygdala, a structure deep within the brain, has the power to override rational thought and orchestrate a rapid, reflexive response to prepare for the worst.

Conversely, an individual's positive emotions enhance learning and memory. While there are still many mysteries about how a new memory is created, Candace Pert, Research Professor in the Department of Physiology and Biophysics at Georgetown University Medical Center, makes it clear that more than the brain is involved. Her research and writing reveal an elaborate chemical communication system that thoroughly integrates the mind and the rest of the body. "The neuropeptides and receptors, the biochemicals of emotion, are, as I have said, the messengers carrying information to link the major systems of the body into one unit that we can call the bodymind...Emotions are at the nexus between matter and mind, going back and forth between the two and influencing both" (Pert 1997, 189).

Attention to the emotional climate for learning is thus critical. Fear and anxiety diminish the possibility of new learning while security, safety, challenge, and a general sense of well-being enhance it.

2. Intelligence Is a Function of Experience.

The brain is designed to make sense of the real world from experiences in it. We are each born with about the same number of neurons. Dendrites are the part of the neuron that makes it possible to receive information from other neurons. Essential collaboration among neurons would be impossible without dendrites. It is highly engaging and memorable experiences that trigger dendrite growth. Thus, "being there" experiences (the study trips outside the classroom) have the greatest power to increase dendrite growth among those in the following hierarchy of learning experiences:

- Being there
- Immersion
- Hands-on with the real thing
- Hands-on with a model/representation
- Second hand (book, video, computer, and similar resources)
- Symbolic (words, numbers) (Kovalik and Olsen 1994)

The richer the incoming sensory data, the greater the likelihood of dendrite growth. Real experiences add power and meaning to every learning option in the hierarchy, while physically changing the anatomy of the brain (Diamond 1998).

3. Multiple Intelligences

Howard Gardner describes eight human intelligences, defined as problem-solving or product-producing capacities. They are verbal/linguistic, logical/mathematical, visual/spatial, body/kinesthetic, musical/rhythmic, interpersonal, intrapersonal, and the naturalist (Gardner 1983). Each person has every intelligence, but in varying degrees. Working in weaker areas can strengthen them, but may not result in transforming the intelligence into a preferred mode for solving problems or creating products. The multiple intelligences provide a framework for creating a wider array of strategies for learning and assessment activity in schools.

4. The Search for Meaningful Patterns

The brain is designed to make meaning out of the barrage of sensory data it continuously processes from inside and outside the body. To do this the brain seeks patterns, any repeat occurrence registered by any of the senses that can be assigned meaning in relation to something already experienced. Every verb and noun in the English language represents a pattern. The richer the **input** available, the richer the patterns detected and categorized by the brain. Language acquisition provides an example of this process. Attentive mothers and fathers do not "dumb-down" language for their newborns. Instead, they provide a rich flow of language during waking hours. The baby detects the pattern of sound that is her name, and soon after come "mama" and "dada." At first, "dada" may represent any man in trousers. But the infant continues to refine and then detect patterns such as uncle, older brother, neighbor, or stranger. Each brain is uniquely shaped by an individual's experiences (Hart 1983).

5. Learning As the Acquisition of Useful Mental Programs

The brain is selective about what information becomes a part of long term memory. Leslie Hart, author of *Human Brain and Human Learning* (Hart 1983) explains that once meaning is detected through pattern recognition and understanding, the second aspect of learning is to build a program for action—a behavior—that allows the learner to apply what is learned. Information that makes it possible for a human to **do** something useful in daily life has a natural advantage over irrelevant information that may linger in the hippocampus or other brain structures and eventually evaporate. Learners require multiple opportunities to manipulate the pattern(s) related to a particular task before a network of neurons with axons (a part of a neuron) encased in myelin align to do the task repeatedly. Myelin is a coating that "insulates" the pathway of the electrical impulse as it travels from neuron to neuron. At that point, the behavior becomes a part of information stored in the long term memory. For example, if I have learned to ride a bicycle and then don't ride for several years, I can nevertheless ride again without having to start over in the learning process.

6. Personality Affects Learning

Beyond varieties of intelligence, personality/temperament differences have a profound impact on learning. Keirsey and Bates describe a useful framework for looking at the impact of personality preferences (Keirsey and Bates 1984). Grounded in the work of Carl Jung, they identify four broad types of orientations to new information and other people, some of which are a better match than others for traditional school settings. Characteristics are depicted as a range of possibilities on four continuums shown in Figure 1.1.

Figure 1.1 _____

Temperament Continuums

		TAKE IN	
1.	SENSING (S) details, concrete	————— INFORMATION —————	INTUITIVE (N) wholes, theory, hunches, future
2.	FEELING (F) subjective, empathetic	————— DECISION— MAKING —————	THINKING (T) objective, logical
3.	JUDGING (J) organized, closure, priorities	————— LIFESTYLE —————	PERCEIVING (P) open, flexible, spontaneous
4.	EXTROVERSION (E) gains energy from being with others	————— ORIENTATION SELF and OTHERS —————	INTROVERSION (I) gains energy from solitary reflection

* Based on D. Keirsey and M. Bates (1984)   © 1997 Susan Kovalik & Associates

While humans can learn behaviors at many points on each continuum, they have strong preferences that are prominent when individuals are in new situations or when learning new information.

Critical for educators is the understanding that teachers tend to teach as they like to learn based on their own temperament. Keirsey and Bates report that approximately 56% of teachers have sensing/judging (SJ) temperaments and that SJ students have just a 25% chance of becoming a school dropout. Revealing is the fact that from 75% to 90% of our schools' at-risk students are SP personalities. For them, "The system is simply too structured, too rigid, too boring, too oppressive." (Olsen and Ross 1995, I-41)

The Research Translated to Practice

Susan Kovalik was working in the field of gifted education when she first became aware of the findings about the brain and learning. She recognized that brain research affirmed many of the practices being advocated gifted youth. She also became convinced that the urgent need was not for gifted programs, but rather for gifted teachers who knew how to create brain-compatible learning opportunities for **all** students. Her great gift to educators is the ITI (Integrated Thematic Instruction) model—the practical translation of the brain research findings into every-day classroom applications.

Finally, the long-time research gap has been reduced and educators now have the framework to build brain-compatible learning.

The Eight Brain-Compatible Elements

Kovalik's eight brain-compatible elements provide a practical summary of the key brain research implications for educators (Kovalik and Olsen 1994). This list forms the foundation for the other two major parts of the model, teaching strategies and curriculum development. An overview of the Kovalik ITI model appears in chapter three. Kovalik estimates that eighty percent of the power of the ITI model to transform learning, class-rooms, and schools lies in the application of the brain research before creating integrated curriculum. Therefore, a deep understanding of the eight elements is a critical starting point. They are:

- Absence of Threat
- Meaningful Content
- Choices
- Adequate Time

- Enriched Environment
- Collaboration
- Immediate Feedback
- Mastery (application level) (Kovalik and Olsen 1994)

Recall a positive learning experience that can serve as a personal reference point as each of the eight elements is explained. Select one still vivid in your mind's eye through which new skills and information came to you almost effortlessly as you enjoyed the event(s).

I recall such an experience I had while teaching third grade in South Bend, Indiana. My students and I were studying trees and their impact on our lives. While details of the classroom-based study have vanished from my mind, I recall many details of a day-long field trip during which we saw things that were as new and fresh for me as they were for my students.

As logs came into the sawmill, we were amazed as huge saws transformed them into boards to meet various specifications. We visited the factory where wood was used to construct the sturdy frame for sofas. Finally, we toured the former Studebaker mansion where master craftspersons had created elegant beauty in the carvings that decorated the magnificent entry hall and stairway to the second floor. As I write these words, wonderfully rich and detailed mental images present themselves.

Such experiences reflect many of the eight brain-compatible elements. I invite you to use your recalled learning experience to personalize your understanding of each element as you read.

Absence of Threat

Full access to the powers of the cerebral cortex for problem-solving and product production is possible only when there is no threat, real or perceived, present in the setting. Relate this information to your recalled learning event as you keep in mind that each element applies to both students and adults.

On the South Bend field trip, I had removed much of the potential threat through advance planning and organization. Parents as chaperones; abundant communication with contact people at each site so mutual expectations were clear; discussing with students what to expect and what was expected at each site; and providing specific ways for students to collect information as they had new experiences were a few of the ways I created absence of threat for me and my students.

This element is so important that without it, little else can be accomplished. It is a vital aspect of any brain-compatible setting. The most elegant integrated curriculum is destined to fail in a threatening learning environment (Kovalik and Olsen 1994).

Meaningful Content

Our brains can take in and recall vast amounts of detailed information with remarkably little effort when the information has personal meaning. As a species, most of our learning occurs naturally through experiences. We observed on the farm, in the woods, on the hunt, in the market, and so on. To acquire a technical skill, we served as apprentices or watched a master artisan, practiced under watchful eyes, acted on suggestions for improvement, and gradually achieved mastery.

The human brain still remains programmed to learn best from the rich sensory input available only in real places outside the classroom. The notion of a formal school is a relatively new idea, with schools organized the way they traditionally are in the United States emerging just over 150 years ago. From such a perspective, the educator's exciting challenges are to discover what is meaningful to each learner, how to connect essential understandings to that, and how to use a rich set of real-world experiences as the foundation for powerful learning.

Reflecting on the South Bend field trip, I realize that each aspect had particular meaning to me first as the teacher. I was eager to expand my own knowledge of trees to be ready to assist and guide my students' understanding. But the topic was also meaningful to me because woods, their beauty and uses, had always been a source of special joy to my father. Biased by my own prior experiences, I absorbed mental images and details as easily as one recalls last night's dinner menu.

Choices

Learners engaging in an activity by choice are more successful because they bring the positive emotional state associated with doing something one wants to do. They will be more interested, thus releasing increased amounts of the neuro-transmitters necessary for activation of long-term memory. Finally, they can select a learning experience that uses their strongest intelligence from among the eight defined by Howard Gardner.

Clearly, the eight brain-compatible elements overlap and enhance one another. For example, when one has some choices about how the learning can occur and experiences increased success, the sense of threat in the setting is diminished (absence of threat overlapping choices).

Considering the South Bend event in relation to the element of choice, making the trip was certainly an act of choice on my part. I happily embraced the preparation and attention to details, and I was full of anticipation for what the day could hold for me and for my students. We took this trip years before theories of multiple intelligence and today's understanding of the human brain existed. Still, I knew that even as the teacher I required plenty of variety and rich input to avoid boredom and a deadening sameness, too often the by-products of a textbook-driven classroom.

Adequate Time

Learning something new, **really learning it so that it can be used now and in the future,** takes time. Furthermore, it takes a different amount of time for different learners depending on a whole range of challenging variations among learners that we are coming to understand and respect more fully. When time is too short, a learner may resort to rote memory, become anxious and lose learning power as described in "absence of threat" above, submit incomplete work, or just give up. Accepting the truth of these undesirable responses means that the teacher must make some very tough curriculum decisions early in the learning process to reduce the amount of material students are expected to master. Susan Kovalik counsels teachers developing curriculum, "Less is more."

It takes time to show that one can **use** new information. For example, a student may create a project to help others learn the information, or may write letters to officials recommending action aligned with what was learned. Either approach requires set up, thinking time, planning time, perhaps collaboration time, revision or quality control time, and time for self-assessment and feedback on the final product. The more one is interrupted by such things as a rigid daily schedule, the more time will be wasted in stopping, starting, and re-establishing the flow of the work. **Adequate time is the most difficult of the elements to honor.**

In reflecting on the field trip with my third graders, we succeeded in some ways and failed in others to honor the element of adequate time. My planning for the trip began well in advance so that there was time to discover and address each ingredient of a successful trip. As I imagined the trip, I believed that I had allowed sufficient time at each location; however, on the day of the trip, there was a sense of rushing about and spending too little time at each site. How much more could have been learned if several trips had been taken instead? Budget constraints prevented that approach, but in retrospect it might have been more fruitful to visit just two places so that a deeper level of knowledge could have been achieved.

Enriched Environment

The human brain is a very aggressive organ, and one designed to handle a large amount of in-coming data simultaneously. It is easily bored. The educator who understands this begins by arranging an attractive and inviting learning environment. This resembles the process for designing a living room in one's home! Limit the plan to two or three colors, give a prominent focus for the key points being studied, and attractively display a variety of learning resources and reference materials. Provide for home-like touches such as potpourri, lamps, plants, and carpeted areas furnished with bean-bag chairs.

Corporations large and small understand the importance of these concepts and do not leave their office environment to chance. They hire interior designers to create the desired impact on clients and workers. While schools are seldom in a position to hire an interior designer, they can observe and learn from office and hotel environments.

Enriched environment also means providing the body and brain with access to experiences in the real world, varied resources to explore, and the opportunity to interact with real objects. Frequent field trips (even to visit a part of the school grounds), access to the Internet and to information stored on CD-ROM, many books on a variety of reading levels related to the topic, regular visits from community persons to share their expertise, and the chance to work often as a member of a cooperative group all reflect an enriched environment.

Looking back to South Bend, I recall rich detail from the field trip because I, too, benefitted from the experiences. For example, I had never seen logs becoming boards or wood frames becoming sofas. The environment in the places we visited provided ample stimulation for my brain and created vivid, lasting mental images.

Collaboration

Collaboration is simply working together effectively to accomplish something of importance to the individual and group. The most important projects in business, education, religion, government, medicine, or just about any other area depend on collaboration. Employers generally list the ability to work effectively as a member of a team as an essential qualification for employees.

The brain needs the opportunity to manipulate and explore new information and find ways to connect it with what is already known. When this process occurs in a threat-free setting and accompanied by positive emotions, information is more likely to move from short-term to long-term memory. Learning as a member of a congenial cooperative group creates the opportunity to manipulate information in the necessary emotional environment.

Immediate Feedback

When humans are involved in learning, the sooner we know how we are doing, the better. Knowing results of our efforts early in the learning process increases the opportunity to make prompt corrections and avoid learning something the wrong way. Trying to forget incorrect information and replace it with correct learning is a frustrating and time-consuming process! The most difficult thing for the brain to do is to forget an old, well-learned mental program. Knowing how we are doing as we learn also helps us to value the progress we are making, thus increasing motivation to continue investing effort toward achieving the learning goal.

When feedback is automatic as a part of the process, that is ideal. The real world usually provides built-in feedback. Did I choose the right coat for today's weather? Yes, I feel comfortable. Did I improve my ability to make baskets in a game of basketball? Yes, today six of my eight shots went in, whereas last week only four of eight hit the mark. And so it goes.

Thinking back to my field trip, I can now understand that the experience provided immediate feedback for me as a teacher in several ways. First, I could both ask and answer questions to check my understanding of what I was seeing. As students asked me questions, I tested my ability to restate what I had learned. By observing my students and their responses to the lumber mill, furniture factory, and historic home, I could readily detect their level of interest and involvement and know if the field trip were adding to their understanding.

Mastery

The real test of learning success is what the learner can DO with what was learned. Mastery in the ITI model means being able to apply what one understands in a real world situation. For example, if the learner's goal is to write an effective business letter, producing one to send demonstrates mastery. It takes coaching (immediate feedback) to achieve correct first learning and subsequent mastery. Mastery takes time and practice.

Mastery for me as the South Bend teacher came as I used the information I gained on the field trip to plan follow-up learning activities for my students. I knew I "got" it when I could discuss with confidence what we found out about wood and its uses. I knew that the information was mine to use as I created letters to thank our various hosts. I continued my own demonstration of mastery as I prepared documents to test my students' mastery. See Figure 1.2 below for a summary of the elements.

Figure 1.2 _____

ITI Brain-Compatible Elements

Absence of threat: being free from fears or anxiety about physical or mental safety, experiencing a general sense of well-being and positive emotions with respect to learning experiences

Meaningful content: selecting topics that interest students and have power to help them understand and influence their world

Choices: providing options as to how learning will occur, with attention to multiple intelligences, higher level thinking, and personality preferences

Adequate time: having enough time to thoroughly explore, understand, and use ideas, information, and skills

Enriched environment: providing a healthful, inviting, homey setting with many resources from which the student can learn, and special emphasis on real places, people and objects

Collaboration: acting on the belief that two heads are better than one to solve problems, explore, and create

Immediate feedback: providing coaching to promote correct initial learning and sustain motivation toward more learning

Mastery (application): ensuring a curriculum focus so that students acquire mental programs stored in long term memory to use what is learned in real-life situations

* Based on Kovalik and Olsen 1994

Brain-Compatible vs. Brain-Antagonistic

To test mastery of what is meant by a brain-compatible learning environment in terms of the eight elements, consider any teaching strategy and document evidence of the elements in action. In fact, ITI coaches strongly recommend that teachers use the eight brain-compatible elements as a structure for peer coaching and for self-assessment. When a lesson or series of lessons fails to engage learners, the difficulty can be found in a missing or neglected element. Absence of just one brain-compatible element undercuts potential learning.

Let's consider the middle school teacher who opens with a written agenda for the day's class followed by ten minutes of direct instruction (lecture) about the reasons for recycling trash. Students then select a learning activity from a list of five possibilities. Individually or with a partner, they create a product reflecting what was learned to share with the class. The classroom resource area is stocked with a wide variety of supplies for creating a product, as well as reference materials including computer software, books, models, and items related to the potential chemical impact of landfills. Students have the remainder of a ninety-minute block of time to do their research and planning. They know that there will be additional time available the next day to put finishing touches on their creations. As the students work, the teacher circulates and interacts to insure correct understanding and reinforce the established criteria defining a quality product.

Imagine that you are observing that classroom. You can use the template of the eight brain-compatible elements to gauge the likely effectiveness of the learning opportunity for the students.

Absence of Threat	Yes. Students like the security the agenda provides so that they know what will happen today. They feel more comfortable choosing the activity and whether to do it alone or with a partner.
Meaningful Content	Yes. The community has just implemented mandatory recycling that will change the habits of each student's family for handling trash disposal.
Adequate Time	Yes. Students have a block of time in which to conduct research and create the product described in the activity.
Enriched Environment	Yes. Rich resources and supplies are available.

Collaboration	Yes. Partner work is an option, and the teacher is available to advise and to assist.
Immediate Feedback	Yes. The teacher is available to answer student questions, clarify, and make suggestions.
Mastery	Yes. Mastery is demonstrated when students present the final product to classmates.

Based on this analysis, the students in this classroom are on their way to powerful, brain-compatible learning.

Importance of a Brain-Compatible Environment

Educators must know and be able to articulate why they are doing what they are doing. One could say, "It just feels right." However, the most defensible rationale for professional decisions is the ability to show the connection to a compelling research base. The research base that relates the biology of human learning to events in classrooms is now available and continually evolving.

Through an understanding of research about human learning one can make informed judgments about what constitutes best practice. If an innovation emerges, but can't be shown to support what we know about the human brain, it goes. A new approach to assessment of student learning that flies in the face of the biology of learning is not adopted. We analyze the traditional and keep only those practices that are consistent with a brain-compatible setting and subsequently a brain-compatible curriculum. Educators are finally freed from the all too familiar pendulum swings carrying them from one hot innovation to the next. The parts and pieces that result in systemic change are unified by, and grounded in, the brain research describing the biology of learning.

Let's take a brief look at how an understanding of applications of the brain research creates a defensible rationale for selecting strategies to assess student learning. Susan Kovalik believes that there are two central questions regarding assessment of student learning:

1. What do students understand?

2. What can students DO with that understanding (Kovalik and Olsen 1994)?

These questions relate directly to descriptions of the brain as a pattern-seeking organism and a builder of useful mental programs (Hart 1983).

Understanding something demands more than the student parroting back memorized information on a paper, test, or quiz. Genuine understanding could be demonstrated as a student teaches an idea to a fellow student. It could be demonstrated in a thoughtful essay or a visual model showing how the new idea relates to or supports previously learned ideas. The presence of useful mental programs will be visible when a student orchestrates a letter campaign related to a significant local issue. Mental programs are essential when the student participates in a service project that benefits the school and/or community, or behaves in a more mature and respectful way.

Whatever the focus of the educational decision or question, the most productive responses are grounded in an understanding of the research about the biology of human learning. In the research is the powerful lens through which the leader can confidently examine current behavior in a school and then determine constructive next steps on the path toward becoming a brain-compatible school or school district.

Conclusion

Students and their effective learning are at the heart of each school's mission. While it is true that adults who work in a brain-compatible environment develop professional competence beyond what they may have imagined possible, the most exciting results for brain-compatible schools is the powerful learning done by students. Students in ITI schools discover that learning makes a positive difference in their daily lives NOW as well as in their preparation to achieve future goals.

II

Leadership and the Change Process

by Susan Brash and Jane Rasp McGeehan

Introduction

"I'm thrilled to see the positive changes in our school!"

"I'm absolutely exhausted!"

"I think that they really get it and are committed to working as a team despite their differences."

"I'm discouraged and so is the staff in the face of community resistance and the slow rate of change."

Ah, yes! You recognize the human roller coaster ride that attends major changes in a school.

This chapter flows from experiences of leaders embracing change through implementing the ITI model. The stories appear in six broad categories:

1. Getting everyone involved

2. Getting to know the community

3. Determining the school's vision and mission

4. Establishing a system to reach the aim

5. Creating a culture that embraces continuous improvement

6. Avoiding and learning from pitfalls others have experienced.

The experiences we relate provide specific examples of strategies related to each broad area. Other examples of leaders' work in these areas will be seen in subsequent chapters.

Background About Change

A leader seldom faces more resistance than when she tries to change an organization. Humans favor the comfortable, the familiar. Change is often difficult and unpopular. People inside and outside the organization argue that the change will be hard to achieve and expensive. The person spearheading a change effort is often at the center of a controversy.

Lasting change comes slowly even when it is urgently needed. Failures are an inevitable part of the process. While such failures along the way carry valuable lessons for all, they also come with emotions such as self-doubt that are uncomfortable. Not only that, sustaining personal energy levels and a healthy perspective is tough when one is immersed in change. Participants' emotions and closely held beliefs are tested and questioned—always a difficult process. And when the successes show up, so does a new mountain of work as the leader figures out how to sustain and nurture an organization focused on continuous improvement.

We do not intend to present theories of either leadership or change in this chapter; however, the work of three admired authors creates a useful frame for the stories of change experiences that follow. Seymour Sarason prevents us from viewing proposed innovations through rose-colored glasses with his gloomy reminder about schools and change: "The more things change the more they remain the same—that is a recurring statement in this book, which in part is devoted to trying to understand why this is so" (Sarason 1990). One explanation for this result according to Sarason is that the intended outcome of the change is rarely stated clearly. We would add that even if the outcome is stated clearly, the words can have vastly different meanings if there hasn't been much discussion. The school staff may express agreement with the intended outcome, and not realize that they have different pictures in their minds of just what that outcome might look, sound, and feel like once in place.

William Bridges, in *Managing Transitions*, provides valuable insights into the impact of change on those creating it along with practical strategies for addressing its complexities (Bridges 1991). In the Bridges framework, change is an external event that simply occurs. For example, the new computer system is installed on December 13. He defines transition, however, as the ". . . psychological process people go through to come to terms with the new situation" (Bridges 1991, 3). Transition is the hard part. The first step in the transition process, he writes, is an ending. Something new is replacing something familiar, and a loss is suffered. The leader must bring such losses out into the open so that people can celebrate what was and even grieve for its passage. The school leader has to understand both personal and organizational losses and honor their importance.

This aspect of change ties directly to the brain-compatible element of adequate time. Transitions for individuals and for organizations cannot be rushed.

The third author who helps to set the stage for this chapter is Thomas Sergiovanni, whose writing has informed many leaders. In his 1994 book, *Building Community in Schools,* his definition of community and its importance is inspiring.

"Community is the tie that binds students and teachers together in special ways, to something more significant than themselves: shared values and ideals. It lifts both teachers and students to higher levels of self-understanding, commitment, and performance—beyond the reaches of the shortcomings and difficulties they face in their everyday lives. Community can help teachers and students be transformed from a collection of 'I's' to a collective 'we,' thus providing them with a unique and enduring sense of identity, belonging, and place" (Sergiovanni 1994, xiii).

Without taking the time to build a strong sense of community, any significant effort to bring change is doomed. Leaders must have a deep understanding of community and know how to create and nurture it.

Get Everyone Involved

If organizational change were a solo event, we would see much more of it. It takes everyone's involvement and support to give birth to something important and new at the school. So, who is "everyone?" The leader must identify all stake-holders in the school community. Some are obvious while others can be easily forgotten until they organize later to block the change.

Obvious	**Don't Forget!**
• Students	• Support Staff (food services, custodians, bus drivers, etc.)
• Parents	
• Teachers	• Community business people
• School Board	• Neighbors with no school children
	• Area senior citizens

Within the school's key planning groups, whether a School Improvement Planning Team, a Steering Committee, or a Site Council, generate the list of stakeholders. Describe what you already know about each group's potential stake in the school's success.

Then make a plan for talking with representatives of all stakeholders. Pursue their perceptions of the vested interest they each have in the school's success. Ask such questions as:

- What do you want this school to stand for?
- What are some things you hope never change?
- What is your most reliable source of information about what is happening at the school?
- What could make this school even better?
- In what ways would you like to become more involved with the school?

The list could go on, but should be tailored to your community and limited to the five or six best questions.

Get to Know the Community

Whether the leader is a long-time resident of a closely knit community or a newcomer to a large, impersonal one, a critical first step when change is contemplated is to check one's own knowledge of the community with respect to the mission of the schools. Who holds formal and informal political power? Who is active in the schools? Who has been active in the schools? What special interest groups have the ear of which school board members? Which future plans for growth and development in the community will have a direct impact on the schools? Do community members value some school goals over others? Is there general agreements about the top school priorities? Are there negative impressions of the school to address before initiating change?

The leader can uncover essential information about the community in many ways. For example, one suburban superintendent asked several long-time residents inside and outside the school organization to give him the names of community leaders. Over the next three to four months he took each individual named to breakfast or lunch for informal dialogue. In a rural setting, a high school principal attended community meetings, such as the Chamber of Commerce, to observe and listen. Another principal in an urban community joined a service club to establish new relationships. Yet another hosted monthly morning coffee meetings at the school for informal dialogue with community members. A suburban school district with 18,000 students hosted a community forum about proposed changes. It was widely advertised and well attended. The event provided for two-way communication as the keynote speaker's remarks focused the subsequent small group discussions and formal feedback opportunities.

Determine Mission

It is impossible to reach a goal together if each person on the team has a different mental picture of that goal. The vision statement sets forth the ideal for the school—the best result that can be imagined. Effective vision statements derive from extensive community dialogue. As distilled into a brief summary, a school's vision statement might read, "ABC school provides a brain-compatible environment where all people learn successfully what they need to know and be able to do to become responsible citizens of a democracy and of the world." The mission statement then defines what the school community will **do** to move toward that ideal state. It specifies active involvement by stakeholders to work toward making the vision a reality.

The following vision and mission statements illustrate the **dreaming** and the **doing** as they provide a common frame for the work of continuous improvement:

Amy Beverland Elementary Vision Statement
(Actual)

The Amy Beverland Family is committed to academic excellence and the cultivation of individual potential through a cooperative, enriched environment where each person feels equally significant and appreciated.

Mission Statement
(Illustrative)

The Amy Beverland Family uses teaching strategies and curriculum design grounded in current brain research so that each learner experiences regular success academically and personally and develops the basic skills needed to be a productive citizen of a democracy.

Fluvanna County High School Vision Statement
(Actual)

The administration and faculty of Fluvanna County High School, students, parents, and community members share the responsibility for the development of youth into adults who can stand confidently, participate fully, learn continuously, and contribute meaningfully in their world.

Mission Statement
(Illustrative)

All who play a role in the education of Fluvanna County High School students act on an expanding understanding of the current brain research to design curriculum and use teaching strategies that ensure each student's success in mastering the social and academic skills needed to be successful in reaching personal and societal goals in a democracy.

The most efficient and least effective way to create either a vision or a mission statement is for the leader to write it. The statements themselves will play a critical role in motivating and sustaining the change effort ONLY if the stakeholders believe that they and their views were a part of the discussion leading to their creation. In fact, the rich and honest discussions that precede writing vision and mission statements are as important as the statements themselves in clarifying what the collective picture of school will be. Adequate time plays a key role and the steps in the process cannot be rushed or undervalued. It is through the dialogue that commitment to the mission or aim is achieved. Everybody associated with the school has to be prepared to act on the school's stated mission.

Even more important is the conversation that follows the creation of vision and mission statements to translate the "big picture" into specific, daily actions. What do we mean by the brain research? What is our picture of success for each student and how will we know it is happening? What are the specific teaching strategies and curriculum designs that align with the brain research? How will we learn to apply these tools in our classrooms and on a schoolwide basis? Questions such as these demand detailed action plans to bring the vision and mission into reality, leading this discussion to the next broad category for leadership.

Establish a System to Reach the Aim

Starting with the mission, the leader next sets up a system of people with defined functions to reach that aim. Creation of a threat-free environment for youth and adults is the first step. Only in such an environment can each person do his/her best work and thinking. Everything comes back to the brain-compatible elements reviewed in chapter one. Consult chapters four, five, and six to learn about specific strategies for nurturing a threat-free, productive classroom and school.

Working within a threat-free school community, create a plan that shows how each person plays a part in bringing the vision to life. The planning process generates the specific goals and strategies. Taking an innovation, such as the ITI model, to the schoolwide level demands time for thoughtful planning. It won't happen by itself. As Susan Brash, principal of Amy Beverland Elementary puts it, "You could have 34 brain-compatible classrooms and not have a brain-compatible school!" She recognized that the ITI brain-compatible elements provided a workable framework for the rest of what needed to happen. Further, the Deming Total Quality Management principles complemented the direction the school established while providing a format for focused collaboration (Deming 1986).

Founded upon the staff's beliefs in shared leadership and decision-making, the system that emerged from planning had three key structures:

1. School Improvement Planning Team (SIPT):
   A planning team with broad-based representation

2. Quality Circles (student services, staff development, wellness, curriculum coordination, curriculum enrichment): Each circle consisted of teams of teachers representing each grade level with the authority to make budget decisions and initiate activities.

3. Grade Level Teams: Teams of teachers within each grade level collaborated to make curriculum decisions and share teaching strategies.

People comprising each of the three kinds of groups interacted based on a clear understanding of their group's function. The School Improvement Planning Team directed schoolwide planning with the benefit of representatives from each grade level and quality circle working side-by-side with parents and administration. The statement, "As good as we are, we can always get better!" helped to inspire a culture that embraced a commitment to continuous improvement.

The direct impact of the quality circles is so powerful at the action level that their work merits a closer look. They are doing some of the work that principals at other schools try to do along with a myriad of other tasks, usually with too little time. Brash gives testimony to such delegation as she comments, "I don't need to know everything all the time. That's why we have good people!" Each quality circle establishes specific annual goals within their area that support the overall goals for school improvement stated in the school action plan. In addition to carrying out plans to reach the goals, the quality circle is also responsible for collecting data to share with the school community about what actually happened during the course of each school year. In addition to a printed annual progress report, the School Improvement Planning Team coordinates a reporting day on which each quality circle reports on their year's accomplishments.

The richness of those accomplishments is apparent in the 1994-1995 report. The goal for one circle as stated in the school's action plan was, "The Staff Development Quality Circle devises and oversees the organizational plan for development in areas of stated need." The annual report listed the strategies planned and completed under the leadership of the quality circle. Examples include the following:

1. The Staff Development Quality Circle organized biannual "tantalizing tips" sessions. Staff members presented fifteen-minute, small group presentations on instructional and classroom management tips.

2. Staff members received release time to observe their peers in the following areas: behavior management, teaching strategies, and individual student needs.

3. The Student Assistance Team (SAT) was expanded so that each teaching team was represented. This generated a wealth of ideas and resources including some specialized training for the staff.

The complete list of training sessions involving one or more members of the Amy Beverland staff that year is extensive. All were applicable to the skills and knowledge needed to create the brain-compatible classroom. It is significant that the principal didn't hold primary responsibility for these activities—the quality circle accepted that assignment.

The breadth and depth of the staff development is characteristic of a school that has focused on ITI implementation for several years. Early implementors need to emphasize ITI training events including all staff members.

Create a Culture That Embraces Continuous Improvement

Once the system is in place, the administration and staff can sit back, right? Wrong! Now the really hard work for leadership begins—sustaining the culture, climate, and system to nurture continuous improvement. Everyone involved must committed to on-going improvement. The work is never done because we are working with human beings, about whom we are constantly enlarging our understanding, and who present themselves at schools in ever-changing combinations requiring differing responses.

One characteristic of a school committed to continuous improvement is the willingness to ask the question, "What is working and what needs to be dropped or improved?" At Amy Beverland they also ask each year, since a settling in after year two, whether the quality circle structure needs refining or changing. So far, there hasn't been a perceived need for change in that structure.

Meetings are a regular feature of life at Amy Beverland Elementary. As staff members worked together, they became increasingly aware of how to make meetings more efficient and effective. The grade level teams brainstormed attributes of their best meetings and captured these ideas as recommended meeting procedures. These lists are shared among the various teams and circles, acting on one of the school's beliefs, "Transport best practices." What improves one then has the chance to improve all, or as Deming puts it, "reduce the variance" between the best and worst meetings (Deming 1986). As a result, the staff has greatly enhanced their productivity at meetings. Examples of such procedures appear in Appendix D.

In six years Amy Beverland grew from 450 to 900 students, presenting the challenge to build the sense of community among a growing staff. From the start, the staff agreed that ground rules for interacting with one another over difficult issues were needed. They agreed to seek first the support and advice of a "balcony person" about upsetting information. The "balcony person" is a trusted person who typically provides encouragement. The larger the staff, the more vulnerable they became to the very human activities of hearing, believing, and passing on gossip and rumors. In Amy Beverland's sixth year, three different people came to Susan Brash with incorrect information relating to total inclusion of special education students at the school. She traced each piece of information directly to the source and provided correct information to the whole group at once.

To prevent such things from undermining their strong sense of community, new ground rules were needed. The plan for sharing personal and professional expectations developed by John Champlain (Figure 2.1) was used to continue and deepen the process. Susan and her staff realized that without stating openly what they expected of one another AND having a plan for confronting others in a caring, professional way, fragmentation and lack of trust would be likely.

The new ground rules prescribed what an individual should do if he/or she heard something upsetting. Essential features of the new agreement were as follows:

1. Give it time, and if appropriate just let go of it.

2. If the comment requires a response, go directly to the person involved to clarify and resolve the issue through professional confrontation. Champlin (Figure 2.1) suggests, "We agreed...I saw... Help me understand," as a general formula for such confrontation.

3. If not able to do step #2, or if it was not effective, go to the principal. The principal is committed to listen, ask questions, give an opinion if solicited, and help the person determine the next step. The principal

serves as the mediator where needed, but only with the understanding that she would not judge any individual differently for having the courage to come to her with the truth.

These ground rules arose out of a specific incident and eventually were embraced by the entire staff.

Obtaining each staff member's commitment to continuous improvement comes about in a variety of ways, depending on the school's traditions and culture. Once obtained, people must talk in open and specific ways about how they will nurture the culture that supports such a commitment. In the specific examples shared, the reader can begin to appreciate the time and caring involved.

Figure 2.1

Expectations of Peers

PROFESSIONAL	PERSONAL
What does it look, sound, and feel like?	
1.	1.
2.	2.
3.	3.

WE AGREE I SAW HELP ME UNDERSTAND

Courtesy of John Champlain

Pitfalls to Avoid

There are many pitfalls for the leader who aspires to facilitate organizational change. Because the mistakes of others are instructive, this section focuses on pitfalls to avoid. Not only must leaders be prepared to recognize and help remove barriers to ITI implementation, they must avoid being the construction engineers building the barriers!

Susan Brash provides some solid advice for avoiding pitfalls based on her experience at Amy Beverland:

1. Don't make assumptions. Talk directly to the person(s) involved.

2. Provide a model by using effective brain-compatible teaching strategies whenever working with the staff, a grade level team, or a quality circle.

3. Trust your intuition. If you sense tension and stress, it is there. Check it out! Often you'll sense this exactly when you **don't have the time** to deal with it. As a leader, you must make the hard decision to **take time**.

4. Deal with district mandates by emphasizing the goal. While the activity or event prescribed by central administration may not appear to fit with school goals or processes, the goal itself may be quite compatible. Negotiate for permission to make plans to reach the district goal in your school's own unique way.

5. Give credit to others for their contributions.

6. Don't deal with the whole group on issues that affect a few. Go talk directly with the few.

7. Don't pass the buck. Take responsibility as leader whether or not you feel personally responsible. Get beyond blame to action-planning.

8. Examine your motive. If you intend to do the right thing for students, you will probably make defensible decisions.

Compare these ideas with your own experiences. Use what works for you, and continue to collect advice from colleagues.

In the same spirit, we'd like to share advice based on predictable failures gleaned from Karen Olsen, Director of MCSIP (Mid-California Science Improvement Project) through 1997. The Packard Foundation funded this effort to wed brain-compatible teaching with a deeper understanding of the science content to be taught. During the project's first nine years, key roadblocks to organizational change emerged. The resulting recommendations from Olsen (shared in a small group session for administrators during the spring of 1995) demand thought and the courage to act on one's convictions:

1. Ground discussion and planning in the brain research findings. Avoid getting lost in vague discussions on educational philosophy. People need to be clear about **why** they are doing what they are doing. Some of the teaching tools are not new, but used in new ways. If the **why** isn't clear, people revert to using old tools in old ways, often without even realizing it!

2. Develop tools to recognize and deal with the ups and downs of change. People do not change in a predictable, even pattern. Pressure for change builds, and people lurch forward. Frustration increases and people can slide back a few steps. The ITI Rubric (Olsen and Kovalik 1994) is an excellent tool for guiding forward progress during the implementation process.

3. Be willing to let go of old ways that do not support brain-compatible learning. Likely to be jettisoned are approaches to student discipline based on threat and control by adults, favorite units of study that are not developmentally suited to the students, and familiar, but cluttered, ways of organizing and decorating classrooms.

4. Have one over-arching vision for the school or district—learning based on what we know about the human brain. Avoid a focus on programs or textbooks. Examine the budget and consider reallocating funds that do not directly enhance the implementation of brain research findings.

5. Train, coach, and support teachers continually so that they develop new habits and reach success with ITI implementation.

6. Accompany training about the ITI model with content-specific training to deepen knowledge levels.

7. Know the social structure of the school staff. Who are the informal leaders? How proficient are they in using the ITI model? Know that these individuals can undermine the change effort if it threatens their social role and the leadership they have exerted in the past as "best" teachers in the school. Don't allow factions to develop around the so-called fast runners and slow runners. Implementation is not a race!

We invite you to consider these thoughts in relation to your own experiences. Use them to promote meaningful discussion among the staff so that you can collaborate on ways to prevent and remove barriers.

Conclusion

Acknowledging the power of the status quo, the complexity of coming to terms with change, and the importance of constantly working to develop a strong sense of community among those working to educate youth will increase the likelihood of leading successful change at the classroom, school, and district levels. Success demands strong intention and thoughtful planning by those sharing the leadership for the proposed changes.

Careful planning for deliberate action targets six broad areas: 1) get everyone involved, 2) get to know the community, 3) determine the school's vision and mission, 4) establish a system to reach the aim, 5) create a culture that embraces continuous improvement, and 6) avoid and learn from pitfalls others have experienced. Future chapters will present other examples of action in these areas.

What Is Integrated Thematic Instruction?

by Jane Rasp McGeehan

Introduction

Integrated Thematic Instruction (Kovalik and Olsen 1994) is a powerful model for implementing the brain research findings to create brain-compatible classrooms and schools. For many teachers across the United States, it is the vehicle for making learning important and exciting for students and teachers alike. Teachers, students, schools, and whole school districts are coming alive in new ways as they act on what is known and being discovered about the human brain, an incredible learning organ.

Many people reading this book have prior knowledge of and perhaps direct experiences with ITI. This chapter provides a brief summary of the ITI model and introduces the reader to the ITI Rubrics (Appendix A and B). In cases where greater detail is needed, the reader should consult the listing of books and video material about ITI in Appendix C.

Integrated Thematic Instruction Defined

Integrated Thematic Instruction (ITI) is the area of overlap among three well-defined bodies of knowledge:

1. Biology of learning (formerly brain research)

2. Teaching strategies grounded in the biology of learning

3. Curriculum development that enhances the pattern-seeking and mental program development activity of the brain.

The more a teacher and administrator act effectively in all three areas, the more likely it is that a student is presented with brain-compatible learning opportunities.

Figure 3.1

Integrated Thematic Instruction (ITI) Model

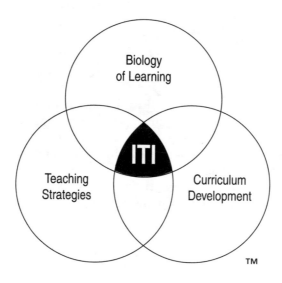

The three areas are interdependent. A solid understanding of the biology of learning makes it possible for a teacher to select teaching strategies that help instead of hinder the brain as a natural learning organ.

An informed high school teacher may decide to limit lectures to fifteen minutes in a high school class and then provide choices for students from among varied learning activities so learners can attach personal meaning to what was said (pattern recognition and understanding) and practice using the new material (acquire a new mental program). The teacher makes productive choices about the workshops to attend or avoid. If the strategy being advocated at a workshop definitely assists the teacher in creating brain-compatible lessons, the workshop merits consideration. For example, knowing that Collaboration is a brain-compatible element, the teacher chooses a workshop to refine her ability to use cooperative learning strategies.

The context and demands of school leadership also illustrate how brain research, strategies, and curriculum are interdependent in everyday usage. Consider the frequent need to plan for a meeting of the faculty or staff. Most people dislike attending such meetings, but does it really have to be that way? Couldn't the regular meeting of such a vital group within the school system be the occasion for individuals to generate creative ideas to move the school toward its vision? Couldn't the meeting help to nurture the fragile and essential sense of being a part of something larger than one's self—part of a community of learners? The answers are yes! If the leader acts on the brain-compatible elements, selects appropriate teaching strategies when learning new information is the goal, and focuses on items that are meaningful to those in attendance, then the meetings will become a highly valued activity.

Compare a brain-compatible meeting with the kind of meetings we all frequently have to endure. Assume that this meeting takes place in a school that has made a commitment to becoming a brain-compatible place for youth and for adults. They have the Lifelong Guidelines and the LIFESKILLS (see Appendix C) in place as guidelines for the interactions among the adults.

You'll know immediately that something is different. There is soft music playing as you enter, and, perhaps, appropriate snacks and beverages to help you both relax and focus. You'll be warmly welcomed by the chairperson and receive the meeting agenda, to which you have had the opportunity to contribute. The meeting begins on time with an opening activity designed to reestablish the sense of community within the group and help people focus on the business at hand. This part is often light and fun-filled so that you are already feeling uplifted.

The chair distributes a handout that presents routine information needed by the group, but not requiring dialogue. How wonderful not to have the leader's voice droning announcements. Several people who were assigned responsibilities at the previous meeting report on action or progress. Each uses professional, quality transparencies and handouts so that the presentations are interesting and easy to follow.

The central issue for discussion is presented by the chair. Part of the introduction is a ten-minute video with accompanying pamphlets that provide background information. Working in smaller groups of three determined by the chair, with each group focuses on a specific aspect of the larger issue. One member creates summary charts or mindmaps for the small group report to the larger group. After adequate time for discussion, people reassemble for sharing.

The chair invites responses to small group reports, clarifies the work to be done before the next meeting, and makes arrangements for each person to receive a copy of the small group reports to consider in the interim. The chair provides information available from the previous meeting and adjourns the present meeting within five minutes of the promised end.

Consider ways in which the ITI model influenced the chairperson's planning and execution of the meeting. Where is there evidence of the eight brain-compatible elements in action?

Biology of Learning Is the Foundation

The content and the implications of the biology of learning are dynamic. New information is emerging on a par with the rapid changes in the technology surrounding computers. Educators can count on increasingly exciting insights as technological break-throughs allow scientists to glimpse the brain at work in a wider variety of settings. If such findings are ignored by educators, it will be at great peril to the goals of education.

The ITI model begins with the biology of learning so that all subsequent decisions are grounded there. In creating the ITI model, Susan Kovalik translated key aspects of our knowledge of the brain into a methodology for teachers. The "Brain Basics" as explained in chapter one are emotions as gate-keeper, intelligence as a function of experience, the brain as a   pattern-seeking organ, multiple intelligences, learning as the development of useful mental programs, and personality affects learning. The implications for educators are summarized in the eight brain-compatible elements, also described in chapter one.

Brain-Compatible Elements

- Absence of Threat

- Meaningful Content

- Choices

- Adequate Time

- Enriched Environment

- Collaboration

- Immediate Feedback

- Mastery (Application)

The brain-compatible elements are the major bridge from research to classroom, school, and district implementation. In being trained to use the ITI model teachers and administrators learn practical steps to bring each element alive in the classroom and the school. Effective educators frequently realize during ITI trainings that a specific practice already in their repertoire is an excellent example of acting on one of the brain-compatible elements. Knowing they have the right idea provides motivation to expand the repertoire.

Instructional Strategies

The ITI model emphasizes selecting instruction strategies that enhance the brain-compatibility of the classroom and the school. Such strategies include those that facilitate academic and social learning. Figure 3.2 provides specific examples in relation to the brain-compatible elements.

Figure 3.2 _____

Brain-Compatible Instruction

Brain-Compatible Elements	Illustrative Instructional Strategies
Absence of Threat	• Classroom environment that calms and creates focus
	• Use of agendas
	• Procedures to state specific behavior expectations for various classroom situations
	• Teacher models Lifelong Guidelines and LIFESKILLS
	• Inclusion and team-building activities

Meaningful Content	• Real experiences through study trips
	• Effective and focused direct instruction
	• Student notebook to learn skills of organization
	• Questions from students help guide the study
Choice	• Students select what learning activities they will do part of the time
	• Teachers write learning activities (inquiries) that reflect multiple intelligences and different levels of Bloom's Taxonomy (Bloom 1956)
Adequate Time	• Blocks of time provided for student work
Enriched Environment	• Lamps and plants added
	• Multiple resources available beyond the textbook
	• Access to at least ten times more input than is typical of a traditional classroom
Collaboration	• Students organized into learning clubs
	• Students taught to work cooperatively and to develop the social skills to do so with success (are not simply placed into groups!)
	• Classroom meetings are held to solve common problems

Immediate Feedback	• Answer keys and specific criteria are available to guide student self-assessment
	• Teacher circulates as a facilitator/advisor
Mastery (application)	• Processing questions used by students after small or large group activity
	• Presentations and products created for real audiences

Teachers who make the leap from traditional to brain-compatible approaches require the courage to let go of the familiar and embrace the unfamiliar, with its attendant risks. It's not easy to try something new, fail at it the first few times, and still persist until the new strategy can be applied with success and ease.

This is where leadership plays an absolutely critical role. The leader must provide strong, steady support.

This support begins with a school environment that is free of threat for adults. If it is good for the students, it is good for the adults. The staff members must provide the model as they "walk the talk" of the Lifelong Guidelines and LIFESKILLS. As advised in chapter two, the staff must invest the time to agree on their expectations of one another, and on the specific ways in which they will confront each other professionally when expectations are not met. They must know what the leader's response will be if a new idea doesn't work. Will the leader listen, understand, help to analyze the pitfalls, and help find ways to insure success next time? Will the leader be willing to stand side-by-side with the teacher to try the new strategy, too? The next three chapters present specific examples of ways leaders have supported new and veteran teachers as they begin their personal ITI journeys.

Curriculum Development

ITI curriculum is grounded in a real location or significant event. The year's study is organized around an over-arching theme that has the power to illuminate student discovery of the connections among the various topics being studied. In this way, meaning is enhanced for the learner. Every aspect of the curriculum is tied to important concepts to avoid requiring students to learn isolated facts of limited usefulness.

The thoughtfully designed curriculum facilitates the brain's work of pattern-seeking and program-building. Brain-compatible curriculum is meaningful to the learner. It is not overloaded so that learners must rush through a unit of study with superficial understanding and little opportunity for application.

The brain-compatible curriculum answers Susan Kovalik's central questions of "What do you want them to understand?" (pattern recognition) and "What will they **do** with it?" (mental program mastery).

Traditional curriculum often lacks meaning for the students. The learner seldom uses the new material for any purpose beyond passing a test or impressing a younger sibling with his or her esoteric knowledge! The important connection to living everyday life may lie undiscovered by the student even if it is obvious to the teacher.

Textbook-based curriculum too often consists of such a quantity of information that superficial memorization is the only realistic option for students. We know that being able to master and apply the information usefully—developing a mental program—requires time and practice. Lecturing and reading alone do not result in useful mental programs stored in the student's long-term memory.

ITI curriculum is centered on locations that can be visited easily and frequently by learners—locations that illustrate the curriculum topics. Starting in the real world capitalizes on the brain's natural power to learn. ITI teachers recognize that each community offers rich opportunities for meaningful content. Few professions are more dependent than education on the rich human context of the immediate surroundings to achieve goals successfully. It is the classroom teacher who knows that context most completely, including personal knowledge of the students themselves. What topics are appropriate for the students to pursue because they are age-appropriate and aligned with students' developmental levels? What topics can be related to the experiences the students are bringing to school, and what locations can be studied regularly that will extend each student's competence? The answers to these questions provide fertile ground for meaningful curriculum.

ITI teachers naturally refer to state and local curriculum guides as they create meaningful curriculum. The more conceptual the focus of such guides, the greater their usefulness for the teacher as curriculum developer. It is the teacher's responsibility to insure student mastery of essential skills and knowledge. It is also the teacher's responsibility to advocate on behalf of "less is more" when the prescribed curriculum consists of far too many topics and skills.

Does this mean that all thematic curricula are brain-compatible? Unfortunately, the answer is no. The curriculum must be carefully designed to spotlight essential patterns and increase the likelihood that learners will observe the connections among them. Many thematic curriculum products fall short of this goal.

Observing in an ITI Classroom

My own experience as a principal provides a perspective on the ITI model in a real setting. Visualizing this classroom vignette and comparing it with your own experiences will help to increase your understanding of how the three parts of the model work together.

Come with me to a biology class of ninth and tenth grade students. They are also part of a group of around 100 students, a school-within-a-school, whose teachers share a commitment to implement ITI.

I'm seated during the class break as students arrive. The day's agenda is a mindmap entitled, "Thinking Thursday." The yearlong theme, W.A.L.L.S. (We Are Life-Long Students) is prominently displayed. An interesting fact related to the current study topic is posted. The classroom is arranged with six large tables for students; a carpeted corner with beanbag chairs; numerous plants; several small animals in cages; student work on display, inquiry boards with a variety of potential learning activities described; and a wealth of resource materials. As students enter the classroom, they greet the teacher and one another in a friendly way that implies that they are glad to be there. Without direction from the teacher, and before the bell signals the official beginning of the period, students take out their three-ring binders. They copy the daily agenda and interesting fact into the designated section. The mood in the room is relaxed, but business-like. Shortly after the bell, the teacher sees that most students have completed the opening procedures and briefly explains the daily agenda. Gaining student attention seems effortless. The teacher then launches into fifteen minutes of lecture, the overhead projector and appropriate transparencies providing strong visual support.

The students pay close attention, taking notes in another section of the binder, and asking several questions for clarification. There have been no interruptions for discipline. Now students have the remainder of the period to work on their chosen learning activities (inquiries) about the topic. The teacher reminds them where special supplies are located that they might need. Within a few minutes, the classroom has settled into the productive buzz that accompanies twenty-eight students at work singly or in groups. Excepting three off-task students who appear to be catching up on the latest news, all the students are actively engaged in a variety of tasks. Some are designing posters, others writing letters. One group has plans to make a video production to be shown to the class. Others read the textbook, pamphlets, encyclopedia, or news articles. The teacher is busy as the consultant and advisor. She talks with students one-on-one or in their small groups answering or posing questions to help students reach the standard of their personal best. She is also available to review completed inquiries, note completed work in her grade book, and suggest possibilities to students for their next inquiries.

The time flies by for the students and for me as the observer. No one seems ready for the period to end, but the teacher signals that it is time to observe the procedures for the end of the class.

Efficiently, materials are placed where they belong and students gather up personal items, ready to move to the next class. I leave knowing that student learning is thriving in this brain-compatible, ITI classroom.

(Note: The desire for adequate time pushed this high school to a modified block schedule and eventually to the four-period day.)

The ITI Rubrics

The ITI Rubrics describe what to expect over the three to five years it takes to transform a classroom or school from highly traditional to brain-compatible using the ITI model. They were developed under the leadership of Karen Olsen, who worked with ITI teachers and coaches to tap their personal observations. These observations were distilled from over five years of coaching in more than one hundred ITI classrooms. The Rubrics have proven to be invaluable tools for understanding ITI, for training, for coaching ITI beginners and veterans, for planning, and for assessment. The more first-hand experience one has with ITI, the more useful the Rubrics become.

Please refer to the ITI Rubrics, in Appendixes A and B, to see how they can assist one in gaining a deeper understanding of what ITI looks like at various points in the implementation process. The Schoolwide Rubric is the starting point and describes targets for leaders who seek to create a brian-compatible culture throughout the school. Looking at the Classroom Rubric, begin with Stage 0 and read each of the columns under the heading, "curriculum." You can see how the teacher begins by teaching the students how their brains learn and then gradually works toward curriculum organized around the yearlong theme. In the same way, begin with Stage 0 and read all columns with the heading, "Instructional Strategies." The classroom becomes more and more brain-compatible and thus more likely to inspire powerful student learning as real experiences become a central focus. The atmosphere is safe and inviting. The student has a variety of options that lead to mastery of the curriculum's key points. A thorough reading and re-reading of the ITI Rubrics provides a summary of the ITI model in a handy, practical format.

Using the ITI Rubrics to Focus Energy and Sustain Motivation

Let's imagine a hypothetical situation in which you as administrator or peer coach meet with an ITI colleague who has fully implemented Stage 1 of the ITI Classroom Rubric. You begin the session by looking together at Stage 1. As you talk about this stage, you place a "plus" by most items to indicate that they are characteristic of the teacher's classroom. You then turn attention to Stage 2 of the Rubric, and ask the teacher to share any things listed there that he is already doing some or all of the time. He says that he is using a wide variety of resources to support learning, including classroom speakers and field trips. At this point, they are not all related to a theme, as the teacher may not have selected a yearlong theme. However, further discussion reveals that the teacher has identified both content and skills that will be mastered by his students during the year.

You recognize what has already been achieved and relate it to any observable changes you may have noticed in student attitude and learning. Through dialogue, you work together to determine two areas listed on the Rubric that will be the target for the teacher's continuing growth in competence with the ITI model. They are:

- the development of a science theme connected to the nearby park as a starting point for curriculum integration, and

- the creation of inquiries for each key point identified.

You find out what the teacher thinks will be needed for him to be successful in the target areas, and indicate what specific support you'll be able to provide while also pointing to other sources of support.

You agree on a time next month to meet informally over coffee to discuss about how things are going. The teacher expresses appreciation for the feedback and suggestions. You both leave the conference feeling satisfaction, enthusiasm, and renewed energy.

Conclusion

The ITI model bridges the gap between research and classroom application. The overlap among the research on the biology of learning findings, instructional strategies based on knowledge of the brain, and curriculum that facilitates pattern-seeking and program-building is where ITI is born.

Creating a Brain-Compatible Elementary School

by Susan Brash and Jane Rasp McGeehan

Introduction

Brain research findings, Kovalik's ITI model, Gardner's multiple intelligences, cooperative learning strategies, Deming's Total Quality Management—in combination, a truly exciting and brain-compatible vision for the elementary school where all students are successful learners emerges! The story of one school's move from vision to reality provides one path and illustrates options that may work for others. This chapter tells the story of the creation of Amy Beverland Elementary in suburban Indianapolis, Indiana.

The steps taken by principal, Susan Brash, and her staff do NOT consist of a formula for others to follow; rather, they suggest discussion of the question, "What will we do here in our school with our unique school community?" All plans must flow from an honest and unhurried dialogue about the beliefs held in common by the administration, staff, and parents of the school community. If others come to visit our school, how will they recognize our core beliefs in what they see?

Amy Beverland Elementary School opened in the fall of 1989 as the ninth elementary school in the Metropolitan School District of Lawrence Township in suburban Indianapolis. The attractive, inviting school is located among a collection of retail businesses and professional establishments, with wooded and lakeside residences nearby. While it opened with approximately 400 students, the school presently serves over 900 youth.

Throughout, the students have been a diverse population with regard to ethnicity, learning needs, and socio-economic status. At this writing the students are 18% African-American, 16% qualified for free or reduced lunch, and 14% identified to receive special education services.

The children of affluent families living close to the school are joined by children of low-cost housing projects, apartments, and mobile homes to form the Amy Beverland Family.

Getting From Zero to Brain-Compatible

The best way to create a brain-compatible school is to apply the tenets of brain-compatible learning to every aspect of the school environment. Building trust and creating a climate and culture that are absent of threat constitute the essential starting points. Just as the effective teacher builds community through procedures, the daily agenda, consistency, and team-building activities, so the effective principal must build a cooperative team of stakeholders who decide together what they really believe about children and successful learning.

At Amy Beverland Elementary School, each step was tested against Kovalik's brain-compatible elements to insure that it stayed consistent with those beliefs. Susan Brash attributes much of the school's on-going success to this practice.

Giving Birth to a New School

Rapid growth in the school district dictated new construction. The site was secured and a committee formed to work with the selected architect to design a state-of-the-art elementary school facility. The committee was co-chaired by the two assistant superintendents, Ed Williams and Jane McGeehan. Committee members represented all adult groups who would inhabit the school, including teachers of regular and special education, teachers of art, music, and physical education, parents, and support staff. General budget parameters made a quality building possible to consider. The new facility was to blend attractively with the surrounding residences, be an inviting place for students and community members to gather, have plenty of natural light, and meet the practical needs of students and staff.

Visitations by committee members to four or five other schools in the state produced clearer pictures of what was and was not acceptable. The architect translated the group's ideas into potential floor plans.

A professional interior decorator from the architect's firm made suggestions about colors and wall treatments that would minimize the institutional appearance of the school and make it more similar to home-like spaces. The color schemes featured soft blue, grey, green, mauve, and beige. The classrooms had bay windows with levelor blinds. Hallways were carpeted and classrooms were partially carpeted.

Working from this base, the principal made the final interior finishing decisions during the eight months before the school was to open, shortly after she was hired to open the new elementary school. (Note: Most leaders do not have the opportunity to create a brain-compatible learning environment from scratch, but as renovations and updates come along, many of the same ideas can be used in existing facilities.)

Year Zero

Staffing the new school was a top priority for the newly appointed principal. She hosted two receptions in the spring, before the school was to open, to greet interested candidates from inside the school district and to share her personal and professional ideas. Over 150 teachers, assistants, and substitute teachers expressed the desire to become a part of the Amy Beverland staff.

All such internal applicants were interviewed personally by the principal. Since students would be coming to the new school from the five existing elementary schools, the principal was expected to choose some teachers from each of those schools. Susan Brash set out to choose a diverse group of caring teachers, instructional assistants, and support staff who would meet the needs and interests of the diverse student population. In choosing the new staff she looked for these common characteristics:

- genuine concern for others
- passion for teaching
- commitment to "workplace family" and cooperation
- understanding of the time and work involved in creating an effective school.

The new staff met for the first time in May of 1989. Meeting at the construction site, the staff saw floors of sand and the skeletal steel beams that would be their school. Inspired by the possibilities of the new facility, they planned summer activities to begin with a retreat.

In June before Amy Beverland opened, prospective students and their parents coming from existing elementaries were invited on a field trip to their new school. Parents received personal invitations to accompany their children to meet the principal and tour the not-quite-completed school. School buses provided transportation. During the bus ride, the principal and students sang songs and became acquainted. The principal suggested two ways that the students could prepare for their new school:

1. Practice good courtesy.

2. Read, read, read!

The students and principal shared examples of good courtesy and ways to enjoy reading. The principal gave each child a small box of raisins to remind them of their visit and their summer preparation pledge. They were challenged to eat the raisins, and return the empty box to her on the first day of school as evidence of their efforts.

In addition, the principal made a concerted effort to identify potential business partners to collaborate with the new school. Susan Brash's personal visits led to invitations to become a part of the Amy Beverland Family. See chapter eight, "Beyond the General Fund," for more detail.

Year One

The Amy Beverland staff gathered for a two-day planning retreat in August, a month before the school was to open. Their primary goal was to create the school's mission statement.

The question, "What do we want Amy Beverland Elementary to stand for?" elicited lively discussion. Brash reviewed the guidelines for effective brainstorming and for creating mindmaps. Then, working in cooperative teams with roles assigned, the staff took five minutes to generate 75 descriptions of the school. Even today the memory is fresh. Brash declares, " It was so exciting! I'll never forget it as long as I live!"

Brash then invited the groups to look for natural clusters among the descriptions. In an amazingly short time, they had agreed on thirteen organizing clusters. During the break following this work, Brash invited each person to choose one of the clusters on which he/she would want to work. People couldn't wait to sign up for the one they wanted! The clusters then became the first Quality Circles. The Quality Circles then brainstormed objectives for the year, a timeline and activities to meet those objectives, and an estimated budget of monetary and human resources needed.

When they reassembled, Brash charged the Quality Circles with the responsibility of leading the new school. This, she said, would be the "try and see" year. The work of each group would be reviewed at the end of the year to discover what the school would really be about. The two-day retreat energized and defined the work of the staff.

The result? By the end of the year, several Quality Circles had dropped out and others had combined work with a closely related circle.

What emerged were five circles that still operate to this day. More details about their structure and work can be found in chapter two.

To continue the work of the staff prior to the school's opening, two three-day work sessions were held after the retreat to address follow-up activities established as priorities by the group. Teachers were paid stipends to attend. They worked in cooperative groups by grade level teams to create a brochure for parents to explain the curriculum for each grade level. Although varied and creative, the brochures had one common denominator—a center portion for each grade level to list the skills and knowledge that would be the focus for student learning.

The school logo, first year motto, school colors, and school song were also produced at these workshops. They were the result of a patient consensus-building process. The STARS acronym, Sparkling Thinkers Achieving Remarkable Success, led to the star design for the logo. Blue, green and white became the school colors. The first year's motto would be "Courtesy is contagious...Please pass it on." The STAR logo and the school song captured the school's essence as a place where each person was equally significant, valued, and appreciated.

A School Improvement Planning Team was established to oversee the school's progress. Its membership consisted of teachers, administration, parents, community, and support staff. They worked with the topics of the thirteen Quality Circles to generate the school's mission statement. The process took much time and effort, listening, and caring. Finally, the day arrived to consider possible mission statements. One person's ideas captured the essence of the group's ideas, and the following statement emerged as a consensus:

> *Amy Beverland Elementary Mission Statement. The Amy Beverland Family is committed to academic excellence and the cultivation of individual potential through a cooperative, enriched environment where each person feels equally significant and appreciated.*

Although the wording is reviewed each year to ensure that what it says is still what the school values most, this statement (without change) has inspired the work of the school during its seven years.

Building the school culture and climate to support the mission statement provided the focus for year one. Tribes training, an approach to cooperative learning created by Jeanne Gibbs, prepared the faculty with a common language and method that fostered teamwork and team spirit among students. All adults worked to provide a warm, caring, nurturing environment. All made a commitment to include special education and identified gifted students in the regular classrooms. The school's mission and first year motto were highly visible throughout the school to rein-force the behaviors that create the desired culture.

Parents became valued partners right from the start. Before the school opened, the principal hosted a coffee in every neighborhood that housed potential Amy Beverland students. Flyers and letters were sent to parents to invited parents to meet the new principal and allow her to begin to assess their needs and interests. Each parent was invited to a June meeting to create a parent-faculty organization. They elected officers and determined the organization's structure. The elected officers recruited board members and wrote a constitution and by-laws accepted by the membership. Their first activity was "Sundae on a Sunday," the day before the school year's first Monday. Over 1,200 sundaes were served. It has become a tradition—an annual opportunity to meet the teachers, see classrooms, and conduct other school business.

Year Two

While the first year was challenging, it also provided many rewards and nurtured the motivation to continue getting better. At regular meet-ings, the principal introduced several video tapes by Susan Kovalik that presented the ITI model. The staff became convinced that ITI was a match for their school's curriculum needs. They determined that becoming a brain-compatible school was an exciting and worthwhile goal that would push the school family closer to realizing its mission statement.

Grant money provided a week of summer ITI training for each staff member. Coordinated by Susan Brash, it was offered at Amy Beverland Elementary with Barbara Pedersen, Director of Indiana's C.L.A.S.S. project to implement ITI on a statewide basis, as the primary trainer. Demonstration classrooms created the possibility for teachers to see the model in action as experienced ITI teachers showed how to create brain-compatible learning. That training prior to the school's second year was followed by another two-day retreat. Teachers met as grade level teams where a high level of trust existed as a result of their first year of work together. Focusing on the eight brain-compatible elements, each team reached consensus to concentrate on Absence of Threat and Enriched Environment. They delineated the following specific strategies:

1. Respond to the need for a calming environment, by adding lamps, plants, and by playing classical or other soothing music. Organize the classrooms to provide structure and security.

2. Use welcome boards with morning procedures to let students know procedures to start the day and the agenda for the day's activities.

3. Select just three colors to create a feeling of continuity in the class-room, and remove clutter so that students feel calm and able to focus attention on learning.

4. Post in the hallways and in each classroom the Kovalik Lifelong Guidelines and the MegaSkills developed by Dorothy Rich. (Subsequently Kovalik developed a more comprehensive list termed the LIFESKILLS.) Use the behaviors we want students to use, facilitate activities to promote them, and reinforce the same desired student behaviors. A strengthened sense of community resulted from the decision to share a common focus. The positive, non-threatening atmosphere in the school could be felt immediately by students, parents, and visitors. Teachers got support from visits and feedback from experienced ITI teachers. This coaching process involved periodic visits from December-June to ensure continued teacher growth in ITI implementation.

Nurturing community partners and strong parent involvement con-tinued to be a central focus for the school. The details about these efforts can be found in chapters two, seven, and eight.

Year Three

The Quality Circles continued their work, and by sticking with the process established, Meaningful Content and Choices emerged next for special attention. **No one was expected to implement a yearlong theme right away.** Instead, the pursuit of meaningful content was approached through increased emphasis on taking field trips and building related curriculum. It was also pursued by looking for natural connections in the existing curriculum. The administration and teacher leaders invited staff to create new connections, to try a theme for a day, a week, or a month, or to experiment with the integration of two, three, or four traditional subject areas. "Have fun! Play with the power of themes tied to real places," they exhorted.

The message to teachers, in sum, was to discover, try something and evaluate it, and move forward in one's own time toward using and devel-oping all seven intelligences.

The approach to incorporating choices for students was similar. Teachers considered Howard Gardner's multiple intelligence theory (Gardner 1983) to help plan for student choices and to add variety to learning activities. The staff began by assessing their own areas of rela-tive strength and weakness with respect to the multiple intelligences. They shared this information with colleagues and team members to deepen each other's appreciation of the importance of bringing a team with multiple talents to address a task.

As understanding of ITI increased and relationship among the parts and pieces of the Model was clearer, a kind of synergy occurred as a powerful energizing force. When teachers had first-hand experiences that confirmed what they had learned about the human brain, they became even more convinced of the value of the brain research in relation to their work as educators. Because their own learning as adults was happening in a threat-free way where collaboration and positive feelings were essential components, they felt renewed commitment to create the brain-compatible learning environment for their students. Experiences transformed some beliefs about learning and affirmed others.

It was clear that the dramatic changes occurring in the curriculum would require parent support, and that such support would only come from an understanding of what the school was doing and why. Parents were brought into the process through periodic presentations and discussions in addition to regular communications from their children's teachers. See chapter seven.

Year Four

During the summer before the fourth year, most teachers participated in another week of training in the ITI model, as they were now ready to learn at a more advanced level. At the subsequent summer "advance" (retreat), the staff evaluated the previous year's efforts in relation to their growing picture of the ideal brain-compatible classroom and school. They reached consensus about collective commitments through dialogue in small groups and processing in the large group.

Everyone was ready to embark on a yearlong theme that integrated at least three subject areas. Teachers chose whether to work alone, with a partner, within a small group, or as part of a grade level team. State and district proficiencies (essential skills) were embedded meaningfully within each theme. Teachers posted the proficiencies appropriate for each grade level around the upper perimeter of the classrooms as reminders for themselves and to serve as a guarantee to parents that they would be addressed throughout the year.

Parents continued to be actively involved in the affairs of the school, including ITI implementation. The Staff Development Quality Circle planned and conducted formal parent workshops so that parents could learn the ITI model along with their children and the staff.

Year Five

By now, the staff could see a pattern of continuous improvement based on their planning and team effort. As brief descriptions of activity during years five, six, and seven of ITI implementation reveal, significant change **requires sustained, thoughtful attention.**

- Quality Circles reviewed and evaluated achievements to date and set their next goals.

- Writing effective inquiries became a goal for everyone.

- The Curriculum Coordination Quality Circle raised the need to communicate about curriculum across the grade levels and generated ways to improve such articulation to avoid fruitless repetition or unintended omission.

- The Staff Development Quality Circle continued to present parent workshops.

Year Six

- Staff identified the need for stronger collaboration among teachers and continued focus on communication about curriculum across grade levels.

- This was the "try and see" year to explore better methods for assessing student work.

- Teachers practiced and shared with one another to create better descriptions of a quality product (rubrics) to guide student work

- Parent workshops continued.

Year Seven (1995-1996)

- Teachers refined and expanded uses for specific classroom procedures as described in the ITI model.

- Staff challenged themselves to write key points at a conceptual level and lively learning activities to promote student mastery.

- Understanding and application of Gardner's multiple intelligence theory moved forward.

- Staff reviewed basic beliefs about children and brain-compatible learning.

Why Change is Happening Successfully

A number of intentional steps, many of which come under the influence of the principal, continually work together to nudge and nurture change at Amy Beverland Elementary School. The phrase, "As good as we are, we want to get better!" summarizes the attitude supporting change at the school. Primary among the intentional steps favoring change at this school are:

- Living the model individually and as a staff.

- Regularly revisiting basic beliefs.

- Personalizing the ITI model to match Amy Beverland Elementary's circumstances.

- Involving everyone in the positive excitement of change.

- Monitoring progress toward goals, and formulating new goals based on that information.

- Providing the time and support necessary for adults and youth to learn new skills and habits.

Living the Model

Living the model is the most essential ingredient for successful implementation, and is arguably the umbrella idea under which most other strategies fall.

In planning curriculum, teachers begin with the question, "What do I want my students to learn?" Likewise, the principal and staff plan for staff meetings, retreats, and staff development presentations with the parallel question as a starting point—"What do we want the staff to learn?".

Next the meeting planners create a mindmap to illustrate the parts of the meeting and how they relate. A two-day retreat can be like living a miniature year-long theme. At one summer "advance," for example, Amy Beverland teachers immersed themselves in the schoolwide theme for the coming year, "Celebrating Our Tapestry of Talents." As reminders, they set up figures of a child representing each of Gardner's multiple intelligences. A conceptual key point was the focus for each activity for the teachers while they used the multiple intelligences to enhance learning. The staff moved, sang, talked, and reflected in just the ways that they in turn plan to provide variety for their students.

One of the greatest challenges for the staff in an ITI school is the need to live by the Lifelong Guidelines and LIFESKILLS. In an ITI school, the public face and the private face must become one. Knowing that children learn as much from what they see the adults **do** as from what the adults **say** demands a high standard of behavior from the adults.

The philosophy of teaching by example is so essential that it even includes the principal's commitment to build a personal relationship with all 900 students. In addition to countless informal interactions as Susan Brash moves throughout the classrooms, dining room, and media center during a typical day, she builds in a series of formal steps so that no child is missed. She visits each classroom within the first three days of school. During the visit, she personally and publicly greets each new student with a handshake and conversation. She welcomes returning students in the same warm manner. Teachers know generally when to expect the visit that typically takes no more than ten minutes of instructional time.

During the year, the principal builds on the relationships in additional ways. Each student's birthday is celebrated with an announcement on the P.A. system, a visit to the principal's office, a card and pencil, and a handshake or a hug (student's choice). During the December holiday season, the principal delivers greeting cards personally to each child with a small gift to commemorate her special love for each one. Finally, during the last two days of the school year, the principal says farewell to each child when she visits the classrooms. In addition to the customary handshake or hug, each child receives a small memento of the year, such as a STAR eraser or pencil.

Revisiting Basic Beliefs

Staying focused demands revisiting basic beliefs at regular intervals. At Amy Beverland, each proposed improvement is tested against the eight brain-compatible elements and the school's mission statement. If a proposed workshop or program doesn't support those essential guideposts, and by definition the underlying brain research, the staff doesn't have time or money for it. Activities proposed by the School Improvement Planning Team or any Quality Circle must be connected in a meaningful way to the brain research and core beliefs. Sometimes, the staff just needs time to consider and discuss. The rich dialogue and/or journal entries resulting from such reflection returns the group to center, enhancing balance. Further, it suggests ways to address problems and remove barriers. It is—and has been—time well spent.

Personalizing the Model

Starting from ITI's three primary parts, biology of leaing, teaching strategies, and curriculum development, the staff of an ITI school must discover specifically how the model will work within the unique context of their school. Such discovery is guided by thoughtful questions:

- What teaching strategies do we already know that support brain-compatible learning? What can we teach each other?

- What does applying the brain research findings really mean for us?

- What is active listening among adults? What does it look, feel, and sound like?

- What procedures capture our expectations for an effective meeting?

- What are the locations to which we can readily take our students?

- How will we meet the learning goals stated by Indiana and the Metropolitan School District of Lawrence Township through themes based on these locations?

The staff at Amy Beverland asks themselves these and many similar questions as they work to align the ITI model with the needs and expectations at Amy Beverland Elementary. They see the importance of spending time together on this task, and make the commitment to do it.

Two Examples of Personalizing the Model

The principal considers what absence of threat means for the faculty. Susan Brash believes that it must be clear that a choice is really a choice. If she presents options to the teachers, she is careful not to convey any mixed messages that there is a "preferred" choice that would please her. A choice is truly a choice, so that all possible threat of making a "wrong" selection is removed. When everyone needs to comply with a directive, it isn't presented as a choice in the first place!

"If it's good for the classroom, it is good for the school" is frequently heard in staff conversations at Amy Beverland. So, another way in which the ITI model is personalized is by creating procedures for grade level team meetings to generate a common set of expectations just as the teachers create student procedures for classroom routines. The effectiveness and efficiency of these meetings have improved as a result, as has each person's understanding of his/her personal responsibility to the group effort.

Involving Everyone

All stakeholders at Amy Beverland Elementary know the school's mission and contribute suggestions for their personal contributions to it. As one custodian stated, "We want to be positive role models for these kids." Such commitment to the school's mission has grown naturally out of regular investigation of the needs and interests of students, staff, and community. The principal repeatedly asks what resources are needed and what barriers people are experiencing that she could help to remove. Her methods include small-group discussions with parents, teachers, students, and support staff plus occasional surveys. Additionally, the quality circles conduct annual reviews of their work as a part of the on-going school improvement process.

All along, the Amy Beverland school family has shared what they were learning and doing as the changes unfolded. From secretary to bus driver to parent to business partners, the Lifelong Guidelines and LIFESKILLS are part of daily living and talking. Each role group involved with the school has the chance to learn about what the school is doing so that they can become an active part. For many of these individuals, Kovalik's Lifelong Guidelines and LIFESKILLS are a shared part of daily life. Monthly "spirit days" invite students, staff, and parents to wear any combination of blue, green, white, stars, and smiles as a reflection of their commitment to the Lifelong Guidelines. Members of the Amy Beverland school family are not ranked by someone's perception of status. One of their core beliefs is, "Educating everyone takes everyone!"

The results can't be overstated. The students see that every adult role is as vital as every other, and thus their role as students is vital to Amy Beverland's success, too. The teachers feel valuable and appreciated because they are empowered to make choices and decisions about their curriculum, the school's special events, and how the money is spent. The instructional assistants, secretaries, food services personnel, custodians, and bus drivers, feel appreciated and honored by the VIP (Very Important Person) Days that are set aside for each group. On these days, others assume the duties of the persons being recognized while honorees enjoy and long lunch followed by gifts and written tributes of their contributions from students and faculty. Parent volunteers are thanked daily, but their role is specially celebrated at the end of the year when the entire staff hosts a formal candle light dinner for all the volunteers, complete with music, gifts, and entertainment.

Monitoring Progress

The only way to demonstrate that a school continues to get better is to monitor and document progress in systematic ways. At Amy Beverland, each quality circle gathers data to chart progress toward stated goals. These reports, gathered into a booklet, are available to the school board and community members each year. That progress report also becomes a part of the school's Performance Based Assessment documentation required by the State of Indiana. The informative booklet presents a rich description of goals set and the methods used to achieve them. Several kinds of test data combine with a broad list of staff development experiences and countless other plans carried out by quality circles to describe a school culture that takes on-going growth and self-monitoring very seriously.

At the beginning of each school year, the school publishes to its community the Amy Beverland Elementary School Report Card summarizing the accomplishments and honors attained by students, staff, parents, and community. It is a document that celebrates monitoring progress and the commitment to getting better.

Providing Time and Support

Finally, the change process flourishes at Amy Beverland Elementary because its faculty, staff, and students receive the time and support they need to let go of old ways, identify new patterns, and develop new mental programs to guide their behavior. It's accepted that people will grow and change at their own rates.

For example, teachers come to consensus on schoolwide improvement goals, but have wide latitude to set additional personal goals. Asking for help is the norm and is strongly encouraged, especially when one faces difficulties and feels discouraged. It is safe to fail. Coaching by experienced ITI teachers is provided so that questions and concerns about ITI implementation can be addressed. Teachers can admit that a new strategy didn't feel comfortable, receive advice from a colleague who has used it more often, and go on to practice until it does feel comfortable.

Significant change occurs successfully, or fails to occur at all, for complex reasons. As the Amy Beverland experiences show, the strategies embraced and lived by one school helped to insure that the ITI model worked to benefit both the children and the adults.

Sustaining Systemic Change Over Time

It is fairly common to read of this or that innovation making a splash in a school, perhaps earning extensive media coverage, only to watch it subsequently fall into oblivion. The innovation may have been grounded in research, may have supported community beliefs and goals, may have created excitement initially, may even have been a genuinely positive change. None of those attributes guarantees that an innovation will survive past birth into adolescence, let alone reach maturity. So, what did the people at Amy Beverland Elementary do to make sure that after seven years of effort, people would continue to strive for improvement? The critical strategies for this school include:

- Training and re-training
- Communicating and more communicating
- Selecting new staff based on clear criteria
- Orienting new staff and students
- Holding school family celebrations
- Working toward a state of personal and professional balance while remaining sensitive to each individual's differing needs
- Developing a formal process focused on continuous improvement.

The specific ways in which other schools might approach each of these areas will naturally vary. But for Amy Beverland folks, each strategy played a critical role in sustaining motivation, interest toward becoming an even more brain-compatible place to learn and work.

Training and Re-Training

Learning never ends when one models the behaviors of the lifelong learner. We humans naturally love to learn when the learning is meaningful for our lives; so, teachers are excited about understanding the power of brain-compatible learning for themselves and for their students. As one Amy Beverland teacher put it, "This approach brings out individual student strengths, such as the normally shy animal expert in our class. The students validate each others' strengths."

Reflecting on the steps taken to become a brain-compatible school, it's clear that training for staff is always a high priority. Everyone has the chance to be trained to work with the ITI model. Furthermore, everyone has access to coaching so that implementation challenges can be addressed with specific support and advice. Re-training after having worked to implement the approach brings out a deeper level of understanding. With prior experience, teachers hear more and pick up different ideas because they have acquired new patterns and programs to which the information can be connected in a meaningful way. Affirmation that they are indeed making progress increases motivation to continue.

Brain research findings themselves are constantly being updated to incorporate new information, so re-trainings also bring the most current knowledge and the corresponding classroom applications to the teachers.

Communicating and More Communicating

Rumors, gossip, and misinformation are the enemies of systemic change. The antidote is heavy doses of communication to ensure that people are immunized with accurate knowledge.

Using agreed-upon procedures and sharing expectations of one another in specific and open ways leads to agreements about communication as well. For example, the Amy Beverland staff have agreed on ground rules for dealing with conflict. The first response is simply to let go of the problem. If that is not warranted or possible, the next step is to go directly to the person or team involved and openly address the concern. An alternative to direct confrontation is to seek assistance from the principal. The principal gives advice or facilitates mediation, if requested. The point is that at this school it is not acceptable behavior to talk about others and situations in a negative way. Building and maintaining positive relationships is a high priority.

A powerful tool to promote daily connections among staff is the "Elementary Energizer." Everyone looks for the bright yellow "Energizer" in mailboxes each day and depends on it for getting essential information.

All may contribute announcements of upcoming meetings, changes in the routine schedule, special events, opportunities, and the like. The principal also contributes information about district level needs or events.

Adding New Staff

The reader might be tempted to credit the strong sense of community and uniform focus on the mission largely to the fact that teachers sharing a similar philosophy of education were selected to open the school. That would be a correct assessment of the early years, and is undeniably an advantage for anyone building organizational culture. However, within the first four years, Amy Beverland grew from a school of about 400 students to one of over 900. Without strong attention to the way in which new staff was chosen, the initial advantage would have quickly disappeared!

The existing staff and the administration choose the new staff members from the principal's talent pool of possible candidates. For all on the talent pool list, she has made at least one personal contact and has reviewed background and qualifications. These individuals **must** be caring toward others, able to make a commitment to goals beyond personal ones, and possess a strong work ethic.

When an opening occurs, the principal calls for volunteers from staff and parents to serve on interview teams. All who are interested can serve on at least one interview team. The best candidates from the pool receive a letter about the position that also provides information about the school, informs them about the interview process, and invites them to an interview. In addition, candidates prepare a written response to one of several school situations describing how they would be likely to handle it. The principal prepares interview questions and folders with pertinent information for each interview team member.

Arriving early on the day of the interviews, the principal orients the team by sharing interviewing tips and the areas to be avoided from a legal standpoint. The team then conducts the interviews. Afterward they choose to discuss the candidates or to provide feedback in written form. Finally, the team ranks the candidates and all information goes to the principal for her input. The finalists are invited to return to the school to meet with the grade level team with whom they would be colleagues if chosen. Based on the results of that meeting and comments from each candidate's references, the principal makes the final selection. In this example, effective teamwork among the administrator, teachers, and parents produced excellent new staff choices. As Susan Brash says, "Teamwork is the only non-negotiable."

Orienting New Staff and Students

A variety of formal and informal events bring newcomers into the Amy Beverland family. Almost half of the professional and support staff at Amy Beverland Elementary today were **not** part of the school at the time it opened. Rapid growth has resulted in annual additions to the staff. Although carefully chosen to be in tune with the school philosophically, they have had little or no training in the ITI model.

When hired, each new person understands the expectation and commits to attend the summer institute that provides a week of training in the ITI model. See the description under "Year Two" in this chapter. When the teacher is hired after the June institute, everyone pitches in to assist him/her in creating the classroom decoration and furniture arrangements conducive to brain-compatible learning.

The principal also meets with the new teachers to be sure they understand the Lifelong Guidelines and LIFESKILLS and their role in creating a threat-free learning environment. She places a top priority on building relationships with students, parents, other school staff, and community persons. The principal clearly states that the person is **not** expected to integrate curriculum using a yearlong theme during the first or even the second year of working with the ITI model. She protects new people from extra school-wide responsibilities, respecting the energy and attention required to grasp the patterns and mental programs inherent in implementing ITI effectively.

To capitalize on teacher-to-teacher learning, Susan Brash assigns each new teacher a mentor. She seeks a match based on addressing the apparent needs of the newcomer through the known strengths of the mentor. She meets with each of the new teachers and their mentors to ask specific questions such as, "What are you doing to prepare for the upcoming parent night?" Such exchanges give the principal a chance to get specific information while also assessing the appropriateness of the match.

A mobile and rapidly growing student population creates a need for on-going student orientation as well. Although the majority of new student orientation takes place within the classroom, some administrative attention is also needed. A Student Support Specialist (trained in counseling) meets every week for one month with a "Lunch Bunch" comprised of students who joined the Amy Beverland family the prior month. She asks students about their feelings toward their classroom, the curriculum, and various schoolwide beliefs. She then arranges for any additional support that the new children need to feel "significant and appreciated," as stated in the school's mission.

Holding Celebrations

School-wide celebrations focus attention on what's important and nurture the sense of family and community. Several specific examples illustrate how this works for Amy Beverland Elementary.

Each school year features a new schoolwide theme. For the 1995-1996 year the theme, "Celebrating Our Tapestry of Talents," helped pull everyone together to affirm aspects of the school's climate, culture, and curriculum. The theme affirms what is working, and helps to sustain motivation at high levels. In the case of the tapestry theme, the staff began the year celebrating the power of differences in the multiple intelligences that students and adults bring with them to the school. The theme underscores the school's belief that as talents are celebrated throughout the year, those talents will become more effective for learning. They celebrate—and create—a self-fulfilling prophecy. Celebrations take on a variety of forms:

- "Round-ups" can be called by any staff member for after school and are for the purpose of sharing something exciting or asking for help addressing a serious need.

- "M&M³," or Marvelous and Motivational Monday Meetings, are held once a month for all staff. Since the "Energizer" communicates all one-way information, the "M&M³" days are valued for school family meetings. Topics range from pragmatic issues such as a crisis intervention program to "Tantalizing Teacher Tips" and "Win with Wellness." Refreshments, inclusion activities, music, surprises, and meaningful content are regular ingredients in "M&M³" days as the staff continues its commitment to model brain-compatibility.

- A monthly staff breakfast celebrates birthdays.

- Faculty retirement receptions celebrate careers dedicated to enriching the lives of children.

- The Parent/Partner Appreciation Dinners treat volunteers to an elegant evening.

- Student celebrations include classroom attendance recognition, lunch with the principal, and a Rainbow of Rewards that honors academic excellence, musicians, artists, creative expressionists, fitness, and LIFESKILL accomplishments.

Initially, the principal struggled to help others understand the importance of taking time and spending money to celebrate. The issue of balance is always present as the Student Services Quality Circle plans for student celebrations and the Wellness Quality Circle plans for adult celebrations. Today, though, the system for planning celebrations is working so well that the principal is not directly involved.

Celebrations, although well-planned, are not necessarily elaborate or expensive. Their aim is to strengthen the culture and climate of the school.

Developing a Formal Process for Continuous Improvement

Recall a central school belief, "As good as we are, we can always get better!" So strongly does Susan Brash believe this that she has established a formal process to ensure that planning and actions focus on continuous improvement. As a result, several formalized groups periodically assess needs and interests of stakeholders, create specific plans to move the school toward its ideal vision of itself, act on the plans, study results, and begin the cycle again. Those groups are:

- School Improvement Planning Team (SIPT)
- Quality Circles
- Grade Level Teams
- Amy Beverland Family Association.

Refer to Figure 4.1 for a visual representation of how the various structures are a part of the whole and are grounded in the school's mission statement.

Team-based leadership is the term that Susan Brash and her staff use to describe how they make decisions and run the school. Leadership is truly a shared responsibility. In some areas, the principal retains primary responsibility. An example is the evaluation of teacher performance described in chapter eleven, "Systemic Change and Assessment." Most functions related to the school's goal of continuous improvement, however, are handled by the Quality Circles and the grade level teams.

By the school's second year, five quality circles had emerged as the most essential for becoming a brain-compatible school:

1. Student Services
2. Staff Development
3. Curriculum Enrichment
4. Curriculum Coordination
5. Wellness.

As illustrated in Figure 4.1, the various groups interact to provide leadership. For example, annual goal statements developed by the School Improvement Planning Team are given to the appropriate Quality Circle. Members of the circle do the creative work of listing the exact strategies to be used to accomplish the goal or goals. At monthly meetings, the circle fine tunes plans and discusses what has been accomplished since the last meeting. Each quality circle reports regularly to the School Improvement Planning Team (SIPT). At the end of each school year, the circles document what was achieved in each goal area.

Figure 4.1 _____

Leadership for Continuous Improvement
Amy Beverland Elementary School

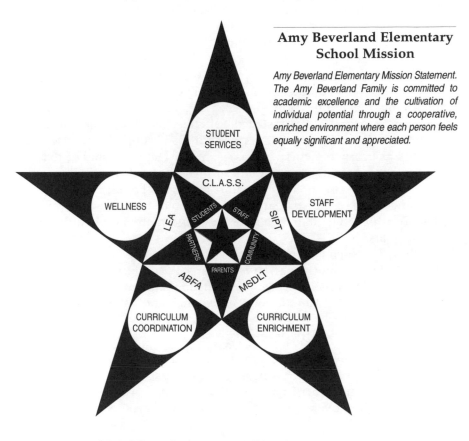

Amy Beverland Elementary School Mission

Amy Beverland Elementary Mission Statement. The Amy Beverland Family is committed to academic excellence and the cultivation of individual potential through a cooperative, enriched environment where each person feels equally significant and appreciated.

C.L.A.S.S.	State supported ITI project
SIPT	School Improvement Planning Team
MSDLT	Metropolitan School District of Lawrence Township
ABFA	Amy Beverland Family Association
LEA	Lawrence Education Association

The regular assessment of needs and interests informs the work of the SIPT in creating or affirming the proposed goals for the subsequent school year. All parties provide input for the creation of goals for the new school year.

Finally, the details of the goal-setting and action-planning processes are reported in the annual School Action Plan that paints the exciting overall picture of what students and adults achieved for the present school year and hope to achieve in the coming one.

The principal's perspective on the process is important to understand. Susan Brash doesn't enter into the work with the SIPT and Quality Circles with a desired outcome in mind. The work is about realizing the school's mission, **not** the principal's own agenda. Rather than the agenda setter, the principal is the instructional cheerleader and servant leader. She defines her primary role as providing of support and removing obstacles as everyone works on his/her part. Her role could be to bring in additional training; it could mean providing release time; it could mean raising money; it could mean re-doing a schedule; it could mean realigning some of the staff support; or it could mean new roles and/or rules. Brash has facilitated each of these and more based on the needs and the goals.

Whew! In such a busy and ambitious setting the hazard of running out of energy and motivation must be constantly considered as the pace is set. Those responsible for providing leadership must remain vigilant and sensitive to the human need for balance and variety while implementing ITI. Balance is addressed in several ways that could suggest strategies for others to try or modify:

1. Consider the whole person, and each individual's personal needs for growth. If a teacher believes a particular workshop will address those personal growth needs, and it is related in some way to the overall mission, the principal tries to arrange for the individual's participation.

2. As an administrator, use the same techniques you want teachers to use with their classes where appropriate. Be vulnerable and do this even if you must admit that using a different technique feels a bit awkward at first.

3. Create the opportunity to fail safely. Use failure as a roadmap for growth.

4. Develop realistic procedures for handling difficult-to-hear feedback about one's professional performance. Does it fit? If not, let it go. If it does, use it to improve.

5. Make wellness a part of the formal process, as seen at this school in the Wellness Quality Circle charged with enhancing and monitoring the health of the school and staff.

6. Recognize as a high priority the parenting done by staff. At ABE, staff members are always released to attend an event involving their own child at another school during the work day. The message to staff? That parent involvement in a child's learning is essential for the child to be as successful as he or she might be.

Conclusion

It takes hard work and collaborative effort by all involved to create a brain-compatible elementary school. Starting with a similar set of beliefs is only the beginning, because the school will be constantly changing as the context and students and families served changes. Systematic planning and team-based leadership have not been left to chance at Amy Beverland. They are built into the life of the school. The culture and climate to support humans as they embark on systemic change must be created thoughtfully and nurtured with intention. Once the seeds of change are planted and spring to life, the demanding challenges of nurturing them begins. Any principal or leader who starts over in an existing school or helps to open a new school must be willing to ask for help on a regular basis. There is too much for even the most gifted leader to take on independently. Through the synergy of collaboration, many can accomplish what one or a few cannot.

V

Creating a Brain-Compatible Secondary School

by Marilyn P. Kelly and Geraldine Rosemurgy

> *If you want to change teachers' behaviors, you must change their materials, their practices, their daily routines, and the fundamental beliefs they have about children, about learning, about teaching, and about knowledge.*
>
> Larry Cuban
> 1996 ACSA Superintendent's Symposium

Introduction

The high school basketball coach in our district believes that it is his job to share all of his experience, knowledge, and enthusiasm with his players. Even though he knows more about basketball than any of his players, he understands that he will never score a basket, make a rebound, or steal a ball during a game. His success comes from preparing his players to be successful. He tries to identify what it will take to improve their individual skills and what he will need to do to make them each better team members. Each year he has a different team and he has to start over. Some years he has more talented players than others. But regardless, his success is measured each year by his ability to take the players he is given and help them win games. It is probably no surprise that his program is now the envy of the countywide basketball league. He has taken the program farther in championship play than any coach in the history of the high school.

The leader of change must use the same skills as the coach if she wants to develop a winning team. She must embrace the role of leader of instructional leaders focusing on how to directly support teachers, students, and parents. Such a leader must be allowed to spend major portions of her time being present throughout the school, sharing the culture and vision, seeing first hand the problems of the school, and interpreting the vision.

In this chapter we'll share how we helped one middle school to implement brain-compatible strategies.

School Background

Several years ago Altimira Intermediate School was a "mini high school" of 7th and 8th graders that many of us would recognize from our own experiences as students. Students were grouped according to skill levels and changed classes each period. Teachers were organized by curriculum departments.

When the school board took action in 1988 to restructure Altimira into a 6-8 middle school, a planning cycle was born. To kick off this effort, the board recruited over 100 parents, staff, students, administrators, and community members to diagnose the pressing issues for student learning at Altimira. Three common threads emerged: 1) the relevancy of the curriculum, 2) the lack of student connection to the school, and 3) the need for more ties between the school and the community.

The traditional measures of school success failed to provide an accurate reflection of the actual situation. For example, although standardized test scores had been improving dramatically, conversations with all role groups in the school revealed many serious concerns about teaching and learning.

The group also found that staff, students, parents, and community persons had problems communicating with one another. True, a high percentage of parents and students participated in student orientation, open house, back-to-school night, parent conferences, and graduation. However, each group felt estranged from the school, or resentful.

Many parents felt that no one listened to them. They weren't sure what the school wanted them to do, and they didn't know how to operate in the school system to get information and desired results. They were usually contacted only when the school wanted money, volunteer support, or to report problems with their children.

Many teachers believed that parents didn't support them when they tried to hold students to high personal and academic standards, and they felt threatened by the proposed changes.

Community members saw too many of the school's graduates unprepared for high school. Not only did students fail to apply what they had learned in 7th and 8th grade, some said they had never learned some of those essential skills in the first place.

Students were unhappy as well, and many said they felt powerless. A general malaise seemed to stifle student pride in work and love of learning. They perceived their school work to be boring and meaningless. They reported it wasn't safe to disagree with teachers. They saw peers needing extra help but failing to get it. The discipline policy didn't work for them.

The principal was at the top of the school hierarchy. Most people said that she listened to them, and treated them humanely—but still, they added, it was clear that she controlled the organization. Parent participation in issues related to curriculum programs was minimal.

The school board mandate to convert Altimira from a 7-8 intermediate school with 600 students to a 6-8 middle school with 1000 students became the impetus propelling the entire organization toward systemic change. Although we changed the name to Altimira Middle School nearly immediately—a clear message that new education practices were going to occur—we knew that every group involved with the organization had to be involved in bringing about fundamental changes at the center rather than superficial changes around the edges. We talked about "turning our school upside down."

The changes weren't to happen overnight. Indeed, for the next two years, the staff set about to study and analyze the best ideas we could find, both in written form and from people active in the education field. We perused such seminal works as *Caught in the Middle*, published by the state of California in 1987, to name but one (CA. Department of Education 1987). The result was a complete transformation of Altimira.

One of the most important changes was in how students were grouped—heterogeneously, into teams or "families" of 150 that shared four core academic teachers in mixed ability classrooms. Each team selected an adult leader to meet weekly with other team leaders, office staff, counselors, and administrators to confront problems and to share program successes and failures.

Teachers still had support from curriculum departments, and as part of a quartet of teachers could work out steps toward integrated curriculum as well as concerns about "their kids."

Using this weekly meeting of leaders, our school had moved from hierarchical to collaborative decision-making. Team leaders were a conduit to the total staff, both imparting and receiving information.

Parents also had more meaningful access to the total school system. Teachers began to call parents or to write notes regularly "just to check in," and the school developed a school outreach problem that included parenting classes, a weekly bulletin of school events, and homework hot-lines that allowed parents to monitor class assignments on a regular basis. In addition, the Steering Committee, a decision-making group of parents and staff, was formed. Parents became more actively involved in program and curriculum design, along with other decisions, thus increasing their meaningful partnership within the school.

As in any endeavor, luck sometimes plays as big a role as planning. While writing a school restructuring grant, administrators and members of the staff attended a workshop to broaden our outlook on the subject. One focus of the workshop was current advances in brain research and creating a brain-compatible environment using Susan Kovalik's ITI model (Ross and Olsen 1995) to enhance student learning.

The information on brain research was a major "aha" for us. It provided a rich, integrated, comprehensive framework for the planning process and we scrambled to educate ourselves further. This investigation led us to the very core of how humans learn. It made sense to us that just as a heart surgeon needs to understand how a heart works, a teacher must understand how the brain functions. From that moment on, brain research and the elements of a brain-compatible environment, were the lenses we used to screen the myriad of ideas and proposals being considered. This commitment to brain-compatible learning became the foundation upon which all our programs were built.

As any good coach or leader knows, it is important to lead by example. It was clear to us from the very beginning that brain-compatible elements were as important to practice as a staff as they were to successful student learning. It made sense as well, that these elements should be applied to create a brain-compatible organization and that they should be used now as the framework to reflect upon what worked and what didn't work in implementing brain-compatible strategies using ITI at Altimira Middle School.

Absence of Threat

A critical role for the leader is to monitor and influence the environment inside and outside the school. She must try to find the balance between research and local values and norms. She must help the school to develop a clear vision of what it is trying to accomplish and then communicate that vision to the wider community in order to engender support and obtain additional resources to support the vision.

One of Altimira's first tasks was to develop a formal mission statement with parents, staff, and community members. It reads: *Altimira values its students and is committed to helping them achieve their social, emotional, academic, and physical potential in a safe, nurturing environment.* Informally, this statement soon came to mean, "doing what's best for kids."

How to do that, however, is where the disagreements arose. It is important to remember that there is no "one size fits all" in school reform or in addressing diverse student needs and talents. It is critical to create an environment in which diverse perspectives can exist and the leader can demonstrate tolerance and patience while the organization undergoes change.

For example, one of the recommendations in *Caught in the Middle* was to schedule advisory periods for students. However, our teaching staff was overwhelmingly against taking time from the instructional day for such an advisory period. They did, however, strongly support the concept of providing meaningful adult relationships with kids. Instead of an advisory program, we decided to allow teams to develop strategies to provide these adult relationships with kids that better matched their personal teaching styles.

At the same time, the principal looked at ways to develop more counseling time through the reorganization of the master schedule. An "Alternate Day" in-school suspension program was also instituted to keep kids in school when suspended from the regular program for misbehavior. The principal had to work with the district to enable a classified staff member to monitor the Alternate Day setting as part of the campus supervision program. As part of the Alternate Day program, staff spends part of the day on one-to-one interaction with students.

In addition, a specialized study skills class was formed for students at-risk of failing academically. Students were assigned to participate in lieu of one of their other classes. The teacher took time to build a respectful relationship with each student while also developing the study skills vital for school success. The result is that these alternatives have worked because, instead of forcing the advisory period into the school day, the staff discovered alternate ways to reach the goal and create a meaningful relationship for each student with at least one adult.

Taking a hard look at all facets of a school can be threatening to teachers. It is vital that the leader ensure an environment in which teachers are free to learn, create, and fail. As new ideas are tried, the leader must be constantly vigilant to create a "buffer" to allow for programs to fully mature. She must also understand the local school board and the district office and manage the external politics associated with change. No matter what change is being considered, some staff, parents, or community members will resist. At the same time, the organization must be open enough to hear when changes are not working and to tolerate failure so that it can learn and then move on.

During the change process, we began using a term called "fast failures" to encourage staff and parents to communicate when something wasn't working so that it could be modified or changed quickly. As an example, Altimira had originally scheduled team planning time on Monday mornings. While teachers were meeting, parents and community members planned to run the school's enrichment program. It was clear after only a month that the plan was not working. Volunteers were inconsistent and students preferred to hang out in common areas rather than take an enrichment class. Thus, as quickly as possible the student and bus schedules were rearranged to allow for students to be released early on Wednesday afternoons so that teachers could use that time instead for planning. This continuous monitoring and adjusting kept the school in a constant state of fluctuation for the first year.

Change is difficult. If, as Larry Cuban says, the way to effect change is to change the "fundamental beliefs they (teachers) have about children, about learning, about teaching, and about knowledge," then the leader must provide a safe environment in which to do so (Cuban 1996). Challenging the staff's beliefs about themselves will create conflict as each member of the school community brings his/her own biases and beliefs to the change process. Staff members who have been friends for years may suddenly find themselves on opposite sides of issues. Problems or resentments that have been buried for years may come bubbling to the surface.

The first year of implementation at Altimira is now rather affectionately remembered by the staff as "The Year From Hell." At the time, however, feelings were not affectionate. Emotions ran high as people struggled to implement new practices and new school structures. Virtually every system had been revamped to develop the new middle school program. The ripple effect on systems like bus schedules or printing report cards for trimesters in a semester district created daily snafus. A six period schedule in 7th and 8th grade and a seven period schedule in 6th grade meant that scheduling every rally, every student activity, or even the annual magazine sale had to be rethought.

All of these details were stressful for the staff, so as a response, the Team Leaders began meeting weekly for an hour to resolve the day-to-day problems. This provided an immediate forum for raising issues and voicing concerns for all staff. Today, the Team Leaders' meetings have become an institutionalized part of school governance. This forum gives staff a safe place to raise issues while they are trying out new ideas and programs.

Absence of threat also enhances staff creativity. Two examples come to mind. Altimira's students are primarily bused to one campus from throughout a fairly large, rural valley. Many times the buses ran late and the office would be filled with students trying to get late passes. At the end of the day there were 15 minutes between the last bell and the departure of the buses, which allowed plenty of time for students to begin to get into trouble. The creative solution, once we knew the transportation times couldn't be changed, was to simply set the clocks ahead by five minutes! Suddenly most of the late students were on time in the morning, the office situation improved, and students quickly realized that they needed to move promptly into position at the end of the day or risk missing the bus.

Another example of creativity was the decision to eliminate bells. In the past there was a highly evolved system of tardies with a series of consequences. Much instructional, administrative, and secretarial time was wasted on this process. However, assigning teacher teams to classrooms that were physically located next to one another and eliminating bells helped resolve this problem. Teachers within teams communicated directly with one another about schedule adjustments. A calmness on the campus also resulted in a much more collegial atmosphere. The only bells needed were those to start and end the day, to signal break, and to mark lunch period. Naturally, there were a few raised eyebrows throughout the district when these solutions were implemented, but because staff was able to think safely in nontraditional ways, the solutions worked.

The leader must understand that conflict is inherent in the change process and that it will be her responsibility to confront and help to resolve these conflicts. This can be very lonely and exhausting, as much of the anger and frustration is often focused on the leader of change. It requires personal stamina and the strength to remain the observer and facilitator of the process instead of getting sucked into the conflict. We recommend that the leader develop a small external support group, whether it be family, other professionals, or friends, who can offer positive support during all of the conflict surrounding significant change.

Meaningful Content

"Relevant, meaningful content which is tied to real-life experience increases the effectiveness of the learning experience" (Kovalik 1994). Remember that basketball coach? He had to know each of his players well enough to be able to provide them with the skills that they needed. And so it is with the leader of change. At Altimira the principal would sit down periodically and think about staff members. Where were they regarding changes? What were their concerns? What kind of support did they need? Was it personal or professional? Who were the leaders, the followers, or the resistors? Who needed a pat on the back? Who needed a nudge forward?

This understanding of the individuals and the organization allowed the leader to develop strategies to meet the various needs of the entire school community. It is our belief that schools are highly symbolic organizations which reflect our most deeply held beliefs about ourselves and our communities. Using symbols is an effective way to meet organizational needs. One strategy the principal at Altimira used was to select a theme prior to the beginning of each year based on her evaluation of where the staff was overall in its change process. The "kick off" for the theme occurred at the yearly two-day staff retreat held prior to the beginning of school. The principal used themes to spark ideas for team building and staff development activities.

In the second planning year the theme was "Blasting Off to Middle School," using the idea of beginning a trip or a journey as a symbol. At the retreat, the staff analyzed taking a trip into space. What would we each pack? What would we leave behind? What would this adventure feel like? Would it be exciting, frightening, or scary? What would we end up wishing that we had brought along? What surprises would we encounter?

The principal used the metaphor of pruning a rose. Each winter a gardener must sometimes prune healthy vibrant wood, even a rose, for the bush to survive and bloom in the spring. We then developed a "keep and prune" list of those things that we felt were absolutely essential to keep on our journey from junior high to middle school, and those things that could be left behind. As part of ending the retreat, each of us then pruned a rose bush and planted it on campus as a symbol of what was left behind and what would continue to grow.

Each year the theme built upon that of the previous year. In the first implementation year, (the year from hell), the theme was "Sticking Our Necks Out For Kids," with a giraffe as the symbol. A safari setting provided the backdrop for thinking about risk taking.

In the second year, the theme was "Pulling Together" and the symbol was a train in the spirit of *The Little Engine That Could.* Many of the day-to-day systems were in place, and adjustments in planning had been made. People were feeling a little more comfortable since everything was no longer new and they were able to begin refining their practices. "Pulling Together" placed our professional relationships at the center as we reconnected with each other.

In the third year the theme was "Focus on Excellence," with the symbol of a camera with frames of film spilling out where the space ship, the giraffe, and the train could be seen. By this time the systemic changes were becoming institutionalized and staff was ready to move to higher levels of application of brain theory and brain compatibility.

Throughout the year, staff, parents, and community members were reminded of the annual theme. The principal created posters, banners, tee shirts, and note cards. Sometimes it could be as simple as a note saying, "Thanks for sticking your neck out for kids when you organized the fundraising for the sixth grade Outdoor Education Program." Activities at staff meetings throughout the year reinforced the theme.

The theme was also actively used at public meetings, drawing examples from current experience. To illustrate, an introduction to parents about survey results during the "Focus on Excellence" year began, "In response to parent interest, Altimira is currently 'Focusing on Excellence.'" The intent was to continually remind the school community of the year's goals so that they could better understand the change process and learn from it. It was our way of providing meaningful content to the tasks at hand.

Choices

Believing that "humans learn best when they are able to select the ways in which they problem-solve and create products" (Kovalik 1994), then a variety of opportunities for staff growth are essential. During the planning process, some staff and parents visited other schools, attended workshops, and sat in on typical classes. Experts on diverse topics spoke to a variety of school audiences. Staff members were encouraged to develop their knowledge and skills and become "staff experts" in areas of interest. The staff development budget allowed people to select the type and style of training experience that each needed.

One year, for example, several staff members attended the ITI training at Granlibakken Resort at Lake Tahoe during the summer. This helped us see the need for and arrange monthly visits for an ITI coach obtained from Susan Kovalik & Associates. Through this coaching, which we consider to be an essential element of success, individuals and teams had the choice of observation with feedback, demonstration lessons, or guidance in curriculum development.

As each new change was discussed, the staff and leadership continually asked ourselves, "What will it take to make this work?" or, "What support will staff need if they are expected to implement this strategy effectively?" In this environment staff members were freed from thinking that "nothing will ever come from the planning" because it was clear that changes were going to happen and that staff would have access to varied types of support.

In the second year, the staff developed a new choice for students and parents. We formed a multi-grade team open to 6th, 7th, and 8th graders that came to be known as the Integrated Core option. Its teachers were interested in an in-depth focus on integrated curriculum using the ITI model. Families could select this team or the regular program of interdisciplinary teams at the different grade levels for their child's placement. On the multi-grade team, students who learned best from a primarily project-oriented, demonstration style environment thrived on the opportunity to learn outside of the traditional system. On the other hand, students who needed more structure benefited from the interdisciplinary teams where brain-compatible strategies and interdisciplinary, thematic units were primary tools.

Adequate Time

To plan and implement systemic change, adequate time must be allowed. Teachers need time to think, to explore, and to create. They need time to consider alternatives and to develop implementation strategies. They need time for training and for curriculum development. Altimira's principal made clear to the district and the school board that resources must be made available for purchasing new materials, conducting research, and providing released time for teachers to think and to plan.

She received the needed support, and set in place ITI training over a three-year period. And over the years, new staff members complete the training prior to the beginning of school.

The support for adequate time is evident in other areas. During the summers, extra pay for curriculum development is provided so that staff can create or refine curriculum for the next school year. Released time is also provided during the year for each team to work on curriculum priorities.

The principal herself must also have adequate time to plan for major change. The Altimira principal lobbied the district for additional help. She knew that there was not adequate time in her day to continue to run the school and plan a major reorganization at the same time. Instead of simply reorganizing existing personnel or adding tasks to people who already had full-time jobs, one person was added to focus solely on planning. The principal also took advantage of slowed growth in the district. When the enrollment figures in district elementary schools stabilized after the first year of planning, she delayed the implementation for another year so that the staff could plan changes in more detail. "Go slow to go fast" became a mantra at the school.

Team planning time was a recognized priority from the onset. To meet this need, the student's school week was reorganized so that four days of the week were longer and one day was shorter. A two-hour block of time was created for curriculum planning, team activity development, discussion of student needs, and contacting parents. This reorganized week is now so valued that it has been adopted K-8 in the district as a way to allow teachers time to plan together.

Enriched Environment

An enriched environment provides the physical resources and information needed to solve problems effectively. It helps individuals to "see connections between things, observe subtle similarities and differences, use metaphors that are useful in understanding how things work and how they can be used in new settings or for new purposes" (Kovalik 1994, 82).

We realized from the beginning that we must focus every available resource on our new priorities. One key element in managing this change has been to provide all staff, interested parents, and community members with the best information and research available on every issue. We established a staff/parent research library. We provided copies of the most important books and documents to every team. One major concern of teachers was that the team concept would dilute curriculum expertise. In a departure from common middle school practice, the school decided to have curriculum departments and teams at the same time. Department chairs would be subject area leaders and trainers, while team leaders would focus on team planning and school-wide issues. Budgets were expanded to provide stipends for both leadership positions and money to support team and department activity. In addition to weekly team meetings, teachers continued to meet regularly in their departments to develop their curriculum expertise.

Much time and effort targeted effective communication with staff and parents as planning continued. Staff newsletters and Team Leader minutes contained the day-to-day, nuts and bolts information previously reserved for staff meetings so that these meetings could focus instead on issues that affected all staff, and new ideas. The staff meeting became a place to share successes and failures. In return, staff agreed to be accountable for the printed information. A running agenda for Team Leader meetings was posted in the staff conference room so that any member of the staff could place an item on the agenda. Minutes were distributed to staff promptly so everyone was updated on the policy and program decisions.

Clear, prompt communication with parents was also a priority. It was closely aligned with the need to define the parents' roles. The overall purpose for defining the role of the parent in the school was to recognize the fact that the school needs to be responsive in a real way to what it can do for parents, instead of always asking them to do things for the school. The parent newsletter was changed from a quarterly letter to a weekly update to inform them quickly about events and schedule changes while also educating them about middle school practices. Meetings and parent conferences were changed to consider the needs of working parents in an attempt to re-engage those parents who had lost interest or who were feeling isolated or unimportant to the life of the school. Opportunities were expanded for parent involvement in curriculum planning through the Steering Committee, a joint parent-staff group, which served as the middle school experts and "think tank" for the school. This group was responsible for all middle school program recommendations and played an active role in leading the school through the change process.

Collaboration

Since the organizational changes at Altimira have been so comprehensive, it has taken time and positive experiences to transform the culture of our school. An atmosphere of trust is beginning to develop since the school community has been trained and participates in decision-making through a consensus-building approach. The consensus model of decision-making is one of the single most important factors in the successful implementation of changes at Altimira. It has had an enormous impact in the way people feel about newly implemented programs and practices. Instead of conflict and turmoil, we are now experiencing less resistance to new ideas. People trust that they will have a meaningful voice in innovations and that changes will not be made for the sake of change or to punish someone, but rather to create a better school for student learning.

Staff are most productive in organizations when they are free to think and to effect changes. People need to feel that they have choices that can influence the direction of their work. We can address more of the human needs of members of our school as a result of the consensus processes employed. Veteran teachers are now re-energized, growing, and stretching in ways that they could not have imagined several years ago. At our school it means that innovation and creativity are now welcomed and celebrated. It also means that, although individuals may not have been actively involved in choosing the "what" of decisions made, they will have the professional freedom to choose "how" the decisions are to be implemented as long as they honor the consensus decisions.

The school's redefined culture has fundamentally changed how problems are solved, how decisions are made, and how people are treated. After the first year of implementation it was clear that two different schedules for 6th, 7th and 8th grades were making everyone crazy. However, the sixth grade teachers loved their seven-period day because it allowed time for a transitions class for sixth graders. The 7th and 8th grade teachers liked the six-period day because it allowed more class time and they felt it better met the "adequate time" needs of 7th and 8th graders. Twenty-eight staff members elected to participate in a consensus group to find a solution. After days of meetings they decided that the school would share a six period day schedule. However, the consensus process that teachers experienced, where all concerns were heard and considered, allowed them to find a solution that was best for the school. After this one major experience, it no longer was necessary for everyone to participate personally in future group issues. It was clear to staff members that there were ways they could make their interests known and they were confident that their concerns would be genuinely considered and incorporated into the solution. The consensus model became such an important part of staff life at Altimira that all new staff members are now also trained in the consensus model based on interest-based bargaining principles.

The consensus process also helped to guard against "group think." It allowed everyone's interests and concerns to be heard and it forced a group to consider every concern. This was particularly important after a few years of using the consensus model. It was becoming too easy to reach consensus because we had become too like-minded. We made a conscious effort to include new staff members or parents into issue groups, particularly if they felt strongly against a proposal. Involving those with different view points forced groups to consider ideas to which they might otherwise be blind. In the beginning, this was a bit of a struggle. After the "year from hell," staff welcomed a little smooth sailing and they were not anxious to consciously invite criticism. The commitment to seeking diverse views has, however, truly improved the quality of the decisions being made.

Immediate Feedback

Learners of all ages need to receive constant information and feedback in order to update continuously and modify decisions in the process of problem-solving. Because we had undertaken such comprehensive change, we needed a formal way to monitor the success of different programs. We were interested in having reliable feedback to guide our decision-making instead of primarily responding to loud, vocal critics. One way we constantly monitored the school was to periodically ask staff, parents and students to give us feedback on "What's working?" and "What's not working?" This allowed us to hear about brewing problems before they could become full storms.

The Steering Committee also recommended a formal survey of all students and parents to gather statistical data upon which the school could rely. Surveys would also provide a way to compare progress throughout the years. The survey, developed by staff and parents, tested many of the concerns that had been voiced during the planning process. Did students feel safe at our school? Were they being challenged in each of the subject areas? Did students and parents feel welcome? Did they know where to get assistance? How responsive were the office staff, administration, and nurses?

Two skilled and trustworthy parent volunteers tabulated results by team, grade level, gender, and student classifications such as GATE, high-achieving, special education, bilingual, and low-achieving. In the first year over 85% of students and 58% of the parents participated in the survey. (The student survey was conducted in language arts classes.) Ninth grade students and teaching staff at the high school were also surveyed to determine if students were prepared in a variety of ways for high school.

This annual survey has become integral to assessing the progress of the school. Initial results told us there was widespread support for the direction of change at Altimira.

Each year, however, prior to the survey being conducted, the anxiety level among teachers perceptibly rises. There is always the natural human fear that the results will be negative followed by a sigh of relief when the results come in. Altimira regularly receives approval ratings averaging over 85% and considers anything below an 80% approval rating as a demand for thoughtful attention. For example, one year 85% of students indicated that they felt safe at school. However, many of the bilingual students in the 7th and 8th grades reported not feeling safe at school. These data allowed the staff and parents to further investigate and resolve the problems for this specific group.

We have also been able to use the results of the annual survey as a public relations tool. For example, if someone says, "Those kids at Altimira are having a really hard time in math at the high school," the principal can document that students and teachers at the high school feel that students are prepared for math at that higher level. The survey also validates the teachers' work. They are receiving clear feedback about the perception of quality associated with their work by students, parents, and high school staff. Although the data are reported to the public by grade level, team-by-team data are also confidentially available so that each team can pinpoint individual strengths and weaknesses.

All students participate in the district's nationally-normed tests in reading and math each year. Teachers also use performance assessment strategies such as writing samples. These data are tabulated and compared to identify trends. For example, one year it became clear that students needed more experience in writing. A program of writing was developed in each of the disciplines to ensure that students had increased experience in all of the types of writing required.

Altimira has also received feedback from the state level. In 1991 it was selected as a California SB1274 restructuring school and in 1994 it was recognized as a California Distinguished School. All feedback, both positive and negative, continues to guide on-going changes at Altimira.

Mastery

Joel Barker in *Future Edge* describes three keys for any organization that wants to participate fully in the 21st century: anticipation, innovation, and excellence (Barker 1992). Excellence will be required simply to enter the marketplace. Understanding this has helped Altimira support the high expectations and high standards needed for producing a quality school. We have had to anticipate, innovate, and strive for excellence to create the winning team our community demands.

We believe our "key to excellence" is our teachers, the heart of the school. They are at once the true decision-makers and leaders, as well as the most important link to the community. All planning has been based on a fundamental belief that teachers are good, hard-working people who really care about kids and who have the skills and expertise to be excellent teachers. Just as the coach or the fans may think they know more than anyone about how to win, it is the players, or in this case the teachers who play in the game. They must be treated respectfully if they are to become masters of all of the new programs that they are expected to implement.

The principal must become a master of change. For further reading we suggest *Change Forces* by Michael Fullan (Fullan 1993) and *Managing Transitions* by William Bridges (Bridges 1991) on change; *The Winner Within* by Pat Riley (Riley 1993) on team building and coaching; and *Credibility* by James Kouzes and Barry Posner (Kouzes and Posner 1993) on leadership. True change will put teachers in vulnerable positions. The leader has the ethical responsibility to ensure that the change process won't expose them while they are learning and trying new ideas. The leader must also be a learner and must give up some of the "I am the king, the all-powerful, the all-controlling keeper of the purse strings" attitude. Remember the coach. He will never score a basket or defend against the other team. It is the same with the leader. She will not be the one to implement change; her success will depend on her ability to prepare the staff who do.

It is also the job of the leader to ensure that she becomes a master at coaching and decision-making during the change process. At one point in planning about 80% of the staff had agreed with the proposal to reorganize into teams and it was clear that no amount of information was going to change the opinion of the other 20%. The leader had to take a strong stand and "call the play." She had to decide that teaming was a fundamental program element and that everyone would participate. In addition, she determined that it was important that she form the teacher teams to ensure that they were balanced. This required a fundamental understanding and mastery of the elements of leadership such as when to direct, when to coach, when to support, and when to delegate. Even though Altimira valued collaboration, when the leader determined that strong leadership was required, she acted, rather than allowing 20% of the staff to sabotage the entire planning process. Further, it was a high priority for the principal to remain constantly vigilant throughout implementation to watch for the phenomenon of the vocal few trying to block the will of the majority. She knew from experience that the force of the status quo can become powerful enough to overcome new programs and stifle creativity.

Conclusion

The change process at Altimira was demanding, challenging, and exciting all at the same time. We learned and experienced many things. The ITI brain-compatible elements made a real difference in the success of this middle school. Altimira is not just a better place to work, it has become a better place to learn.

Epilogue

We left Altimira almost five years ago. The principal now serves as superintendent of the same district and her assistant is the district facilities planner. The first principal hired lasted two years. He did not support or practice the ITI brain-compatible elements. The current principal is in her second year. She has been successful in rebuilding the school's brain-compatible environment in a short amount of time. The lesson to be learned is that when a major change process includes brain-compatible elements in a meaningful manner, it can survive in the face of challenges.

Journey to a Brain-Compatible School

by Barbara Pedersen

Remember every journey begins with the first step.

Introduction

Life's journey is one grand learning experience. We learn in a multitude of ways: personal and shared experiences; elementary, secondary, and professional schooling; and perceptions taken in through our senses. We are all different in what we become during our lifetimes—unique individuals. What makes us the same is that we all process information through our brain, the organ for learning.

As a teacher, I became interested very early in how several students could be given the same information and yet each would perceive it differently. I could not create meaning for students; only they could create their own meaning from what I was teaching. At the same time each would gain and understand certain commonalities from the same information. Knowing this, framing education so it was meaningful and useful for all students became a challenge. I know now that understanding how the brain "learns" and adapting teaching techniques to the biology of learning are essential tools to meet this challenge. In this chapter, I share the perspective I have from my visits with hundreds of schools across Indiana as the director of the C.L.A.S.S. (Connecting Learning Assures Successful Students) project.

Thinking About the Journey

Implementing brain-compatible learning is like taking a journey. We must do some preliminary planning:

1. Where do we want to go?

2. Why are we going on this journey?

3. Who will be traveling with us and how do we arouse and sustain the interest of our traveling companions?

4. What do we need to pack for the trip to make our journey a success?

5. How long will the trip take?

Let's discuss each of these questions in greater detail.

1. *Where do we want to go? What is our destination?*

We must envision realistic goals that reflect high expectations such as:

- developing a mind-set for students to want to learn

- creating a pleasing learning environment

- creating cooperative relationships between teacher-student, teacher-teacher, teacher-administrator, and teacher-parent

- knowing and applying basic principles of brain-compatible learning.

Achieving each of these goals in the classroom and school will lead us to achieve our ultimate goal: helping each student to become a well-prepared adult who is able to function in our society as a responsible and productive citizen.

2. *Why are we going?*

We cannot wait any longer for the system to change. All educators have a responsibility to improve the learning process for students if society is going to prosper. Students today deserve an outstanding education based on current brain research. I don't suggest that everything we have done is wrong, but rather that we have new information about the brain that we must use to create outstanding schools.

3. Who are we taking with us, and how do we arouse and sustain the interest of our traveling companions?

The staff, students, parents, and community will join us. But before we can travel together, we must decide that we all want to go to the same place. Some may choose a different route, but we must share a common destination and a commitment to support each other. We must build relationships with the staff, parents, and community, and create opportunities to bond. It is easier to travel with people we trust.

4. What do we need to pack to make this trip successful?

A. Seeds of Knowledge: Brain-Compatible Learning

We need to have a belief system about education. Knowledge will enable us to know what we believe. Our resources will include:

- *ITI: The Model*, by Susan Kovalik with Karen Olsen (Kovalik and Olsen 1994)

- *A Celebration of Neurons*, by Robert Sylwester (Sylwester 1995)

- *Human Brain and Human Learning*, by Leslie A. Hart (Hart 1983)

Shared knowledge and dialogue create a common language and clear focus.

B. Respect

We must show respect at all times to children, staff members, parents, and to anyone else who is going on the journey. We can do this by acknowledging the ideas and accomplishments of others. Respect will help keep us on the path.

C. The ITI Lifelong Guidelines and LIFESKILLS

These tools remind us of the ways in which we agree to interact, and will enable us to move forward in any situation. If we behave as we believe, we can climb any mountain we find on our journey. The Guidelines and LIFESKILLS must be visible and modeled constantly.

D. Protection

We must have a plan if we meet a conflict along the way. A well thought-out, organized plan that supports the way the brain learns will withstand any controversy. Brain-compatible education works because it is based on research, matches common sense, and teaches the way students learn. We should remember that we have the support of those who have gone before us and weathered the storms. We will be proactive. We will anticipate barriers and meet them head-on with the LIFESKILLS of courage and responsibility.

5. *How long will the trip take?*

Remember this is not an overnight trip; it is a lifelong journey. It will require adequate time to master mental programs. It is the process that will get us where we want to go. If we watch along the way, we see that spring follows winter. Growth follows the dormant period. It takes time to get through the slow growing period to get to productive growth. The seed does turn into a flower, but sometimes it takes faith and time. Be patient and enjoy the trip.

The Indiana ITI Project, C.L.A.S.S., and the Process of Change

Overview

My journey toward sharing ITI on a state level started with the creation of C.L.A.S.S. (Connecting Learning Assures Successful Students), a professional development model supported by the Indiana State Department of Education. Thanks to visionary educators such as Dr. H. Dean Evans and Phyllis Land Usher at the state level, and Dr. David H. Hutton, Superintendent of Lebanon Community Schools, at the local level, C.L.A.S.S. was born. It took people who were convinced that instruction can be improved.

Based on ITI, the brain-compatible model designed by Susan Kovalik, C.L.A.S.S. started out with five schools in 1990. Participating teachers attended five days of ITI training followed by coaching over the next three years.

By 1998, we were working with 250 schools and over 5000 educators.

Personal Experiences Developed Leaders

All of us involved in launching C.L.A.S.S. had taken part in various attempts over the years to improve schools. Each year we added innovative ways to teach, buying into each new reform as it came down the pike. We finally realized that we didn't need any more quick fix programs; we needed a whole new approach. We needed to change the entire mind-set about what education should look like and sound like!

In the early 1980's, I was exposed to a new concept of teaching through Susan Kovalik and Associates that was designed to achieve brain-compatible learning. Called ITI, the program made sense to me. It was a realistic approach to the teaching-learning process. I believed it should be the foundation for C.L.A.S.S. Since then ITI has been successfully adopted by the school where I taught, and many schools throughout Indiana. In each case where successful implementation has happened, there was a change agent who stepped forward to take the lead in guiding the school through change.

"The love of life is necessary to the vigorous prosecution of any undertaking."

—Dr. Johnson

Those of us who initiated C.L.A.S.S. discovered that we had developed a collective conscience about what was the right thing to do. For the first time we asked ourselves, "Why do we do what we do in our schools?" What was our rationale? Surprisingly enough, many of us had **no reasons** why we taught the way we taught. We began thinking about what could really happen in our classrooms to make them better. How could we teach so it would be meaningful to all students? We pictured interested students eager to learn. We pictured excited teachers eager to teach. We were not sure how we were going to make that happen, but we knew what we wanted to see in our schools.

Susan Kovalik had a way of letting teachers know that we could be more than we thought we could be. I knew that if it had happened to us, it could happen to other teachers. If we all started doing what was right, the schools would change. I knew that creating learning experiences that allowed my students to experience success really worked. I knew that doing something that was successful allowed them to feel good about themselves. If it was really that simple, we needed teachers to experience success so that they would have the confidence to keep getting better, too.

"We didn't all come over on the same ship, but we're all in the same boat."

—Bernard Baruch

We knew we could make a difference in our own classrooms, but if we were going to change the school, we would need the collaboration of everyone on the staff. Collaboration didn't mean that we would all do the same thing at the same time as we walked hand-in-hand down the road to change. It meant that we each would have a personal vision about what our classroom could be. It meant that we could talk about

"People become house builders through building houses, harp players through playing the harp. We grow to be just by doing things which are just."

—*Aristotle*

what we wanted to see and come to a common understanding of how to accomplish our mission.

We soon realized that we were not just talking about improving our classroom, we were talking about improving society in general. The concept grew, and what was initially perceived as a way to improve teaching strategies suddenly became a mission to improve life. We were on our way. This was more important than we had first realized. Reading everything we could about the brain and observing our own experiences working with children gave us the knowledge we needed to get started. We felt a new responsibility. We had direction, and we began to see the vision of a brain-compatible school.

Getting Started

At the beginning of C.L.A.S.S., four elementary schools were invited to join Central Elementary in Lebanon, Indiana, on their mission to create brain-compatible schools: Amy Beverland, Pleasant View, Lowell, and River Forest. The success of these schools depended on the educational leader who guided each staff. At Amy Beverland, Lowell, and Central the principals, Susan Brash, Susan Howard, and Linda DeClue, led the march. At the other two schools, a third grade teacher, Gayle Smriga, and the gifted and talented program coordinator, Peggy Buchanan, were the advocates for change. Such leaders, we realized, could be anyone in the school who had a clear view of the mission and the skills to help the others see that there can be a better way.

"If you have knowledge, let others light their candles at it."

—*Margaret Fuller*

However, someone in each school had to be the designated leader—the champion for change. She/he was really a change agent creating other change agents. The leader understood the implications of brain biology and was able to share with others in a non-threatening way.

We also needed people from various levels of the organization, including all staff members, to be a part of this change—bus drivers, custodians, cooks, assistants, secretaries—everyone! We needed every-one's input to make this succeed, and we needed to all work together.

The work began with teachers and choice was the first criterion for teacher involvement in C.L.A.S.S. Only teachers who **wanted** to be a part of the training and coaching participated. We knew we could not mandate change. The teachers involved had to understand and be committed to what we wanted to do. After an orientation about brain research findings, teachers signed up to be a part of a three-year program to create brain-compatible classrooms. It was their choice. We found educators in every school, dedicated to helping children find their way in the world. These were the teachers who chose to grow.

The full staff participated, including support personnel, at both Central and Amy Beverland. These schools moved further and faster than the others. At Lowell, everyone didn't opt in, but after the three-year period, the entire staff was involved. It showed us that people will move when they are ready, if it is for a good purpose.

The other two schools didn't ever achieve full staff participation. One reason I observed was the constant change in programs and personal beliefs that I will address later when I discuss conflict. Another was that the principals lacked the strong vision and desire for ITI to go forward.

Teachers opting into C.L.A.S.S. had to be willing to view the process of change as the journey. We wanted them to appreciate the trip and not to focus on the end of the journey. At that time we who were leading the way were not sure ourselves exactly what it was going to take to get where we wanted to go. We stayed focused on our goal. We were honest from day one. We explained that the change would not be easy and that we would have our highs and our lows. We didn't want to crumble when problems occurred, because solving problems would provide us opportunities to grow. We also stressed that if problems arose, we would know that we were really doing something different.

Our belief in what we were doing kept us moving, even on the roughest days.

The strong message to teachers was to ask how much more effective they could be if their methods and skills were based on knowledge of the biology of learning. It was **not** that they were wrong in their teaching methods. No one was asked to discard what worked for them but rather to be willing to try a new approach and share their experiences in brain-compatible learning with their fellow teachers. Teachers were not pressured into immediate, radical change; they could control their personal timetable. Each school would create their own approach based on their shared beliefs, climate, and culture.

From the beginning, we saw ourselves as professional educators who could change the world. Our careers became our mission. The mission was to give students the education they deserve to be successful in today's world.

We had schools on board. We had teachers who chose to make a difference. We were on the way to creating the best schools in the world with the belief that we would eventually share what we learned with other schools—so that all schools could achieve the best. That belief kept us growing so that others could learn from our successes, and from our mistakes.

Living the ITI Schoolwide Rubric: Pedersen ITI Patterns of Growth

With the Kovalik ITI model as a guide, schools in the C.L.A.S.S. project became more brain-compatible places during three years of direct project involvement. But with the change some interesting patterns emerged. I began to see these patterns as predictable patterns of growth in the pursuit of ITI implementation. Figure 6.1 on the following page gives an overview of the descriptions of those patterns.

The ITI Schoolwide Rubric (Appendix B) provides a road map of the ITI journey when whole schools undertake to become brain-compatible learning communities. I have clustered my descriptions of the patterns I observed according to the Stages of that Rubric. My intent is to share the kinds of experiences people have on this journey so that others who follow may take heart and know that the path has been traveled before. Within each cluster, I share both **patterns** I've observed and **best advice** based on what is working for others. Most of the experiences I've selected are tied to Rubric Stages 1, 2, and 3 because it is at those stages that people must embrace new ideas and habits while letting go of the old—hard, but exciting, work.

Individual schools will see many of these patterns in their own unique sequence while skipping others altogether; however, there is comfort in knowing at the outset that others who are committed to systemic change have worked through challenges similar to those you will meet.

Figure 6.1

Pedersen ITI Patterns of Growth

	Patterns Observed	Best Advice
ITI School-wide Rubric Stage **1**	• School opens to systemic change, commits to ITI, visitation and training begin • Leaders emerge, visible changes occur at varying rates • With implementation still superficial, some want to try other things—workshop "hopping" and window dressing • Effective implementation by some sprouts saboteurs—friction and factions	• Build trust and shared, brain-compatible culture • Respond to individuals in a framework of balance, focus on success of students and self-assessment • Focus on brain-compatible learning, provide coaching and feedback, encourage staff collaboration • Meaningful staff discussion on shared beliefs and goals for students, refocus on the brain-compatible elements, emphasize inclusion and team planning based on ITI Rubric
2	• Critical mass moving forward creates energy, school climate reflects ITI brain-compatible elements • Implementation process, self-propelled, has a life of its own and teachers ask for more information and training • Loss of focus underscores need to collaborate, dissension threatens focus • Parent/community questions and concerns arise along with controversy and confrontation requiring special attention	• Teachers gain confidence and professional self-esteem as a member of a team • Provide resources, nurture trust , and maintain focus • Clarify expectations using small group process, restate and discuss the vision, do more inclusion, create JOY
3	• Commitment renewed to honor brain research and one's experience, sense of excitement grows, desire for more time and resources • Shared leadership results in outreach as empowered teachers share with colleagues and community	• Accept controversy as likely part of change, leave ego behind, focus on brain research and what is right for students, listen and be firm • Martial district support to increase planning time and access to resources
4, 5	• Staff requires time and experiences to update knowledge, they want book talks, more training opportunities • Synergy created, staff recognizes connections among skills/content and each other • A few individual hold-outs, negative comments hold others down • Staff networking with other schools, making formal presentations, initiating peer coaching	• Encourage visitors, hold parent closures, share successes inside the school and in the wider community • Celebrate and appreciate • Create the climate to support staff learning, and invite parents as well • Create more ways to share with others outside the school • Counsel negative teacher to a different school or profession • Encourage peer coaching and creation of documents about successful strategies

ITI Schoolwide Rubric: Stage 1

Patterns: Commit to systemic change; acknowledge that our schools are not getting the results needed.

In working with teachers during the last few years, I know that they truly want to do it right. They want children to learn. However, many teach as they were taught in spite of the different needs of today's students. Some rely solely on the text and the manuals.

Others create incredible programs, using their own experiences, common sense, and intuition about how children learn without fully understanding why it works. Still others hop from strategy to strategy, trying to keep up with the latest fad in educational reform.

It is imperative, therefore, that we create a whole new plan. We can't apply the "quick fix" to an educational program that doesn't work. Rather, we must start over connecting teaching strategies to how the brain takes in information.

To create vivid pictures of what is possible and how to begin, our teachers attend ITI workshops and visit brain-compatible schools. They are excited about what they learn and begin to share what they hear and see with their colleagues.

This is the beginning of significant change.

Best Advice: Build trust

Before you jump to a new curriculum and teaching strategy, you must help your staff come to know and trust one another. I can't over emphasize the importance of developing trust among the teachers. You can't expect a team to collaborate if they've never had a meaningful conversation together! Schedule inclusion activities at the beginning of staff meetings to build trust and a sense of community.

For ideas about how to do this, read:

- *Tribes*, by Jeanne Gibbs (Gibbs 1995)

- *Yes I Can The Winner's Circle*, by Clare LaMeres (LaMeres 1990)

Quality books about self-esteem or team-building also include activities to get to know each other better.

Too often, administrators give up this piece due to limited time; however, when leaders realize how important it is to keep the trusting relationships growing, such inclusion activities become a high priority. Once your staff understands each other, they are more accepting of differences in beliefs about teaching. It is important to remember that teaching is about relationships among people.

At this beginning stage, remember that the staff needs to be grounded in brain-compatible information. Books about the brain must be readily available for further research. Everyone needs to discover the truth about how children learn by researching how the brain takes in information and makes use of it.

Goal-setting and self-assessment have a specific focus if you work with both the Classroom ITI Rubric and the Schoolwide ITI Rubric. Return to them regularly to chart your course and determine progress.

Now the staff has started! Just taking these first steps shows the commitment. Don't dwell on change. Dwelling on the fact that we must change will actually slow you down. Rather, emphasize the belief that you must build caring relationships with each other and with your students. Develop trust; then you will move ahead with powerful learning. Start the process and let it take you where you need to be.

> *"Life is change. Balance is the key. We don't want to be in perpetual confusion, on the other hand, we don't want to be locked in time."*
> —*Pedersen*

Patterns: Leaders emerge

Some teachers start moving faster than others in implementing ITI. They are more positive about what they are doing because it matches their existing beliefs. They are **responding** to the brain-compatible teaching, not **reacting** to it. They have followed the brain-compatible approach, and now they are ready to start leading others by their examples.

Others may not be ready to move ahead. They aren't sure yet what they believe at this point. They haven't had enough success yet to sell them on this plan.

Some of the most committed ITI teachers don't just use the agenda, procedures, Lifelong Guidelines/LIFESKILLS, and class meetings at school; they also send families ideas to use at home. Classrooms are beginning to look different—not just lamps, plants, music, and pleasing colors, but also displays related to studies and the Lifelong Guidelines/LIFESKILLS. The Lifelong Guidelines/LIFESKILLs are a part of the day regardless of the topic under study.

Other teachers, though, are stressed about just finding a book to go with a LIFESKILL. They are not in the rhythm of the change and may be experiencing a variety of barriers. If they have a tough class, they may be discouraged that ITI isn't a quick fix. They may feel the need to revert back to assertive discipline and control techniques instead of having patience and teaching responsible behavior to each student.

Best Advice: Respond to individuals

Don't publicly praise one teacher over another. This isn't the time to start rewarding top teachers. It has never worked in the classroom and it will never work in the staff room. You don't want to create competition and opposition. Value the integrity of each teacher who is moving forward.

Giving all the teachers some flexibility at this time will foster more trust among the entire staff. In this sensitive time, you need to give both freedom and direction. Balance is the key. Lasting change cannot happen from the top down; it has to move both ways. You must support what is happening, but not expect everyone to do the same thing at the same time.

When teachers believe that they have no control over their situation, they feel powerless and they react in a negative way. If you push your staff too fast, they're afraid. If such fears continue very long, they start to believe that their situation is hopeless. They react instead of respond. Once they believe that they have already failed—and you have hardly started—it will be over.

It is imperative at staff meetings to stress the importance of attitude. Attitude will drive you forward. Reassure the staff that it is O.K. to move at different speeds.

> *"Man is the only animal that laughs and weeps; for he is the only animal that is struck with the difference between what things are, and what they ought to be."*
>
> —*William Hazlitt*

Once a staff realizes that they can all grow together, even if they don't grow at the same speed, it is a major breakthrough.

There are many ways to foster positive attitudes. Encourage your staff to look for successes in the classroom that relate to the brain-compatible techniques. Once teachers experience some success with brain-compatible learning, they feel better about what they are doing, and they are willing to keep going. Show by example what you expect.

Staff inclusion activities also are vital ways to help the teachers feel less threatened that they are changing at different rates. Your consistency will inspire trust that you really mean what you have been saying.

In addition, watch for opportunities to tell each teacher specific ways you see improvement in their children. Thank-you notes and phone calls of appreciation will help at this time. Nurture the growing sense of community.

Patterns: Superficial implementation

As ITI becomes more rooted, some teachers believe that they have done it all, and they are ready to move on to something else. Some teachers may think that they are creating absence of threat and an enriched environment because they have their LIFESKILLS display up in their room and a plant on the table.

There is much more to it than that, however. We are so used to quick fixes in our culture, that too often we don't spend adequate time implementing a new program.

Some teachers who were quick to start ITI, are now looking for other workshops to attend. Often these workshops don't support brain research, and in some cases oppose brain-compatible teaching.

Best Advice: Coaching and collaboration

This is not the time to jump ship. Revisit your goal. In staff meetings ask: "Are we really implementing what we believe? Have we internalized this process? What mental programs have we built for ourselves?" It often takes an entire year or more just focusing on ITI Rubric Stage 1 to do it well! Keep the staff focused on the school's ITI-grounded expectations. Remind everyone that brain-compatible teaching takes time to implement. This was fun to start, but now you have to work at fully understanding and implementing Stage 1 and prepare to move to more advanced stages of the ITI Rubric. The students and teachers haven't had time to create mental programs about the Lifelong Guidelines, LIFESKILLS, and procedures. That is why ITI is not working in some classrooms.

Don't get bogged down in too much discussion, which can make the vision appear exhausting. Keep teachers on a direct path to how children learn. Remind everyone to be patient and keep working to create absence of threat in the classroom and the school.

Encourage teachers to show their individuality in implementing ITI. You don't want a group of clones; you want the classrooms to reflect the character of the students and teachers.

Be compassionate with the teachers who are struggling. Give them some specific suggestions to try in their classrooms. For example:

- The media specialist can locate specific stories and books to support the LIFESKILLS.

- The staff can brainstorm activities to teach the Lifelong Guidelines/LIFESKILLS

- The staff can review the effectiveness of their procedures for students. Do they set clear expectations? Are teachers consistent?

Don't throw up your hands and decide that some teachers need to move out of the building. Intolerance will never bring harmony to the staff. Respect each other for individual progress. Encourage the teachers who are complaining about other teachers to be patient and continue to share ideas to help others grow. Value everyone's ideas. You may find someone unexpected has an idea to help the staff move on. If mutual respect is achieved, you will be amazed how the entire staff will start to move faster.

"The man who goes alone can start today; but he who travels with another must wait till that other is ready."

—*Henry David Thoreau*

It is especially difficult dealing with staff members who have made little or no progress toward ITI implementation. Some may realize that they do need to change some things, and that frightens them. Perhaps when they started they thought this was just another teaching theory; now that ITI is starting to make sense, they're worried that they can't teach this way.

As you move through this entire process of growth, you will find some teachers who should be encouraged to find another career—this is not the time. At this point, work with such teachers to help them improve. I will address the other situation later in this chapter.

Patterns: Saboteurs appear

It is now obvious that some teachers are really moving with brain-compatible learning. It's a sensitive time when some teachers feel they can't be as good as others in the school. The underdog may even feel this program is useless—that there's no way to keep up. This is a critical time for some educators. You don't want a saboteur to step forward at this time.

In one of the C.L.A.S.S. schools, the primary team was working hard to create a brain-compatible school. The local newspaper featured them every week. Parents were thrilled at the extra activities, and the principal was beaming with these incredible shining stars—teachers and students.

Meanwhile, however, the intermediate team was furious that no one thought they were accomplishing anything. Hadn't they agreed to implement ITI with the others? What happened to "move at your own speed?" Didn't anyone notice that they were meeting each week to write the curriculum?

A damaging rift split the faculty. The intermediate team started to sabotage the entire program. Comments included: "This isn't working." "Our kids are misbehaving." "We need to go back to stricter discipline." "It worked better when we were putting names on the board and paddling."

One answer could have been, "Good riddance. Get rid of the students and teachers who can't get it!" But listen to the underlying message. What would happen to society if we all had that attitude? We have to look for a response that creates a sense of the possible and keeps people involved.

Best Advice: Refocus through discussion

You don't want teachers or children to think that they have to be somebody else. You aren't taking them from a comfort level and dropping them into potential failure; rather, appreciate where each teacher and child is and nurture strengths while developing trust. You aren't giving the message that there is something wrong with some teachers. There is nothing wrong with them, you just want to help them to learn new things that will make teaching and learning about life more effective. Model respect.

Openly state that although some people are moving faster, they can also help everyone see next steps. If you have been doing inclusion activities at the staff meetings, this will be an easy stage to go through, because you have set specific expectations of each other.

If you have let the bonding between teachers break down though, this could be a time of serious splits among the staff. For any group to get along, it takes a constant effort on everyone's part. Return to inclusion activities, and, if needed, have some one-on-one conferences to gain insight.

Make time for significant discussions at staff meetings about directions the staff wants the school to go. Continue to build a shared belief system. What is expected of the school? What must happen for students to learn better? Brainstorm teaching strategies that work and relate to the biology of learning. Analyze what is not working, and see what ITI brain-compatible elements are missing. Share specific examples of how to implement those brain-compatible elements.

Each grade level or team should examine what knowledge and skills are important for students at their level. You will see teachers at different stages, and they will have different ideas about what is important. Sharing will keep everyone growing.

Collaboration is not just everyone agreeing. It's being able to voice opinions and come to an understanding. Communication of feelings and ideas is vital. Review and update knowledge of the brain research and provide leadership to decide about the next steps. Provide specific guidelines for teachers based on the ITI Rubric to help them formulate individual growth goals. The leader has to help everyone remember why the decision to implement ITI was made in the first place.

You will see amazing personal growth in the stronger teachers. They realize that they are not doing this to be recognized as the best teacher; rather, they are doing it because they understand how it empowers student learning. Their personal satisfaction will come when they see the rest of the staff working together for a common cause.

"The probability that we shall fail in the struggle should not deter us from the support of a cause we believe to be just."

—Abraham Lincoln

Celebrate the successful teacher, but not at the expense of losing an "up and coming" teacher. There is both strength and humility in collaboration. The stronger teachers will continue to be challenged and move ahead, but it will be for a much more satisfying reason. Instead of resenting the slower teacher, they will look for ways to make that teacher successful, too. This is an incredible growing period for all teachers.

ITI Schoolwide Rubric: Stage 2

Patterns: Reach critical mass, sustain momentum

A majority of your staff, students, parents, and community now share the same belief system: ITI-based education. It may have taken until now to get people on board. Expect a new energy in the building that spurs the staff to keep moving forward. They realize that they are doing something important.

The culture of the school is changing. Negative conversation is missing from the lounge. People are kinder to each other. The school is starting to have an atmosphere of true caring. The LIFESKILLS are everywhere in the fabric of daily school life. It is obvious when you enter the building that this is a school that models respect for all. The custodian warmly greets children, the cook smiles, the secretary welcomes the late children with a sense of compassion. The multiple intelligences are being used in teaching and learning. Amazingly, some of your teachers who took the longest to get on board are now soaring past some fast starters.

Learning displays of the shared belief system are everywhere. The school has become an institution for learning about life.

Best Advice: Nurture confidence

The teachers know that they don't have to fear that they're not doing enough, and they are starting to share what they are doing. Now, even the smallest celebration might be shared in the teacher's lounge or at a staff meeting. Teachers realize that they do have good ideas, and that those ideas are their own. They don't have to get everything out of a text-book or manual. They can create meaningful learning experiences for their students using their important knowledge of students and the context for learning. Teachers start appreciating their individual worth as a part of an incredible team. More advanced teachers see that their patience and sharing is helping to create a dynamic staff.

Specific feedback from the leader reassures the staff that ITI is working. Notes in their boxes, phone calls, and the like, help to nurture the momentum. Everyone has bad days; your reassurance and feedback help to keep these in perspective.

When you started this journey, you took side trips every once in a while. Now you see the path clearly before you, and it is straight and narrow. You just need to keep getting better.

> *"Self-confidence is the memory of success."*
>
> —*Anonymous*

Patterns: Self-propelled growth

The staff is really moving. You are amazed that the teachers are moving ahead without your prodding. At this point success is evident in a variety of areas. Teachers start coming to you for professional material. They want to attend more training about brain-compatible learning and the ITI model.

Best Advice: Trust, resources, focus

If you are attending to each detail along the ITI path, you are leading with ease. You aren't burdened.

On the other hand, if you have been too demanding with your desires for the school, you are probably feeling overwhelmed and discouraged. Think about trust and whether you are doing enough to restore it. If not, incorporate more inclusion activities into staff meetings, and restate the key concepts and improvement goals that might have been neglected.

> *"It is extremely difficult to lead farther than you have gone yourself."*
>
> —*Anonymous*

If the teachers are working in an environment that is absent of threat, they will be more productive. Make certain that any proposed training or program idea supports what the school believes about learning. Don't start new programs that conflict with what you are already doing. Locate funding so that the staff can attend appropriate training sessions. Encourage them to meet and discuss chapters in an ITI book. Continue to learn and grow yourself. Your behavior is always one of the most powerful models, and an important part of your leadership.

Patterns: Dissension at the edges

The staff may forget their purpose and the importance of working together. They may start to feel discomfort at this time. **(If this stage does not happen—celebrate!)**

Human nature takes over and you notice some dissension starting. It may be a small, insignificant thing that appears to be one teacher's complaint. In one C.L.A.S.S. school, I thought things were going very well. When I visited to provide coaching, however, some teachers told me how terrible things were, and said that people were talking behind each other's backs. I was shocked.

In another school, teachers complained about insignificant things that didn't have anything to do with teaching and learning.

I realized that the little things can cause the biggest problems. Staffs can cope with a big crisis just fine, but never underestimate the small grievance.

Best Advice: Focus on the vision and celebrate

At a staff meeting, divide into small groups. Give each group a sheet of butcher paper on which to list their expectations of each other and of the principal. Then post the sheets and talk about the items listed to reach consensus. If a staff member cannot agree to an expectation, cross it out and leave the ones that are acceptable.

Re-emphasize the Lifelong Guidelines and LIFESKILLS. Remind everyone that if the adults don't exemplify these, they can't expect the students to do so. Disagreements and rumors must be addressed truthfully among the parties so trust continues to flourish.

Emphasize the purpose of the school's work with students. If the staff loses their direction, they'll complain to each other.

Keep it simple at this point. Don't put too many expectations on people. Without too many restrictions, tensions will ease. Celebrate things together just for the fun of it. Plan some staff outings. Make time for more inclusion activities for the staff. Let joy visit your school. If what you're doing for children isn't enjoyable, it's time to step back, take a deep breath, and lighten up!

> *"Most folks are about as happy as they make up their minds to be."*
>
> —*Abraham Lincoln*

Patterns: Controversy

If you didn't actively include your parents and community as you planned and implemented ITI, you may be encountering controversy about your program. Even if you did involve them, community and school board politics can raise unexpected questions and stir up confrontation among various groups.

> *"To learn is to change. Education is a process that changes the learner."*
>
> —*George Leonard*

One C.L.A.S.S. school was well on its way when a group of parents and community members from another school district showed up and accused the staff of teaching New Age beliefs. I suggested that they visit the classrooms, then meet with me with examples to illustrate their concern. When we met, a minister said we should not be teaching children to achieve their "personal best" because that was teaching students that they were better than God. Our intention was that children think before they do the math, write the best they can, and take pride in their work. Use what God gave you the best way possible.

In another school, a group of parents objected to stories about imagination. One parent told the school board that she didn't want her child to think until he was eighteen.

In a third school, a group of parents insisted that only stories from the textbook be read; they didn't want any trade books used. They didn't want the teachers using any curriculum that wasn't in the textbook because, they said, the textbooks were written by experts

Best Advice: Accept controversy, listen, be firm

View controversy as a part of change. If we continue to do what everyone has always done, there will be little dissension, but there will also be little improvement. Once schools start making changes, that sometimes leads to controversy.

Sometimes, the controversy is due to a lack of communication or to semantics. Be sure that the school board and the district administration are aware of, and support, your innovations. Their lack of knowledge or understanding can quickly bring an end to your efforts as money follows another initiative.

Whenever a controversy arises, the first thing to remember is to leave your ego behind and don't take negative comments personally. It's difficult to do, but it helps if you keep going back to your belief system. If you believe that what you're doing is right for children, if you have the research to back you up, and if you have the experience that further tells you this is right, then go forward with confidence!

But remember to be proactive too! When school looks different from what parents recall from their own youth, concerns and questions arise. Educate parents, perhaps initiating a study group. Conduct community meetings. Invite teachers and students to share what they are teaching and learning. Parents need to experience what the students are experiencing. Present model lessons to the parents, so that they can experience some of what their children are experiencing. Host workshops for the parents and the greater community to see what brain-compatible learning really looks like.

At such meetings, ask the parents how they learned in school what they still use in their lives. Most adults acknowledge that worksheets and dittos have very little to do with meaningful learning. Giving parents actual experience with a variety of learning strategies will help them to become more receptive to different teaching techniques.

Educators must be good communicators and we need to remember that avoiding controversy does not solve problems. Be flexible and listen to other viewpoints, but be firm about your commitment. Remember that we learn from controversy. It forces us to look at what we are doing. We need to be open to ideas that would improve the program. Can it be improved? Why are we teaching

> *"If I were to read, much less answer, all the attacks made on me, this shop might as well be closed for any other business. I do the very best I know how, the very best I can, and I mean to keep doing so until the end. If the end brings me out all right, what is said against me won't amount to anything. If the end brings me out wrong, then angels swearing I was right would make no difference."*
>
> —*Abraham Lincoln*

the way we teach? What do we want students to understand? What do we want students to do with what they understand?

We live in a democracy, and everyone has a right to his/her own beliefs. However, it is our responsibility as teachers and administrators to develop and implement the best techniques in teaching. Medicine improves every day. You are using better appliances than your parents used. Why shouldn't education improve, too?

ITI Schoolwide Rubric: Stage 3

Patterns: Commitment renewed, excitement

This is a huge turning point, because now you know that your truth is coming from your own experience. You have a responsibility to teach the way the brain learns. This kind of teaching requires ample time to put together as well as different resources.

Examine how much you have accomplished so far. Remind yourself too, that you still have farther to go, particularly if you have reached a plateau.

This is a very exciting time of awareness. The teachers realize that what they are doing is based on their classroom experience, not just on knowledge from a book. They need planning time and money for resources to focus the curriculum on learning from the real world.

I first understood the old saying, "The truth will set you free," at this stage. The truth will now guide the staff to change their school, because they have successfully used brain-compatible teaching methods. Freedom is more than words in a book. The ITI model gives us the knowledge; now experience has given us our truth.

Best Advice: Marshal resources, provide planning time

You finally understand the power of learning and teaching, and they are the same. Progress can't be stopped at this point. The district must be creative to find planning time for teachers and money for resources— critical pieces that enable teachers to put together brain-compatible learning experiences for students.

Schools can find increased planning time for teachers in a variety of ways. Examples illustrate possibilities leaders can adjust and use:

- In the elementary school, put all special classes, such as art or music, on one day for a grade level so that the teachers have a longer block of time in which to plan.

- If the school day is longer than required by the state, ask for a waiver from the state Department of Education to dismiss early one afternoon a month for planning time.

- Sponsor a V.I.P. day. Invite parents and other community members to share their expertise during an afternoon. Topics might include aerobics, gardening, computer games, and board games. While the students participate, the teachers gather to plan.

- Set up a parent substitute day. Begin by establishing an "official" sub list of willing parents. These parents donate a day or more a year to substitute for a grade level team, releasing teachers for a day of planning.

- Parents will be more comfortable and effective if they are oriented to the ITI model before they serve as substitute teachers.

- Set up block schedules to create longer instructional periods and planning periods for teachers.

Schools are creative when it comes to finding the resources they need. For example:

- *Area businesses:* Establish partnerships with local businesses and you'll see your resources for meaningful studies expand. Discuss ways in which you can help each other. For example, their employees could use the school gym one night a week, or a classroom for meetings. For their part, they could sponsor school projects and recruit volunteer tutors. You'll both benefit.
- *Staff and community resources:* Identify the hobbies and outside interests of staff and parents. There is a surprising gold mine of guest speakers close at hand.

Patterns: Shared leadership and outreach

Shared leadership is the most effective way to bring about systemic change. Knowing that their voice will be heard, staff willingly lead and participate on a variety of decision-making committees.

The teachers are empowered and they are sharing their beliefs with other educators beyond the school. Parents are invited to school to see what the students are learning. Teachers' friends ask to visit.

Best Advice: Encourage visitors.

Teachers can take turns as guides while the principal covers their classrooms. Begin each visit with an orientation to brain-compatible learning. During the tour of the building, teachers who are ready for visitors may post a sign, "Welcome Visitors." Afterward, the principal can answer questions. Students can serve as welcome ambassadors. They can greet visitors at the door.

The teachers are empowered. Let them have the credit.

Teachers need to plan "parent closures," events to culminate the study of a component of the curriculum. Invite parents to an evening presentation by the students. The students share the skills, concepts, and knowledge they have mastered. This is a wonderful way for parents to see what is happening in school. Each grade level or learning team can do this on their own night.

Provide times for teachers to share successes at staff meetings. Such sharing promotes collaboration and provides a way for everyone to use the good ideas. "Chew and Chat sessions" can be held monthly in different classrooms after school to enjoy snacks and share ideas.

> *"Enthusiasm is contagious—and so is the lack of it."*
>
> —*Unknown*

Encourage teachers to provide presentations at state meetings where they can share their successes.

ITI Schoolwide Rubric: Stages 4 and 5

Patterns: Teachers initiate knowledge update

Time and experiences need to be provided for continued staff growth and development. As new information becomes available, the staff knowledge base must be updated and methods for application discussed and practiced. Staying on top of emerging brain research prompts continuous growth.

By now, most of the teachers are so excited they are bursting to share with colleagues and learn more together. Teachers want to start book talks to read and discuss the best resources. They want to share ideas in grade level meetings. They want to attend conferences about the biology of learning. Effective shared leadership needs constant nourishment to sustain its work.

Best Advice: Create climate for continual learning

Create a supportive climate that allows the staff to continue to learn and grow together:

- Encourage attendance at relevant workshop

> *"More and more, I used the quickness of my mind to pick the minds of other people and use their knowledge as my own."*
>
> *—Eleanor Roosevelt*

- Help to organize book talks reviewing the latest educational research, and perhaps invite parents, too. Teachers by grade level or team could be responsible for reviewing one book a year. Prepare handouts with key points from the book. Even if everyone doesn't have time to read each book, they will still pick up valuable information.

- Coordinate book talks at the district level and have each school host a book talk per grading period. Educators need to collaborate. All of us are better than one of us.

Patterns: Synergy

The staff, working together, notice a synergy has occurred. They realize that all things are connected in teaching and learning. Content can be interpreted meaningfully with skills and connected to the real world.

> *"Never tell people how to do things. Tell them what to do and they will surprise you with their ingenuity."*
>
> *—George S. Patton*

They also recognize that they are all connected in their work with students. None stands alone any more; all are working together for a common cause. Some teachers that you didn't think would make it, did. By trusting those you doubted, encouraging those who were not on board, and believing in those who didn't believe in themselves, you now see the wonderful results of keeping your vision.

Best Advice: Increase sharing outside the school

Look for ways to expand and share what you're doing with others. Continue to invite visitors, hold training sessions and expand book talks—in short, share the knowledge.

Patterns: Individual hold-outs

This stage may be avoided, but leaders must be prepared to deal with the individual who cannot or will not support ITI implementation. After doing everything possible to help a teacher grow through this process, sometimes the leader must acknowledge that this individual at least doesn't belong in an ITI school and may lack the necessary skills and attitudes to succeed in the teaching profession.

Of all the schools I have worked with since the beginning of C.L.A.S.S., I only saw the extreme happen once. A teacher decided to go a different direction from the rest of the staff and was critical of change efforts. This teacher who didn't enjoy teaching, and wasn't a successful teacher, was pulling down other teachers with negative comments, and was fostering controversy in the community.

Best Advice: Counsel teacher to a different profession

When teachers worked in isolation, with doors closed, most taught whatever way suited them best. Now that you have opened your doors and are working together, you are finding that some teachers have been protected by the system. If a teacher doesn't enjoy working with young people and isn't willing to spend the time and effort to improve education for all students—no matter what the program is—he/she must be encouraged to look for a new career that will use his/her talents in a different way.

You have been patient. While setting clear expectations, you haven't made unnecessary demands. You have given time to learn and implement what the staff believes is right for children. Make it clear that the school is going in a certain direction and you would like him/her to join the rest of the staff. If a teacher can't support the direction agreed upon, he/she needs to look for a different path to follow. The leader(s) will not allow anyone to sabotage the success of the school or proceed without the children's best interest at heart. The educational leader needs to be responsible for the sake of the students.

> *In giving advice, seek to help, not please, your friend."*
>
> —*Solon*

Patterns: Networking and peer coaching

The staff connects with educators at other schools who are trying to improve education.

Teachers and principals create a network to expand ITI implementation to other schools. The teachers start coaching and sharing with peers. They constantly seek ways to improve the future of education. Brain-compatible learning spreads to other schools.

Best Advice: Create time, share networking opportunities, train coaches

Provide time for teachers to share what is working for them with colleagues from other schools. Organize grade level meetings or content meetings to brainstorm ideas for presenting and writing about ITI. Teachers have many answers; trust them to share and learn from each other. Teachers can conduct workshops sharing good teaching strategies. Designate and train the most proficient ITI teachers to be coaches. Teams of teachers can coach each other once trust is built among them. Encourage the team spirit and use a coaching model to keep the staff moving ahead. Such a staff has developed into professional educators working together to make a difference for students.

> *"We teach
> who we are."*
>
> *—John Gardner*

We believe in something!

We created a plan to implement it!

We shared what we learned with others!

How Did You Get Where You Are?

- You led with a plan of action, following the steps in the ITI Rubrics leading to brain-compatible learning.

- You remained calm through the storm. Conflict did not stop you.

- You did not interfere with the growth of the people around you, no matter how painful it was to you or to them. You realized that by letting go, you were giving others the freedom to grow on their own.

- You provided staff development when needed. You realized that knowledge empowers people.

- You were honest, and you had a vision that you believed would work. You had the map and stepped forward to be champion for the vision.

- You remained balanced in your thinking and your expectations. You stopped the pendulum from swinging too far in any direction.

- You served your staff with kindness, remembering that brains work better in a non-threatening environment.

- You provided opportunities for personal development for your staff. Since "you teach who you are," you never forgot that wellness is important.

- You encouraged your staff to stay focused on their vision and not to veer off track into different directions. You kept school programs connected to the way the brain learns.

• You remembered that ITI implementation was about the students and not personal egos or recognition.

If most of these things didn't happen, you'll probably not be reading this page. If you're a visionary leader, you're making a difference in the lives of students and teachers.

Conclusion

The schools that made it through these stages are doing a fantastic job. Others are continuing to move through them, and some are stuck in a stage but working through it. It takes three years to understand what you want to do. It takes five years to start doing it right.

When you begin this process, there's no guarantee that the staff will persevere and fully implement brain-compatible teaching. It takes a very special guide with vision and passion to move a staff. The most important force in the improvement of a school is the principal. If there is an outstanding principal, there will be an outstanding school. I can't overemphasize the vital role of the principal. An outstanding leader in the building can get things going, but if the principal is not with the staff 100%, the movement will be short-lived.

The same is true for the leadership teachers provide. They will have successful, caring students by the example they model. We all need someone to keep us going.

The results of implementing ITI are compelling. Attendance will increase, both for teachers and students. Discipline problems will nearly disappear. Parents will be happier about school, and more visible in the building. The school support staff will be knowledgeable about good instruction.

The students themselves will discuss specifically what they are learning. Their social skills will have improved, and their confidence in making decisions heightened. They'll demonstrate more responsibility for their learning and behavior.

I wish I could say that students' test scores will always go up, too. However, we have found that the learning goals addressed in a brain-compatible classroom often are not measured on a standardized test. Some of our schools have the highest scores in the state, but not all of them. If the teachers identify the skills they are assessing for the year and teach them in a brain-compatible way, the scores will remain stable or rise. By being clear about what is to be assessed, each school can prepare students with the skills they need.

The leader has courage and a compelling vision of the possible. The leader isn't afraid of hard work or controversy. With eyes and heart on the goal of brain-compatible learning, he/she goes forward, a learner among learners, a teacher among teachers.

The journey continues one step at a time, there is no end, only the continuing adventure that lies ahead. Keep traveling, pay attention, and you will find your way while you are guiding others. The further you travel, the clearer the journey becomes.

VII

Empowering Families

by Susan Brash and Jane Rasp McGeehan

Introduction

Family members are the students' first teachers and their role continues to be vital for the educational success of students. Defining the forms of family involvement and persuading families to consider their children's learning a top priority are challenges for education leaders. The more effectively families and school personnel collaborate, the more students are the winners.

This chapter broadly defines family involvement as anything a family member does to promote and encourage the child's success as a learner. Two stories of family involvement, one at a suburban elementary school and another at a rural high school, illustrate the complexities of fostering broad-based family involvement. The stories are organized around the following common topics:

1. Overview of school demographics

2. Making it happen

3. Family roles in school decisions

4. Family members as volunteers

5. Communication with families

6. Families and marketing

Both the similarities and the differences are instructive.

Family Involvement at Amy Beverland Elementary

"We all sing the school song around here!"
"Parental involvement is unbelievable!"
These are the voices of parents from Amy Beverland Elementary in northeastern Marion County, Indiana. Over the seven-year history of the

elementary (as of the 1995-1996 school year), families invested time and energy in school matters with the strong encouragement of school staff. That staff believes in the importance of forging strong partnerships with families to benefit students.

Overview of School Demographics

Located in the Metropolitan School District of Lawrence Township, suburban Indianapolis, this elementary school serves both the children of affluence and of poverty. The school is attended by students in grades one through five, with the kindergarten program provided at a central location and sixth graders attending the middle school. (See chapter four for further details about the diversity of the student population.)

Throughout the school district families traditionally place a high value on education. Expectations are high. The schools reflect such expectations with a number of them recognized as blue ribbon schools by the United States Department of Education.

Making It Happen

The administration and staff begin building bridges with families before the start of the school year. The school's mission and beliefs are clearly defined and advertised, beginning with the first letter sent to families in the summer. Staff attitudes and actions reflect respect for families and trust in them that they hope will be mutual.

On Sunday afternoon at the beginning of the school year, the Amy Beverland Family Association sponsors the popular "Sundae on a Sunday." Families bring the children to school to meet and greet their children's teachers and fellow classmates in a non-threatening, friendly, home-like setting. The event sends the strong message that this school places a high value on merging school and home families. After the classroom visit, families stroll around the school and enjoy conversation and a sundae in the dining room. At the most recent event, 1700 sundaes were served.

A positive beginning is important, but even more important is knowing where you want to go. Just as with other aspects of the school program, efforts to involve families are tied to the school's mission. A primary goal is to introduce families to a climate and culture where all people feel significant and appreciated. The school staff provides many volunteer options. Inclusion is emphasized as all families are automatically members of the Amy Beverland Family Association, with no dues charged. Families are empowered and taken seriously. Obstacles to family involvement are analyzed and removed wherever possible. For example, child-care and transportation are provided when families are invited to attend any evening event at the school. (See chapter eight for funding strategies to support such services.)

Family Roles in School Decisions

The most significant factor in the successful involvement by families is that the school people sincerely value and respect what family members think about the school program in relation to the specific needs of their children. The principal and school leaders constantly see the family member as a valued client. When teachers listen to families and respond to their child's needs, family members feel that they are expanding their sphere of influence by joining this partnership.

The Amy Beverland staff places a priority on direct communication with families. Telephones are located in every classroom so that family members can be in touch at any time during the day.

In addition to one-on-one communication with the principal and teachers, families also play a significant role in formal decision-making. Because the climate at the school and the behavior of staff show that families' opinions are taken seriously, many family members volunteer for formal decision-making groups that include:

- School Improvement Planning Team (SIPT)

- Quality Circles

- Interview teams to recommend new staff

- School district committees, such as those on drug abuse prevention and human relations.

As members of the SIPT, parents and family members have a say in the directions and priorities for on-going school improvement. In Quality Circles, they work with teachers to achieve agreed upon school improvement goals. On interview teams, they have a voice in recommending which people will teach their children. Representing the school on district committees, they articulate its point of view based on its shared culture.

In each case, families are standing shoulder-to-shoulder with school staff to make the school's vision a reality.

Family Members as Volunteers

The first day of school family members are invited to choose from an array of volunteer opportunities by returning the Volunteer Sign-up

Sheet. (See Appendix D.) Typically, there are 25-30 options, many of which can be accomplished at home and during evening hours. Additionally, the special area teachers (art, creative expression, music, physical education, and Spanish) solicit family volunteers for special projects.

Parents and family members are also invited to a coffee early in the year which provides volunteer program orientation for new families and clarification for those returning. At the beginning of the 1995-1996 school year, over 260 people responded to such invitations.

Back-to-school night provides yet another opportunity to encourage family members to volunteer. As busy as people are, Susan Brash says that the consistently enthusiastic response from families rests both on the ability of school personnel to convince them that their participation is valued and on a wide range of volunteer activities.

The Volunteer Substitute Teacher Cadre is one example of an exciting and unique group of volunteers. The Cadre consists of family members who meet the district's requirements for substitute teachers and then volunteer their services at Amy Beverland Elementary. As a result of this Cadre, teacher teams are released during the school day to create ITI curriculum. The released time varies from a two-hour block to a whole day, and all at no cost to the school. The principal orients the volunteer substitutes to the ITI model so that they know what to expect when they are in classrooms. As family members learn about the benefits of ITI for their children, they become even more committed to its implementation.

In this school many people, rather than a tired few, volunteer their time. Consequently, the number of hours given and the variety of tasks accomplished are impressive. In addition to the usual volunteer tasks of providing clerical services, planning parties, chaperoning field trips, and conducting fund-raisers, these family members also assist in teaching roles. They tutor individual students; work in the computer lab, the Writing to Write lab, and the Writing to Read lab; read tests (not tests of reading skills) aloud to students; prepare audio tapes for special education students; make instructional materials; teach trail groups during camping trips; and work in the media center. No family members can doubt that they are key players in the success of the school program for their children.

Communication with Families

This school staff believes that the more family members know about what is going on at the school, the more effective they can be as partners to nurture their children's success as learners. This belief demands a strong commitment to communication that is dependable, varied, and helpful. The school staff offers annual ITI workshops to teach families about brain-compatible learning. Families' first-hand experiences with the learning and teaching strategies typical of their child's school day lead to valuable insights. Such understanding is reinforced by regular notes and phone calls from the staff to provide immediate feedback on student progress. Families see the fruits of the curriculum in action when they attend periodic celebrations of learning (closure events), at which children teach their families what they have learned.

But the communication doesn't end there. In addition to the classroom telephones mentioned above, the school has homework message and voice mail options on their telecommunication system. To help family members learn effective strategies for working with their children at home, workshops are offered on related topics including Family Math, Megaskills (now replaced by LIFESKILLS), and computer literacy.

"Star Search" is a parent-to-parent variation of the Welcome Wagon idea. Families new to the school receive a personal contact from a returning parent so that questions can be answered and information shared from a family perspective.

The Amy Beverland Family Association publishes a monthly newsletter for families, and the principal a weekly one, "Fantastic Friday." The weekly newsletter provides an overview of activities, names of families new to the school, specific strategies to support children as learners, highlights from the school handbook, student awards, and a preview of future events and plans.

Families and Marketing

The marketing of family involvement at the school merits discussion. The school staff designs a marketing plan similar to what one might expect in the business world. In addition to school and classroom newsletters, the staff creates newsletters, designs informative pamphlets, and looks for innovative ways to describe school programs and the families' vital role. Nothing is taken for granted and every family is a priority. Often, families receive as many as six communications to encourage their attendance at major events. As previously mentioned, child care and transportation are always provided.

Not only does the marketing plan lead to more effective communication. It also creates a corps of effective marketers—the family members themselves. The positive school stories shared with non-parent tax payers help to promote wider understanding and support among those who lack their own direct link to the school.

The Amy Beverland Elementary staff consistently responds to the needs, interests, and suggestions of families. The combined efforts of school staff and families give rise to trusting relationships that directly benefit children on many levels.

Family Involvement at Fluvanna County High School

Families at Fluvanna County High School during the four years that Jane McGeehan served as principal represented a range of views about their role in the formal education of their teenage youngsters. Some were active in established groups such as the Athletic Boosters or Band Parents. Others were content to attend annual conferences, read the school newsletter, and know when to ask to see the report card issued every six weeks. Still others relied on their son or daughter to tell them anything essential and assumed that "no news is good news."

Among many families of high school youth there is an incorrect belief, seemingly encouraged by high school students and some school staff, that family members have no active role to play at the school. "Stay away! Your children are nearly grown and do not need your involvement with the school." That is the message believed too often by well-meaning families.

Such beliefs must be replaced by the view that there are significant and essential roles for family members of high school youth so that their involvement could be expanded. The school leadership team realized that the high school must creatively nurture the strong family partnerships that are regularly apparent in elementary schools.

Overview of Demographics

Fluvanna County High School is situated in the pastoral, rolling hills of Virginia between Charlottesville and Richmond. Formerly a farming community, most people now make their living in nearby cities. Tree farming remains a major rural business. The students represent both affluence and poverty, with 8% qualifying for free or reduced lunches, down from 15% when ITI was initiated in 1990. More students could qualify for this kind of assistance, but family pride prevents some from applying for it. The school provides a full range of special education services for which 14% of the students qualify. About 30% are African-American, generally the sons and daughters of families who have lived in the area for generations. Just 1% of the students are from other ethnic groups. A planned lakeside community around beautiful Lake Monticello attracts many professional families to the county, as have new developments that are gradually replacing family farms. There is a tension among those in the community who want things to remain the same in the county and those who promote changes to boost residential and industrial development.

The school population has grown at a steady pace, from 525 students in 1989 to over 700 in 1995. With more students on the way. The high school and its sporting events are focal points for community spirit and pride.

Making it Happen

Upon arriving at the high school, McGeehan set out to learn about the ways in which family members were already involved in the life of the school. The Athletic Boosters organization was the only formal group that regularly called on families (principally of athletes) for active participation. Informally, others were doing what they could to follow up on homework or any calls from the school about problems with a son or a daughter. Family members often began telephone conversations with the principal by apologizing for taking her time.

Believing strongly that family members needed more alternatives for direct involvement and communication, McGeehan and her staff took the following steps:

- Formed a steering committee

- Formed a parent-teacher organization

- Renewed the band parent group

- Resumed newsletter publication to families and community

- Invited volunteers to work in an office or a classroom

- Invited families to the school for more than athletic or band banquets and student performances

- Enhanced teachers' perceptions of family roles as partners and the importance of regular communication.

The school leadership wanted to create new mental pictures of what family involvement could look like at the high school level.

Family Roles in School Decisions

Families needed to know that the new principal honored and respected their expressions of opinion and concern in areas critical to the life of the school. She sent this message in several ways. She invited family members to come for coffee and dialogue with the principal. While only a few attended given a variety of times to do so, it was a start.

The principal made it a point to be available frequently for casual conversation when a family member came to the school to pick up students for an early dismissal. She looked for informal opportunities, such as conversations at a football game, to invite family members to become an active part of the school. It was a time for building trust and rolling out the welcome mat.

Steering Committee

Early in the first year of McGeehan's principalship, she formed the FCHS Steering Committee. Its members were:

- Three family representatives

- Three teachers

- Four students representing each class in the school

- Two or three community representatives

- Two administrators.

The committee initiated planning for continuous improvement. The challenge of the task involved family members directly in lively brainstorming and discussion about what they wanted the school to become. They spearheaded review of the existing vision statement to learn whether or not it reflected basic beliefs of the school community. They validated and supported the statement as written, but also gained a deeper understanding of the school and each other from the rich dialogue required by the process.

The committee welcomed such significant work as assisting in the preparation of the school's instructional supply budget. Families were now a part of the team making such decisions rather than remaining as distant observers. To expand knowledge of the committee's work and to promote the two-way flow of information, each member of the FCHS Steering Committee identified at least five people with whom he or she would personally communicate between the monthly meetings about the group's work. The principal strongly encouraged such networking by making time to report on it at each meeting. The Steering Committee became one of the most effective aspects of the expanded role for family members.

Parent Teacher Organization

The first semester, the principal also initiated meetings of family members and teachers to discuss a high school Parent Teacher Organization and what needs, interests, and goals could be addressed through such a group. Judging from the enthusiastic attendance of 15-20 parents at these planning meetings, there seemed to be genuine interest in creating the new group. Only three or four faculty members attended the meetings, however, an indication that teachers probably did not wish to spend time in that way. Nevertheless, the parents wanted to proceed and the Fluvanna County High School Parent Teacher Organization was born.

For those who were active in it, the meetings and the relationship formed with the principal provided a genuine avenue for input about decisions, including the subsequent decision to change from a traditional schedule to a modified block schedule. The PTO also provided the avenue to inform members about school programs, such as the ITI pilot program initiated in year two of McGeehan's principalship. The disappointing aspect of the group was the generally low participation. The empowering aspect was the group's ability within two years of its inception to plan and carry out an innovative and elaborate after-prom party.

Family Members as Volunteers

Family members can provide many services to high schools that can be performed both at home and at the school. In spite of what students say, most are proud to have their guardian, mother, or father help at school. Students frequently seemed quite pleased when the principal or other staff member privately acknowledged their family member's contributions.

To encourage broader participation, the PTO sent a menu of volunteer opportunities home each fall. A fairly small number were returned. Some who returned the form commented that they were never called after that. Follow-up was not consistent, so that some families assumed that the school wasn't serious about wanting their help. In hindsight, the principal and teacher leaders needed to be more directly involved with the PTO effort to "sell" the school's desire to involve family members and to generate a viable volunteer corps.

On a more positive note, parents did assist with office duties, publication of the newsletter, "Fluco Fanfare," and tutoring. A number of teachers arranged for family members to come and describe their careers or special interests.

With the benefit of hindsight, I recommend more parent-to-parent recruiting. Perhaps if this group of active volunteers, based on their own positive experiences, were encouraged to recruit others the numbers of parent volunteers would have expanded beyond the twenty or so "regulars."

Communication with Families

Communication is always complex and is most effective when it occurs face-to-face. It is also a cornerstone of any family involvement program. We needed to increase communication among school personnel and families about their children's learning success or difficulty. The grant that brought ITI to Fluvanna County High School challenged the administration and staff to communicate in new ways.

When we introduced the ITI model—initially involving six teachers and about 100 students—we wanted to keep family members well informed about the dramatic changes happening in their children's classrooms. The spring before our ITI pilot project began, we held orientation meetings to explain the program and the hoped-for benefits for students. Following these meetings, we mailed out more information about ITI and the pilot project. Once the year was underway, the ITI students published a newsletter for their families describing what they were doing and learning.

The ITI teachers hosted family nights periodically at which the students taught family members what they had just learned. These events were well-planned and under attended. Discouraged by the modest response, these nights were discontinued. Upon further reflection, though, the staff realized that they needed to be more persistent in offering such events, while at the same time exploring with families other ways to accomplish the same purposes.

Meanwhile, teachers who were not directly involved in the ITI pilot project were also renewing their efforts to communicate more effectively with families. Monthly positive telephone calls began to build new bridges of understanding. "The Fluco Fanfare" newsletter provided a calendar of activities, tips for parenting teens, reports of FCHS Steering Committee and PTO activities, and recognition of academic and extra-curricular student achievement.

In addition, the administration and staff created the Student Assistance Team (SAT) to provide a constructive link with family members of students experiencing school difficulties. Those who met with the Student Assistance Team realized that others cared deeply and wanted to help solve problems blocking their children's school success. Conferences with teachers and the principal became more frequent as family members trusted that they would be listened to and taken seriously. Working together, the staff and families invented more cooperative solutions.

Families and Marketing

Both family members and students emerged as valuable spokes-persons in marketing innovations. For example, most families whose children had been directly involved with ITI implementation became avid supporters as they witnessed a son's or daughter's renewed enthusiasm for learning and increasingly mature behavior. When a student panel met with the grant evaluation team from the Virginia Department of Education, they provided convincing testimonials about their learning. Sample student opinions expressed include:

"I like the freedom and field trips we take most, because I just think they're really interesting. I wouldn't do anything different. I love it all."

"We're learning a lot more than we were. Sometimes I feel it's too hard but it's teaching us to take responsibility for our own work and the things we do. The one thing I like most is the teachers. The teachers are helping more than regular teachers would."

"The thing I like most is the trust."

Many ITI students applied positive pressure on all teachers, ITI and non-ITI, as they provided feedback about classroom events and learning opportunities that were not brain-compatible. Students made positive comments to teachers not involved directly with ITI when those individuals created more attractive room environments and provided increased variety in instructional approaches.

Conclusion

Successful family involvement in an ITI school must be grounded in acting on the school's basic beliefs. Every aspect of the school's culture and climate need to reflect the eight brain-compatible components. Even then, there remains much **hard work** to be done. The process can't be rushed. The adage, "Actions speak louder than words," applies. Changing "the way we do things around here" is the reward of consistent action and full delivery on promises.

Where ITI is implemented in a part of the school, as in the preceding high school example, the rest of the teachers and the support staff must spend time and effort to understand the differences between the present school culture and the culture of ITI classrooms. How inviting is the school's culture for family members? If there are barriers, what are they and how can they be addressed? We believe that it is from a strong commitment to becoming a brain-compatible school that the most constructive links with home are made.

Plans for empowering families to become a part of the life of the school and its on-going improvement will be effective if you start by thinking about the eight brain-compatible elements as illustrated by the following examples:

Ideas for Building Family Involvement

Brain-Compatible Elements	Enabling Strategies
Absence of Threat	• Warm environment • Specific, personal invitations • A special place in the school for family members to meet and work • Non-judgmental listening • Positive school communications
Meaningful Content	• Insure opportunities for input into significant decisions • Listen carefully to what families want for their children and what they believe interests them • Solicit ideas for locations and events in the community that can be the basis for curriculum • Provide workshops to enhance skills and knowledge
Choices	• Provide a variety of ways to serve, including some home-based options • Seek to understand and remove barriers to active participation • Orient families to new programs and describe options for choosing not to involve their children
Adequate Time	• Explore ways in which family volunteers can free teachers to create curriculum • Involve family members in creating and producing newsletters

Enriched Environment	• Invite family members to help design and decorate brain-compatible common areas, such as the student dining room • Create a resource cadre responsible for identifying and contacting guest speakers and locations that support the curriculum
Collaboration	• Provide families with needed information to accomplish their children's learning goals • Create home-school committees responsible for planning improvement activities • Prepare families to market the school effectively in the larger community
Immediate Feedback	• Ask families regularly, in formal and informal ways, about what is and is not working for their children
Mastery	• Provide training and practice for families in using aspects of ITI at home such as target talk with the Lifelong Guidelines/LIFESKILLS

Knowing that the brain pays attention to what is meaningful, and that both home and school want students to be successful learners, it is certain that learning goals are more likely to be met when school personnel are in constant, honest communication and collaboration with those at home. It takes the LIFESKILLS of caring, effort, perseverance, and patience, but the rewards will exceed the costs.

VIII

Beyond the General Fund

by Susan Brash and Jane Rasp McGeehan

Introduction

Quality education takes money. Quality education through ITI demands an appropriate level of financial commitment to insure first-class, sustained training for the school staff. The time required for staff to learn, plan, and create together will cost money. Providing multiple resources and "being there" experiences for students also costs money. Money, money, money!

We contend that you can get the money you need. Don't let an apparent lack of finances within your school district stop you from implementing ITI. Money in the general fund can be reallocated to promote a brain-compatible school or district. Even when the general fund has provided the final penny that can be found for ITI implementation, don't despair. There are many options to explore for the financial resources you require.

We suggest three broad approaches:

1. Do more with what you have.

2. Ask for help.

3. Be creative and think as an entrepreneur.

As we describe the revenue-generating activities of other schools, we invite you to recall good ideas from your own experience to adapt and use. Develop a strong sense of "the possible" so that lack of money never stops you from doing what you must to make learning brain-compatible for your students.

Doing More With What You Have

1. Textbook Dollars

Begin with a careful examination of general fund dollars. Many schools have site-based councils charged with preparation of all or a part of the school's budget. If you have control over the money being spent for the purchase and replacement of textbooks, find out how much you are spending. It may shock you! Ask yourself and the committee about the return on your investment in textbooks. Are textbooks helping to make your school more brain-compatible? For example, if textbooks are but one of many resources to support learning, would one classroom set plus several for students to borrow meet the need? If money is saved from that fund, reallocate it to other resources to enrich student learning.

We offer several cautionary notes, however, before you transfer general fund money to another spending category in the budget. Study state law and district procedures governing reallocation. Some states, for example, provide a process for obtaining a waiver. Be aggressive in your research, consulting primary sources. Don't necessarily take the word of someone who insists, "You can't do that!" Ask that person to cite the relevant state codes and school board policy.

Also realize that parents and tax payers often believe that each student must have a textbook for real learning to occur. Changing textbook spending patterns without educating your public is an invitation for trouble. Instead, provide clear and exciting pictures of the many ways students are learning effectively with and without the textbook. Help people understand where a textbook is the most useful tool and where it is the weakest.

Finally, internal politics related to the purchase and use of textbooks often presents challenges. Teachers may lack the experience and skill to orchestrate learning without the textbook's structure. The state or school district may not have curriculum guides that identify the most important concepts and skills students will master. School board members may advocate one textbook per student, believing that it worked for them and should therefore work for today's students.

To meet these and other challenges, you must create adequate time for dialogue among leaders representing all levels of the organization. Starting from the brain research, generate defensible policy based on a rationale that is understood by all.

Beyond dialogue, leaders must present the results of student learning, supported by a variety of resources, to parents and community members.

For example, provide students opportunities to demonstrate their learning with presentations for the school board, central office, and school faculties.

As we have learned so well, the students themselves are often the most convincing messengers.

2. Roving Substitute Teachers

Roving substitute teachers present another example of doing more with what you have. Imagine that you want teachers to meet with an ITI coach, observe a colleague's classroom as a peer coach, or write key points and inquiries with their team. In each case, a weekly block of two hours produces more potent results than is usually gained in a whole day once a month.

A number of ITI schools have hired a substitute teacher who is assigned to the ITI coach for the day. As the coach moves through his/her schedule, the substitute teacher frees the regular teacher to confer with the coach, receiving valuable feedback.

In another example, the principal hires four substitute teachers for a day. First thing in the morning, four teachers receive two hours of undisturbed time to write ITI curriculum. At the end of two hours, a brief break is scheduled for the substitute team, after which they release the next teacher team. Following the final cycle, three teams have had a two-hour block of curriculum development time on the same day; twelve teachers have received the gift of time, the students don't lose a total day with their regular teacher, and new curriculum products are ready to use without "burning the midnight oil."

Another cautionary note. Be sure that you have planned IN ADVANCE with the school district's personnel department procedures for assigning substitute teacher days to specific teachers. Most districts have strict guidelines for hiring substitute teachers and you may need think creatively or ask for a variance to make this strategy work. The pay-offs are worth the problem-solving efforts.

Ask For Help

Too many of us in education have a Don Quixote complex, the main symptom of which is going after the "windmill" alone. While such an approach may work for the short term, it is a recipe for frustration and exhaustion over time. Proceeding alone also fails to tap exciting possibilities that emerge only when collaboration with others inside and outside the school becomes routine.

1. Invitations and Gifts

One elementary school invited key community leaders to visit during a Model Teaching Week by Susan Kovalik & Associates. The CEO of the area waste removal company was so impressed by what he saw that he requested a meeting with the superintendent and principal. He proposed an alternative to a monetary contribution, and one that would yield much greater financial benefit. His company would collect the school district's garbage for one year free of charge if the money saved would be shifted to provide more ITI training. The financial officer for the district studied the proposal in relation to the state guidelines and found a way to make it work. The school was able to increase its staff ITI training.

2. Foundations

Along with today's increased emphasis on private sector support for education, many foundations are funding improvement projects for schools and school districts (Baumgartner 1995). Depending on the size of your school district and its beliefs, a local school district foundation may exist to fund creative ideas proposed by teachers. ITI schools are discovering that their ideas are attractive to national, state, and/or local foundations.

Clearly stated goals backed up by specific action plans can generate funds from foundations or other sources, such as the federal government. Consider developing a small team of proposal-writing experts at the school. Read and discuss several "how-to" books on grant writing.

The three good ones are:

- *Designing Successful Grant Proposals*, by Donald C. Orlich
- *Winning Grants Step By Step*, by Mim Carlson
- *Guide to Proposal Writing*, by Jane C. Geever and Patricia McNeil

Practice applying the suggestions to your specific school situation and its unmet ITI needs.

Create the time for the grant-writing team to write a comprehensive grant proposal requesting a sizable amount of money. It is normal for the grant-writing process to be time-consuming and frustrating. It often helps to capture the group's ideas for each sub-section of the proposal in a series of mindmaps, and then work in singles or pairs to write first drafts. The best writer/editor among the group can review and compile the drafts to ensure a consistent format and correct usage. After the team reviews and discusses the edited draft, have at least one other person who knows the ITI model read and react to the proposal. Put the proposal into final form and submit it.

Now you have a prototype proposal from which you can pull parts to create future grant proposals. Provide released time for a teacher on the grant team to write or provide technical assistance as others write related proposals.

Through grants, ITI schools have funded additional ITI training and coaching, expanded technology, artists-in-residence, trips for students, and a variety of learning materials for classrooms. One key to success is to **submit many proposals**. It would be impossible for the principal alone, or any other school leader, to make the time to accomplish this; however, when a team of teachers has the expertise and the prototype proposal as a tool, it is indeed possible to submit multiple grant proposals.

3. Family Member Volunteers as Substitute Teachers

Substitute teachers are expensive but we learned that many tasks related to ITI implementation are achieved best when teachers are freed from regular duties for all or a part of the day. Family members who meet the standards established for substitute teachers in one community volunteer their time to their child's school, thus freeing thousands of dollars to be spent for other purposes. (Refer to chapter seven for more details about this approach.)

4. Trade Gifts and Talents

Educational leaders belong to formal and informal networks with other educators and with people working outside the field of education. Use those networks and the talents they represent to help meet the needs of your school while you build community understanding and support. Consider the training, keynote addresses, or other services you and your staff would be willing to provide to others in exchange for services that you want to receive. For example, perhaps someone in one of your networks is qualified to provide training in Jeanne Gibbs' TRIBES approach to cooperative learning (Gibbs 1995). Arrange for him or her to train your staff. In return, perhaps a teacher from your school can teach an aerobics class at that individual's school. The possibilities are endless and extend beyond education-only networks.

5. Community Partners

The community served by each school has a vested interest in what does or does not happen in that school. Unfortunately, public schools in the past have sent the message too often to "Leave us alone. We are the professionals and we know what we are doing. Don't bother us!" Of course most educators know better than this now. Still, we haven't built enough constructive bridges from community to school and back. ITI curriculum **begins** with a location or event in the real world, so asking the community for help is a must.

Solicitation is **not** the first step in generating financial or in-kind support from community sources. Just as within the work at school, generating support begins by building trusting relationships. The relationships must be established personally, directly, and face-to-face by the school person. Have in mind specific services that the **school can provide** for the business or community agency. Demonstrate a genuine desire to contribute to a partnership at the early stages of the new relationship.

Amy Beverland Elementary has cultivated the support of six business partners. Each agreement shares the essential guideline that partners will not be solicited by the school or school-affiliated groups for money. The principal developed a document about the school, "Amy Beverland Elementary: A Journey Toward Excellence," to share with each prospective business partner. She used the pamphlet as she talked about the school and invited businesses to forge a relationship. Key questions posed were, "Are there things that we can share that would make each of us better as a result?" and "How can we work together to strengthen this community?"

In the spirit of genuine partnership, the school discovered unique services to offer. Examples include:

- Student art work on loan
- Videos of students singing for the holidays (stop by our business and see your children singing, enjoy refreshments, etc.)
- Free advertising in the school newsletter
- Invitations to school events
- Recognition of business partners in all school publications
- Use of school facilities, including meeting rooms and the gym.

A stronger community is good for business and the response to the principal's invitation was positive. In this case, the strong school became part of the reason the homes were built in half the time developers had estimated.

After two years of school-business partnership, the principal and the partners evaluated the outcomes of their mutual efforts. Partners acknowledged that the school partnership created an increased customer base, a greater volume of business, and positive attention from corporate headquarters. Partners' responses exceeded all expectations. Seizing the moment, the principal invited partners to co-sponsor an innovative fund-raiser to underwrite a new class in creative arts. Each partner enthusiastically accepted the invitation.

The fund-raiser selected was a celebrity roast. With high-profile sports and political figures as the targets, a blue-ribbon event was born— complete with crystal and china. Through energetic marketing by the school, parents, and business partners, they raised enough money to make the creative arts class a reality and the "roast" became an annual event widely anticipated in the community.

6. Community Sponsors

While some businesses will not choose to become on-going partners, they may be willing to sponsor a one-time special event. Think about what you want to do and why, and create the budget required to carry out the plan. Present the event in a simple brochure to help you approach a community business or organization with the invitation to become a sponsor.

For example, let's say that you want to offer a series of six parent/family training sessions so that parents have a more complete understanding of the Lifelong Guidelines/LIFESKILLS. Create the brochure that explains how critical parent involvement is to student learning success and describe just how the proposed sessions will increase such involvement among parents at your school. Explain that the school needs donations in order to provide the workshops for parents. The donor can give money for general support or can take responsibility for a line item in the budget, such as refreshments or copying. In return, the school lists the names of all sponsors and what they provided in the workshop program, provides a free advertisement for the business in the school paper, and distributes various coupons from each business sponsor at the end of the workshop session. Using this approach, other schools have generated the resources needed. It can work for your school, too.

School leaders must be willing to do this work directly themselves. While generating much needed financial resources they are also building relationships in the community to help the school reach its goals.

7. Parent-School Groups

Formal parent groups, such as PTA's or PTO's, are invaluable partners when it comes to generating financial resources. However, we recommend strict limitations on the type and number of direct selling projects by students. Instead, consider sponsoring family fun options that give families an evening to enjoy together **and** benefit the school's programs. Such events have a positive impact on many goals of an ITI school. Examples of such events include chili dinners before school district athletic or arts events, carnivals, "Funniest Home Video" nights with popcorn, arts and crafts nights, and talent shows involving whole families. The events sponsored will naturally vary in relation to community differences and the age of the students.

Be Creative and Think As An Entrepreneur

Use creative energy, collaboration, and the mindset of an entrepreneur to ensure that your school has the money it needs to do its work in the right way. Successful schools involve many people, both inside and outside the school family, to generate essential financial resources that help sustain ITI implementation.

Use group processes such as brainstorming and team-building activities to release creative energy and ideas in your school community. As leader, prepare yourself with some extra tools to help you unleash new possibilities. Resources to consult include:

- *Six Thinking Hats,* by Edward de Bono (de Bono 1985)

- *100 Ways to Build Teams,* by Carol Scearce (Scearce 1992)

- *A Whack On The Side Of The Head,* by Roger von Oech (von Oech 1983)

There are hundreds of books to give you ideas. You may have favorites to which you regularly return. Plant the seeds of new ideas, ensure that they fall into fertile soil, assign responsibility, and then LET GO! As others collaborate and take responsibility, many more things are accomplished.

Most educators never took a course in marketing strategies nor have most of us ever felt the urge to buy a book on the topic when browsing in the bookstore. In the nineties and beyond, that attitude is one we can't afford. Spend some time browsing the shelves designed to appeal to small businesses and entrepreneurs. When you go out into the community to solicit financial support, take solid marketing strategies with you. For example:

- Make your appeal in person, usually with an appointment, and supported by the brochure
- Make the contribution meaningful from the sponsor's point of view
- Provide a specific picture of how the money will be used
- Offer a variety of giving levels related to specific budget items
- Think creatively!

As you acquire essential marketing skills, think of it as another opportunity to practice the skills of lifelong learning.

The Mind of the Entrepreneur in Action: Loving Care

Four elementary principals in one school district accepted the superintendent's challenge to provide child care at their schools before and after the school day. For a year, they visited child care programs, talked to directors, gathered information about fees and wages, and investigated legal requirements. They consulted an attorney and an accountant about the legal aspects of forming a business. They organized themselves as a not-for-profit organization under the auspices of the school district. They agreed that all money generated by the newly formed "Loving Care" service at the schools would be spent to benefit the children being served.

Happily, the principals discovered that the needs of the children who came early and stayed late frequently overlapped with the needs of the children who were at the school during the day—often the same group. These included additional carpeting for the areas of the school used by the program, different kinds of playground equipment, enhanced computer hardware and software, and books on topics of interest to the students.

The principals also discovered that the day care function at the school increased their own responsibilities. However, they found that the benefits accrued proportionally. "Loving Care" is just one example of what creativity, collaboration, and thinking like an entrepreneur can do.

Conclusion

Here's the BIG MESSAGE of this chapter: **Don't let lack of money slow or erode your ITI implementation process!** Through business partnerships and by combining staff talents, school leaders can generate the money they need to build a brain-compatible school. Here is a quick summary of the success strategies we recommend:

1. Build trust.

2. Establish a process that involves others.

3. Know where you are going and plan thoughtfully how to get there.

4. Listen carefully as you share ideas and possibilities.

5. Plan some more.

6. Listen some more.

7. Think creatively.

8. DO SOMETHING!

We know from our experiences that ensuring needed financial resources takes time. One person has just 24 hours each day, but two people have 48 hours, and three people have 72. Enlist the help you need, but know that the money you need IS out there.

IX

What It Takes to Create a Brain-Compatible School District

by Jane Rasp McGeehan

Introduction

It was the regularly scheduled school board meeting and discussion among board members was becoming heated and not always cordial. A parent in the audience rose to speak. She said, gesturing toward two lists prominently displayed on the board room wall, "We are teaching our children the Lifelong Guidelines and LIFESKILLS in our schools. We need more of them here in this discussion." The meeting resumed—but this time with a more positive tone. The issue under discussion was resolved constructively by the end of the meeting.

This anecdote, shared recently by a district administrator, illustrates the power of common language and goals to influence the way things are done throughout the organization. These school board members had attended the ITI training they provided for the district staff, and the district had created opportunities for parents to learn the new ways along with their children. The leadership in this district believes that providing brain-compatible work and learning experiences is everybody's business.

Just as the brain-compatible classroom will wither and fail in a school that is not brain-compatible, so will the brain-compatible school finally wither in a school district that is not brain-compatible. Traditional school district culture, relying on bureaucratic structures, clashes with ITI brain basics (chapter 1, pp. 4-7) and brain-compatible elements (chapter 1, pp. 7-10). A bureaucracy is inherently brain-antagonistic.

Leaders at the district level have the responsibility and the exciting challenge to determine what it means to be a brain-compatible school system, and to set the course toward this goal. It requires nothing less than re-inventing a school system: true systemic change.

There is no prescription for becoming a brain-compatible school district. While the ITI rubrics can provide specific benchmarks, each school system's unique context is determined by community expectations, the present culture of the organization, the special talents and gifts of the people who comprise the organization, and the quality of leadership at all levels. The people within the school district must engage in rich and truthful dialogue leading to agreement about the implications of the ITI brain basics and brain-compatible elements. Under enlightened leadership, people create a new organization specifically designed to fulfill the intent behind the ITI model. Within the newly configured organization, each person—from the student to the school board member—does his or her work in an environment designed to allow individuals the latitude to solve problems and to create products using the full range of personal capabilities.

Imagine what can be accomplished if everyone in a school district uses the Lifelong Guidelines and LIFESKILLS to guide decisions and personal interactions! Such a district can expect to exceed prior expectations for student and organizational achievements. In such an organization people will enjoy their work and be inspired by the learning opportunities.

In this chapter I examine one process for becoming a brain-compatible school district. Grounded in my personal experiences and those of three other district level school administrators with whom I conferred, the recommendations are offered to stimulate thinking about the best approach where you are. Steps I'll discuss include:

1. Ensure a solid knowledge base, beginning with your leaders, about brain research findings and their significance for learning

2. Conduct a personal audit to explore the extent to which your own behavior with colleagues aligns with the ITI Lifelong Guidelines and LIFESKILLS

3. Conduct a climate audit in each school

4. Review or develop a district mission statement

5. Explore and define systemic change to fulfill to that mission

6. Define essential services and functions to support schools

7. Define essential school responsibilities

8. Establish agreements about culture and climate

9. Find out how it's going

10. Determine the next steps.

Becoming a brain-compatible school district is not a "quick fix." Getting there is a non-linear journey of at least three and more likely five years. In the most successful school districts, educators report that it can take seven or eight years to develop a clear and full understanding of what it means to work and to learn together brain-compatibly. Let's take closer look at each of the above points.

Getting Started: The Knowledge Base

The starting point is shared knowledge among school leaders of the brain research findings and their significance for learning. The goal is to extend that knowledge base to the entire school community through dialogue and training. Common sense suggests and brain research confirms that humans understand and use that which they directly experience and practice. Everyone must become familiar with the ITI brain basics and how to apply them. In time, a common language will emerge to describe what research and effective practice suggest. Such a common language promotes essential dialogue among all educators throughout the district.

Establishing the knowledge base requires the district to provide both shared experiences and options. Perhaps consultants can introduce information to the whole group and suggest additional resource materials. Study groups can read and discuss a book about the brain research with the assistance of a skilled facilitator. Leadership teams visit brain-compatible schools and districts, get a clear picture of the possibilities, and return to share with colleagues. Other teams analyze relevant video tapes.

The biology of human learning is compelling. Its importance cannot be ignored. As people learn more and more, and realize how the information matches their own experiences, their excitement increases and spreads.

Conduct Personal Audit

The inconvenient truth is that lasting change in an organization begins as change happens within each individual. As a result, the first place for applying the new knowledge base is within oneself. A personal audit identifies aspects of relationships that are already brain-compatible; it also points the way to growth goals.

Start with the first ITI brain basic, that our emotions are the gate-keepers to performance. If we each fully understand that threatening relationships and stressful environments are counter productive to learning, we will also understand that learning demands a secure, relaxed setting.

Such a setting applies to your co-workers and your relationships with them. The ITI Lifelong Guidelines and LIFESKILLS suggest a fruitful set of questions about the starting points for those relationships.

The first guideline advises, "Be trustworthy." In your personal audit, ask yourself and perhaps a few trusted co-workers such things as:

- Do I follow through consistently on promises?

- Do I keep confidences and avoid gossip?

- Am I punctual?

- Do I maintain an even emotional temperament despite difficult circumstances?

- Do I make fair decisions based on stated criteria?

Appendix E provides one example of a personal audit that may assist as you design your own.

In Figure 9.1, Dean Tannewitz, an associate of Susan Kovalik, has developed an elegant strategy for making behaviors associated with each of the Lifelong Guidelines explicit and representative of the behaviors of a unique individual or group. In making the chart, she incorporated ideas from John Champlain, education consultant on school reform and former school superintendent.

In hindsight I realize that my leadership as a principal seeking to implement ITI would have been much more effective if I had made the time for our high school faculty to complete the chart together. Anyone who states the specific positive and negative behaviors that define each of the Lifelong Guidelines comes to a clearer understanding of the guide-line's meaning in that specific setting. I see now that such understandings and agreements about behavior could have led directly to a more secure and three-free environment within our high school.

Figure 9.1

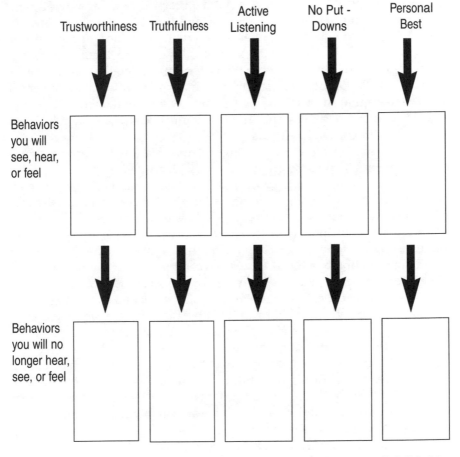

Lifelong Guidelines and Associated Behaviors

© 1994 Dean Tannewitz, Associate Susan Kovalik & Associates

Conduct a Climate Audit; Review/Develop Mission Statement

Successful change requires specific knowledge of the district's present situation in relation and its goals. A school district's mission statement lets everyone know up front why the organization exists, what it's working to achieve, and what its top priorities are. The climate audit provides a rich description of **what** is happening and **how** it is happening in the schools and in the central office as people work to achieve the mission. We'll take a closer look at both.

A meaningful mission statement requires dialogue among all who have a vested interest in the school community. A thorough exchange of ideas yields statements of belief, organizational values, specific goals, action plans, and assessment strategies designed to focus day-to-day behaviors and decisions. Others have written in detail about the planning and collaboration needed to derive a potent mission statement; I won't repeat that information here (Senge 1994). Remember, if a school district already has a mission statement, it must be analyzed in relation to the new brain-compatible goals.

The mission statement of a district that aspires to become brain-compatible must: a) focus on the school as a learning center, and b) serve as the over-arching definition of meaningful content. Fully understood, the successful mission statement gives birth to policies and practices that serve learning first. Additionally, the statement provides the ultimate answer to the question, "Does this (idea, suggestion, instructional strategy) have the power to help us achieve our school district's stated mission in a brain-compatible way?" If a proposal can't meet that test for meaningful content in terms of available research and data, it is dropped.

The process for creating the mission statement and reviewing it on a regular basis provides the format for important dialogue about assumptions that underlie the present school and district programs and practices. What are the often unexamined beliefs about learning? What is the role of teacher, administrator, parent, and community member with respect to fostering learning throughout the community? What are the goals of learning? These and other questions give rise to essential dialogue that opens the door for vital new possibilities. The biggest mistake leaders make at this point is to rush the process. Truly, the process is as important as the final product as the exchange of ideas involving many in the school-community brings people together around common goals and helps them understand their differences.

The district's mission is best pursued in a brain-compatible climate—that's where the audit is useful. The climate audit reveals what is going on inside schools and across the school district. It describes the status quo as seen through observations, interviews, document analysis, and surveys of the various stakeholders. The audit can be conducted by an outside group, such as an organization of retired school administrators, with initial input into its design from district personnel and the school board. It can also be conducted by the district itself if the staff has the time, expertise, and experience. Which approach is selected depends on the desired scope, the sense of trust within the district, and the availability of resources.

The questions posed are designed to shed light on the extent to which individual schools and the school district as a whole act upon the brain research. (See Appendix E for sample climate audit procedures and instruments.) The ITI brain basics serve as organizers for question-asking and for data analysis. The ITI brain-compatible elements are woven throughout the sample surveys and interview questions. While meaningful content, enriched environment, and mastery lead to questions that are more focused on the "what" of the organization, absence of threat, choices, adequate time, collaboration, and immediate feedback lead to questions more focused on the "how."

A few examples illustrate how the ITI brain basics frame the climate audit survey and interview questions. To probe the impact of emotions on the work place for both certified and classified staff, one might ask:

- When you see a way to do your work more effectively, do you discuss your idea with your supervisor? Why or why not?

- With whom do you share complaints?

- Are put-downs generally considered to be "friendly joking?" If so, what is your view of this type of joking? If not, how are put-downs generally viewed? How does the usual joking in the work place affect your work?

- Does anything at work make you angry or upset?

- When and how are you supported in your work?

- To whom at work can you confide that you have made an error and need advice about next steps?

From the data collected, you can recognize patterns that describe a place where people are relaxed and trusting of one another, or one where people are hesitant and/or defensive. Probing the full range of the ITI brain basics and the brain-compatible elements yields specific information about the existing climate in which people work and learn. These rich descriptions clarify the present situation and suggest next steps in the pursuit of the district's mission.

Explore and Define Systemic Change

(Refer also to chapter two discussing leadership for change at the school level.)

The changes required to become a brain-compatible school district *do not constitute an update of the status quo.* As Susan Kovalik has frequently stated, "ITI is not about tinkering." Systemic change is required. Systemic change by definition affects all parts of the school district. At the very least, each part of the district reviews its present status in relation to brain-compatible structures and behaviors.

Figure 9.2

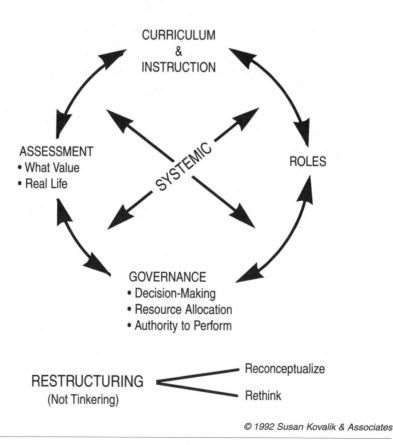

Systemic Change

© 1992 Susan Kovalik & Associates

During a systemic change process, leaders arrange for honest, open dialogue about what brain-compatible, systemic change means for the school district and its employees. The skills of an outside facilitator and pre-established guidelines to govern such conversations increase the likelihood that people are sharing their views truthfully. Challenging a group to design the ideal brain-compatible school district is a useful strategy for encouraging people to "think outside the box."

It is critical at this point for everyone to understand that the school district will not achieve its ITI goals unless it expects more than a few surface changes and innovations. That familiar brand of school reform is simply inadequate to address professionally the application of best knowledge and best practice in relation to biology of learning.

As a clearer picture of the restructured school district comes into focus, specific roles may need to be redefined. For example, a director of secondary education who coordinates the work of teams of teachers to write district curriculum may become instead an ITI curriculum coach. Here she will help teachers write, refine, and strengthen their own curriculum to meet district and state learning goals. She will advocate for conceptual, developmentally-appropriate district curriculum guides and help to identify community resources to ground the curriculum in the real world.

Of course, committed school districts will ensure the training and practice necessary for every coach to excel in their redefined roles while they also reassign or remove people unable to meet new expectations.

Two books by leadership authority William Bridges, *Managing Transitions* (Bridges 1991) and *Job Shift* (Bridges 1994), offer excellent advice about what to expect as changes are implemented. For example, he suggests that leaders create a transition team at the outset to monitor and plan constructively for peoples' responses to change. Such a transition team helps to anticipate and to mitigate conflicts that are bound to occur.

Looking back on personal experiences as a high school principal and an assistant superintendent, I can see that some of the comments and behaviors that I perceived as intentional efforts to undermine were in fact normal expressions of people struggling with the transition from the old to the new. Without question those staffs would have benefitted by understanding and talking openly about their feelings as they faced significant change. A transition team could have prevented painful confrontations in the teachers' lounge and angry parking lot discussions.

Throughout the process, leaders must identify and monitor factors that inhibit change in the school district. Consider the following list developed by Wayne Miller, former district office administrator in Pittsburg, California:

Factors Inhibiting Change

- Concentration of power at the top: the myth of the omniscient leader, management valued over leadership, risk of change in direction with each new superintendent

- School districts governed by persons who frequently are unfamiliar with learning theory and the brain research

- Over-arching concern with bureaucracy: school districts devote time, energy, and resources primarily to management rather than to learning

- Top-down hierarchy and limited role for teachers (Miller 1996).

This list suggests remedies as you consider what the opposite of each limiting factor would be. Your own list may vary, but the point is that by examining and analyzing inhibiting factors, you also begin to focus on how to correct or remove them.

Define Essential Services and Functions to Support Schools

In view of the brain research findings and the school district's mission, what do schools need from the central office so that all schools in the district benefit? The answers vary for different school districts, but a few examples are illustrative. Related ITI brain-compatible elements appear in the parentheses.

District Support for a Brain-Compatible School

- State a continuum of developmentally appropriate concepts and related skills that students are expected to master (mastery, meaningful content)

- Conduct brain-compatible meetings and personal interactions (absence of threat, mastery)

- Articulate clear district mission, goals, and beliefs (meaningful content)

- Monitor written communications to assure alignment with mission and goals (meaningful content)

Note: One district created a rubber stamp to label which brain-compatible element the memo supports.

Brain-Compatible Education								
Absence of Threat	Meaningful Content	Collaboration	Adequate Time	Immediate Feedback	Choices	Enriched Environment	Mastery/ Application	Routine Business
☐	☐	☐	☐	☐	☐	☐	☐	☐

- Provide focus, time, and support to master desired changes (adequate time, mastery)

- Provide assurance that an innovation has support beyond the framework of an individual superintendent's contract (absence of threat, mastery, collaboration)

- Provide resources for field trips and for a variety of instructional supplies (enriched environment)

- Create school schedules and calendars that promote staff collaboration, research, planning, curriculum development, and professional growth (collaboration, mastery, and adequate time)

- Give coaching and direct assistance, including suggestions for other ITI schools to visit (immediate feedback, collaboration)

- Arrange options to sustain professional growth in applying brain-compatible principles (absence of threat, choices)

- Render legal advice (meaningful content, collaboration)

- Supply education research updates, especially regarding brain research and effective practice regionally and nationally (meaningful content)

- Streamline routine reporting (meaningful content, collaboration, adequate time)

- Plan effective district-wide communication strategies that include school board members and build the sense of community (immediate feedback, collaboration, absence of threat, meaningful content)

- Procure resources and training for peer coaching activities (immediate feedback, collaboration)

- Allocate state and local financial resources equitably to provide direct support for achieving brain-compatible goals (meaningful content, enriched environment)

This list is illustrative, not exhaustive. The local discussion that produces such a list in your school district is vital. By asking what is essential, needs may surface that are currently unmet. Possibly, existing district functions and services will emerge as superfluous, especially as you analyze budget items for their direct connection to student learning.

Define Essential School Responsibilities

The whole point of acting on the biology of learning across an entire school district is to produce extraordinary learning results for students. Ultimately, responsibility for creating brain-compatible learning opportunities must rest with the staff at the school—the contact point for students and the school district.

The brain-compatible school district entrusts school-based teams to make decisions based on best knowledge and best practice that achieve learning results. While the district determines the broad goals, monitors, coaches, and ensures adequate resources as described above, heavy responsibility for action falls on the shoulders of teachers, parents, students, administrators, support staff, and community volunteers collaborating within schools.

Examples of these responsibilities highlight their vital nature. The related ITI brain-compatible elements and Lifelong Guidelines appear in the parentheses.

School Responsibilities

- Create integrated curriculum built upon nearby locations to teach concepts and related skills (meaningful content)

- Document the extent to which all students are learning what the district and state expects (mastery, meaningful content)

- Document how the staff is expanding professional skills through participation in relevant training and coaching (mastery, personal best)

- Gather demographic data so that the district can monitor population trends (meaningful content)

- Make requests of the district office well ahead of deadlines (adequate time, personal best)

- Document all expenditures and their link to student learning (trustworthiness, truthfulness, enriched environment)

- Assess and summarize community attitudes and opinions about issues relevant to school improvement (immediate feedback, meaningful content)

- Supply information for routine district reports to the state or other funding sources; and explain how (or whether) such information contributes to best knowledge and best practice at the school (collaboration, meaningful content, truthfulness)

- Engage in honest dialogue with colleagues at other schools and the district office to identify and resolve new or unmet needs that block progress toward achieving district priorities (truthfulness, collaboration, immediate feedback)

With the creation of such lists, some present priorities remain, some are dropped after failing the new tests for relevance, and new priorities emerge. For example, analyzing the school and district budgets through the lens of brain-compatibility is likely to reveal funds that can be reallocated to purposes that are closer to the heart of the district's mission.

The main point is that leaders must have the courage to examine all aspects of the organization so that district services and functions are focused on the intention to provide brain-compatible learning.

Establish Agreements About Culture and Climate

By school culture I mean "the way things are done around here." The prevailing culture of most school districts is resistant to change. The ideas of Lee Bolman and Terrence Deal in *Reframing Organizations* are useful:

"Culture is both product and process. As product, it embodies the accumulated wisdom of those who were members before we came. As process, it is continually renewed and re-created as new members are taught the old ways and eventually become teachers themselves"(Bolman and Deal 1991, 250).

The leaders in a brain-compatible district emphasize dialogue, question-asking, and coaching. They help to create the change-friendly culture essential as the new wisdom accumulates. It becomes the norm.

Climate is the general mood that results from the culture of the school district. It is a subjective thing, yet one that we intuitively sense when we enter a school, the district office, or the superintendent's office. Are people friendly? Cheerful? Business-like? Smiling? Anxious? Nervous? Calm? A brain-compatible culture yields a highly desirable working climate.

The required climate begins at the top: ITI implementation starts with district leadership. Leaders at all levels must show by their attitudes and behaviors what they expect from other staff and from students. That is a tough order when the standards are so high! Teachers who have lost their habit of regular reading must find it. Superintendents must model life-long learning. Principals must collaborate with teachers to design ways for teachers to choose their own professional growth goals. Teachers must engage learners only in content that is meaningful and connected to something about which those learners care. Everyone must incorporate the Lifelong Guidelines and LIFESKILLS into their daily behaviors.

In sum, if learning continuously is to be valued within the culture of the school district, everyone's behaviors must say so—especially those assuming leadership roles and responsibilities. Susan Kovalik shared with me an interesting experience from a recent speaking engagement in Singapore. The Minister of Education sent word that he would be attending the first hour of the day-long event. He ended up staying the entire day, which meant cancelling an important cabinet meeting at the last minute. His participation in the seminar, he decided, was more important. Such a change was unheard of! But what a powerful signal the behavior sent about his priorities.

All too often, though, the situation reported by a teacher at an ITI workshop is typical:

> "Principals need to be here with their teachers. District personnel need to decide either to be here and take full part or stay out. Their pop-in/pop-out, sit in the back/stand-in-the-doorway behaviors are minimally interruptive but more so snobbish and demeaning. They convey the idea that either they don't really need to hear this or that their time is more valuable than ours and they can't afford to be here whole-mindedly. The question lingers: Are they willing to lend more than verbal support to the venture?"(Teacher 1997).

This teacher's words eloquently underscore the need for us all to behave in the ways we expect others to behave.

Agreement to use the Lifelong Guidelines and LIFESKILLS among all personnel throughout a school district is an excellent starting point for creating a more brain-compatible culture and climate. To illustrate some constructive strategies, consider the Lifelong Guideline, "trustworthiness." We too often assume that everyone in the group knows what that means, but the reality is that we have many different ideas. Conversation needs to center on what it looks like, sounds like, and feels like when trustworthy behavior occurs. Examples of trustworthy behavior must be described. Pose the potent question, "What behaviors would we no longer see in our organization if everyone were continuously trustworthy?" Not only does a clear understanding of "trustworthiness" emerge, but also the people involved in the conversation will feel a stronger sense of community for having participated.

Once the group agrees on what is meant by "trustworthiness," they need to practice in advance of an actual situation how to confront a colleague's behavior that doesn't seem to match the group's agreements. John Champlin suggests the following formula with appropriate variations:

"We agreed...I saw...Help me understand"(Champlain 1993).

It is entirely possible that the apparently inappropriate behavior has a logical explanation. If not, the door is open for dialogue to resolve the matter rather than allowing it to linger and further erode the atmosphere of trust and community that is so important. Agreements across an entire school district about how to treat people have tremendous power to build a safe, trusting culture and climate.

Find Out How It's Going

ITI implementation at the school level is a three-to-five-year process when there is strong leadership and appropriate support. It is reasonable to expect that it will take at least that long to become a school district achieving its mission brain-compatibly. At regular intervals along the way, people need immediate feedback to document individual and collective achievements.

The climate audit describes the starting point and establishes a process for marking progress. People involved in their own self-assessment tend to be more interested in the results, so involve many in gathering evidence of progress.

Always return to the brain basics and their practical application in the ITI brain-compatible elements to answer the big questions about goal achievement. The ITI rubrics for classroom and schoolwide implementation provide specific benchmarks against which to measure accomplishments throughout the district. On the other hand, when the data gathered show achievement of rubric benchmarks, everyone can celebrate. When visits to the school by district office personnel are eagerly anticipated where before they were feared, then hooray! Trust and healthy collaboration are thriving.

behavior occurs. Examples of trustworthy behavior must be described. Pose the potent question, "What behaviors would we no longer see in our organization if everyone were continuously trustworthy?" Not only does a clear understanding of "trustworthiness" emerge, but also the people involved in the conversation will feel a stronger sense of community for having participated.

Once the group agrees on what is meant by "trustworthiness," they need to practice in advance of an actual situation how to confront a colleague's behavior that doesn't seem to match the group's agreements. John Champlin suggests the following formula with appropriate variations:

"We agreed...I saw...Help me understand"(Champlain 1993).

It is entirely possible that the apparently inappropriate behavior has a logical explanation. If not, the door is open for dialogue to resolve the matter rather than allowing it to linger and further erode the atmosphere of trust and community that is so important. Agreements across an entire school district about how to treat people have tremendous power to build a safe, trusting culture and climate.

Find Out How It's Going

ITI implementation at the school level is a three-to-five-year process when there is strong leadership and appropriate support. It is reasonable to expect that it will take at least that long to become a school district achieving its mission brain-compatibly. At regular intervals along the way, people need immediate feedback to document individual and collective achievements.

The climate audit describes the starting point and establishes a process for marking progress. People involved in their own self-assessment tend to be more interested in the results, so involve many in gathering evidence of progress.

Always return to the brain basics and their practical application in the ITI brain-compatible elements to answer the big questions about goal achievement. The ITI rubrics for classroom and schoolwide implementation provide specific benchmarks against which to measure accomplishments throughout the district. On the other hand, when the data gathered show achievement of rubric benchmarks, everyone can celebrate. When visits to the school by district office personnel are eagerly anticipated where before they were feared, then hooray! Trust and healthy collaboration are thriving.

Determine Next Steps

The answers to two broad questions will help you choose your future path:

1. How will district office personnel help to identify and sustain the implementation achievements already realized?

2. How will district office personnel contribute to identifying and achieving the next cluster of implementation goals?

My personal experience leading ITI implementation at the high school level taught me not to take for granted what we had already accomplished. I made that mistake when I judged that the strong sense of team spirit and commitment to our goals were nearly indestructible. After all, I thought, the pilot project team had invested hours together during the summer laughing and crying their way through the challenges of curriculum development. Therefore, with time always at a premium when the team met during the school year, we seldom placed a priority on team-building activities.

Gradually, and unintentionally, team spirit weakened. Competing priorities intruded into time that had been reserved exclusively for team planning and assessment. Frustration among team members surfaced— a major distraction from the central tasks.

I learned a vital lesson. Plan in advance of loss or frustration. This is a key area in which district office personnel can help to sustain and build upon existing accomplishments.

While the first "next step" is to avoid slippage, the very important second step is to use climate audit data and other reflections of the present situation to focus energy productively on achieving the next cluster of implementation goals. With the district mission in the forefront, review and adjust action plan time lines.

For example, what are the greatest barriers between where the schools want to be in their ITI journeys and where they are now? How can the district office help them remove, reduce, or go around such barriers?

One thing is absolutely clear from the work that Susan Kovalik & Associates is doing with teachers, schools, and districts: if the school board and district office staff aren't behind the move toward brain compatibility, individual schools eventually give up. Most often people can't find the time and energy to proceed with ITI **and** the latest new program that may or may not complement the school's ITI plans but is expected by the district leadership.

Conclusion: Brain-Compatibility Starts at the Top

Without enlightened leadership any significant change effort is doomed. If ITI is to be implemented on a school-wide basis, the principals must play a key role. If the school district is to become brain-compatible, a highly skilled and visionary superintendent is vital. Roles and job descriptions change when the goal is to implement ITI and operate on the basis of brain research findings, and it must start at the top. The superintendent must have courage, resiliency, and determination. The traditional "big boss" model must go. New roles presenting very different challenges must replace the old, even though they seldom feel comfortable at first.

The superintendent of a brain-compatible school district is:

- A continuous learner and a teacher, a scholar of current brain research findings and their implications for learning and administration

- A facilitator and supporter, ready to be cheerleader

- A visionary who has a deep understanding of change processes

- A resource—well informed, well read, experienced

- A leader who shares vital information

- A coordinator of a learning organization where the growth of each person is valued and expected

- An observer and an analyst who notes important patterns

- A politician who understands dynamics of school boards and community involvement

- An advocate for learning who keeps all facets of the organization focused on student learning

- An ambassador of learning to the larger community who represents the interests of students in talking with the community and in soliciting support for the district's learning program.

I thank Marilyn Kelly, superintendent of the Sonoma Valley Unified School District, and Wayne Miller for sharing their insights in preparing this list.

The good news is that there are highly skilled superintendents and prospective superintendents who know how to serve in these various roles; they know how to choose talented assistants to complement their own personal strengths and weaknesses. Also, with clear pictures of these indispensable characteristics in mind, school boards can more successfully identify and recruit such leaders.

Implementing ITI Regionally

by Ken Horn

Introduction

In Michigan, fifty-seven Educational Service Agencies (ESA) provide leadership, programs, and services that compliment and enhance
the efforts of local school districts. For change to succeed on such a
regional basis across school districts, at least one individual must be the
keeper of the vision. This person serves in a key role, and must be the
project coordinator and facilitator.

It is important that the ESA identify someone within the organization
who understands and supports ITI to serve in this role. Often, this is not
a formal selection process but falls to the consultant whose interests
appear to be the most related to the work to be done. How the facilitator
is chosen is irrelevant as long as he/she has a zest for working with people,
is an avid student of brain research findings and implications, and is
committed to ITI. These qualities are critical to continuously support and
assist teachers and schools as they implement ITI.

Continuous support can take several directions but the key thrust
and focus must always be clear. Continuous support implies three key
ideas. First, the ITI facilitator must be knowledgeable about the various
parts of the model and must have the skills and aptitude to share information while encouraging and motivating others. Secondly, information
must be shared in a multitude of ways, such as coaching, one-on-one
consultations, and small and large group presentations. In addition, it is
critical that teachers make the connections between ITI and other current
workshop offerings. Thirdly, to maintain credibility the ITI facilitator
should only be involved in workshops that connect to the ITI model.
Often, the key task for the ITI facilitator is to assure that teachers attending
workshops can clearly visualize the connections to the ITI model. The ITI
facilitator who offers workshops that espouse a philosophy that is the

opposite of ITI will soon find that he/she has lost all credibility. If a regional service district is serious about actively supporting teachers as they implement the ITI model, then that commitment must begin with the ESA's ITI facilitator clearly focusing upon supporting the ITI model. This sends a strong message that ITI is here to stay and that the ESA is committed to its full implementation.

The Muskegon Michigan Example

As of this writing, five hundred teachers in the Muskegon Area Intermediate School District (MAISD), the Educational Service Agency in Muskegon, Michigan, have been trained in the ITI model of brain-compatible instruction. Despite the diversity of school districts served by our ESA—urban, inner city, affluent, suburban and rural—key components of the ITI model can be found in each one. Introduced in 1992, the ITI model continues to grow in strength and popularity and is widely recognized as the most powerful staff development program ever to be undertaken by the MAISD. Several principals and two school districts now require that new elementary teachers take and implement ITI training as a condition of employment. In addition, many teachers from the counties north and south of us have been involved in ITI through the MAISD training. This chapter will tell the story of how ITI has been supported and fostered within the MAISD.

The Adventure

We started our adventure with the ITI model by having Susan Kovalik come and work with a group of over two hundred educators who filled a large auditorium at the local community college. Concurrent with Susan's presentation we launched an intensive recruitment campaign inviting teachers to give up one week of their summer to attend the ITI Model Teaching Week. Setting a precedent for our county, this was the first teacher training program held during summer vacation. Furthermore, we requested and received a commitment from the twelve local school districts that teachers would not be paid for attending. That agreement marked one of the first times that all twelve districts worked together to support ITI.

To qualify to attend the first Model Teaching Week, all teachers had to come as part of a team. No teacher could attend unless he/she had a partner from his/her school to provide help and support with classroom application of ITI strategies. Eighty-three teachers from ten different school districts attended the trainings.

The following October, about six weeks after the start of school, we invited all eighty-three of the summer's participants to a dinner meeting called, "A Celebration of Success." Each one received a fancy invitation modeled after a wedding invitation. We sent each registrant two post-cards which they were asked to bring along. One postcard asked for success stories and the other asked for concerns, problems, or questions. The concern postcards were for me to use to plan follow-up activities. At the dinner teachers were mixed with colleagues from other districts and were asked to share success stories. After all participants had an opportunity to share at their tables, several tables asked to share with the large group. The most powerful comments came from a junior high teacher who said, "For the last eleven years, I have been blaming my students, their parents, and families for the lack of respect and learning in my classroom. This has been my best year ever and I've come to realize that the problem was me, not them. I can't ever go back to what I did before." By the end of her comments, it was hard to find a dry eye in the place!

After the testimonials, we brainstormed, listing and categorizing their concerns and generating ideas. Based on their requests, I selected and attended workshops across the state to gather information to return and share with this group of ITI pioneers.

I sifted through the workshop materials and concepts, selecting those that supported the ITI model. Thus, I developed my own skills at gleaning information from multiple sources, finding the key concepts, and then creating a workshop to meet the specific needs of teachers working toward brain-compatibility. Among the more popular workshops were, "Making Sense of Learning Styles," "Dittos Don't Grow Dendrites" (brain research), and "Effective Team Teaching" (using ITI to make special education inclusion work). As a result, I found myself in a new role—that of workshop presenter. (See Appendix F for a complete list of workshops.)

We hired Ann Ross, our ITI trainer from Susan Kovalik & Associates for the summer Model Teaching Week, to return to answer teachers' questions and help sustain motivation. By December, in spite of our best efforts, many of the teachers had "hit the wall" and were running out of energy and enthusiasm. I visited as many classrooms as possible, stopping by the principal's office to brag about what their teachers were doing.

Our next step was to start an extensive professional library collection at the MAISD. Teachers were asked to suggest book titles that would be helpful. We ordered almost every book requested and made sure that the requesting teachers were the first persons to borrow each title that they recommended. In addition, I had managed to secure a small sum of money for classroom materials to support the teachers implementing ITI.

Teachers must continuously have opportunities to upgrade their skills to create brain-compatible learning for students. We provided such opportunities with monthly workshops. To be sure each workshop assisted the change to brain-compatible classrooms, we designed them to model the concepts of the ITI model. Common features of all our workshops effectively showed what we were asking teachers to do in their classrooms. They included:

- Posted procedures upon entering the workshop

- A webbed mindmap of the workshop agenda

- A brain-compatible environment including lamps, plants, appropriate color coordination, a choice of snacks, and the use of chimes to signal transitions

- Introductory activities designed to build community and promote networking

- Collaborative activities that used Howard Gardner's multiple intelligences

- Building in processing time using the LIFESKILLS, e.g., discussing which LIFESKILLS helped to complete the task successfully

- At the end, we focused on discovering the connections between the workshop content and the specific components of the ITI model. While this commitment to model brain-compatible learning created more work for us, we remain convinced of its value. The most powerful learning comes from direct experiences.

The workshop contents helped teachers grow in understanding the many components of the ITI model; however, opportunities to network and share ideas frequently proved to be even more valuable. Realizing this, we established a tradition of launching the school year by inviting teachers from across the ESA together for an evening of networking. This evening is extremely important and must occur shortly after teachers have been trained.

Each October, we invite all of the newly trained teachers to an evening program at which the summer trainer from Susan Kovalik & Associates reviews ITI concepts. We continue the tradition of calling the event "A Celebration of Success." It is a three-hour evening program of networking, celebrating, and reviewing. We send a classy invitation, and serve a deluxe meal. The whole event sends a powerful message that we honor what teachers are trying to do, and that we are committed to successful ITI implementation. We continue to ask teachers and principals to come prepared to share one success story with their table-mates. That pattern, established for the initial celebration, continues to be a part of the success formula.

As I began working with teachers and schools trying to support them in their efforts to do ITI, it became clear that I needed to spend more time in their schools and classrooms. I became more visible by visiting class-rooms, teaching model lessons, and providing on-site training. By the second year we had repeatedly heard that **all** staff, certified and classified, needed to be trained. We soon began requesting that secretaries, custodians, cooks, bus drivers, para-professionals, and teachers all be trained together. Such training sends a powerful message that everyone is part of the team and that the expectations for behavior using the Lifelong Guidelines and LIFESKILLS are the same. My relationships with school personnel, especially many of the secretaries, soon changed as we both came to know the person on the other end of the telephone line. Not surprisingly, this resulted in better communication.

As I became increasingly involved with classroom teachers, I discov-ered that many of them were looking for one more set of eyes, or a colleague outside their classroom to notice what they were doing. When visiting classrooms, I worked to be perceived as a non-judgmental supporter. I tried not to interrupt teachers but instead to leave a short, written note of encouragement identifying things that were going well. I avoided criticism, unless the teacher asked for specific feedback focused on suggestions for improvement.

When teachers did ask for specific feedback, I learned to pose reflective questions until they identified the concerns. My golden rule has become, " If in doubt, be quiet!" However, I have also learned never to miss an opportunity to tell teachers what they are doing well.

After teachers master a concept, I ask them if they would feel comfortable serving as a resource for other teachers at the same grade level. Two things usually happen. Teachers usually ask for the name of a peer who can help them in their own self-selected area of need, and because someone has recognized what they are doing well, they feel encouraged to continue ITI implementation.

As I grew more involved in the local schools, I seized every opportu-nity to talk about key concepts of the ITI model. Every workshop that I did on multiple intelligences, reading, or inclusion, ended up with my helping the staff see the connections to the brain research. I also delivered a short commercial for the summer's week-long ITI training.

Responding to numerous requests, I also trained interested teachers and support staff members in the ITI model during the school year. I attempted to use teachers as mentors on their own campuses. My initial effort involved a whole school where the principal gave us all of the staff's school improvement time, a total of 5 1/2 days. Our training sessions were conducted during the school day and were attended by the whole staff. The results were disastrous, as the rest of the staff acted very belligerent and testy, and each session became increasingly negative. In spite of the best efforts of six people, this training was a complete calamity. We learned two lessons: It is totally impossible for teachers to be prophets in their own buildings, and training a staff to implement ITI isn't as easy as it looks.

It was a whole year before we again provided ITI training using local educators. I structured my second attempt differently. This time we offered an introductory class with graduate credit for teachers interested in learning more about ITI. We made it clear from the start that this class was not intended to replace the summer training but was designed to pique interest and acquaint teachers with the concepts. Luckily, the local district superintendent and three principals decided to attend the class. In connection with the class, the superintendent agreed to give teacher participants one-half day off to observe in another ITI classroom within the county. This method of introducing the concepts of ITI to teachers has been refined and has now been repeated in three of the twelve school districts within our county. The format for these sessions is a series of four, four-hour evening presentations on the brain research, multiple intelligences, creating a sense of community, and curriculum integration.

Some 70% to 80% of the teachers who take the overview class go on to participate in the week-long intensive summer training. The school district paid for one hour of graduate credit for each of its participating teachers in the most recent class that was offered. This wasn't as expensive as it may sound, as I returned to the local district the money that the MAISD received from the university for sponsoring the class. The final result was a win-win scenario for two reasons: 1) The superintendent, curriculum director, and principals attended, and 2) a large number of teachers from the graduate class attended our intensive week-long summer training. As a result, at the request of two of our superintendents, I am planning to offer a similar introductory class for secondary teachers. This class will be open to secondary teachers from both districts. The districts will pay for the graduate credit for teachers attending.

As we trained more and more teachers it soon became clear that it was essential for me to support the progress of those already trained.

Unable to do that alone, I began to look for ITI classroom teachers who had the skills and ability to share with others. We developed a cadre of mentor teachers, and some remarkable things happened. I discovered that recognizing teachers for their expertise and giving them opportunities to share with peers paid some wonderful dividends. The more teachers shared, the more they improved their own skills and strengthened their convictions. Both mentors and trainees felt more confident.

Sharing with peers can be difficult, so we created several safeguards. No teacher would serve as a mentor in his/her own school district. Instead, the MAISD would coordinate all mentoring on a cross-district basis. All of our attempts at cross-district mentoring and sharing have been wonderfully successful and positive. I feel that our experiences have made it clear that mentoring in another district is far superior to trying to mentor in the homeland.

In addition we developed a cadre of experts who serve in a variety of roles. Taking a page from the Susan Kovalik & Associates training approach, teachers in this cadre work with colleagues as demonstration classroom teachers, small group facilitators, learning club leaders, ITI coaches, and presenters. Now, when I do presentations in local districts, I introduce concepts, and these experienced teachers lead small group follow-up activities and processing. This format allows us to share our expertise in a non-threatening way and give plenty of support.

Experienced ITI teachers also become part of the staff for the summer Model Teaching Weeks. In addition, we provide three local classroom teachers with additional training to set up the model ITI classrooms. For each of the last two summers, nine to ten experienced ITI teachers have served as learning club leaders. These learning club leaders provide grade level discussion opportunities for new teachers who are going through the intensive Model Teaching Week. They share their own experiences and help teachers visualize how the ITI model looks at their specific grade level.

We recently added another eighteen teachers to serve as ITI coaches during the school year. These master ITI teachers are released from their classrooms one day a month to coach four teachers in another district. I provide training and coordinate the coaching program. Expectations for the coaches were established in advance and agreed upon by coaches, principals, and superintendents.

Figure 10.1 _____

Expectations of ITI Coaches

- Coaches will receive feedback to improve their own ITI applications on a monthly basis.

- Coaches will be released from their classrooms one day a month in September, October, November, January, February, March, April, and May to coach in another district. Coaches will be assigned to one building for the entire school year.

- The MAISD will reimburse the local districts for substitutes. ITI coaches will receive $20 a month for mileage and meals.

- Coaches will attend training in August and county-wide coaches' meetings every other month from 4:00 - 6:30. A stipend of $200 will be paid for attending coaches' training.

- Coaches will participate in an on-going support network and will be trained in Cognitive Coaching concepts.

- Coaches are expected to model absence of threat at all times.

- Coaches will not be involved in the evaluation process.

- Coaches will be asked to choose the same day (not Friday) each month for coaching. Districts will make every effort to provide the same substitute every month.

- The MAISD will work with coaches to determine a monthly focus, and provide tools for coaches to utilize in the coaching process.

- Have fun! This is a growing experience for everyone!

_____

Two criteria were also established to determine the schools where coaching would occur: The building principal must actively support ITI; and the building principal must have been trained in ITI. I meet with the coaches on a bi-monthly basis to facilitate networking and problem-solving. The coaching project has been very well received by all stake-holders and is an asset to our ITI implementation.

When looking for teachers to develop into your own local cadre of experts, don't forget recent retirees. They not only have the time, but also have lots of practical experiences to share. For the last two years we have been contracting with a recently retired teacher who serves as a coach, my right hand and often my left hand as we plan, present, and discuss ideas for supporting our ITI teachers. As a veteran classroom teacher with thirty-four years of teaching experience, she has instant credibility when discussing practical classroom issues. We complement one another to make an effective team.

Conclusion

As I reflect on our progress, it seems absolutely incredible that, in less than five years, we have achieved the results that I now see. We have signs of the ITI program in almost every elementary school in the county. LIFESKILLS are being used by students, and people in the community have noted the positive difference. Parents, museum personnel, bus drivers, school photographers, and many other community members comment about how well our students use the LIFESKILLS. Students seem much happier and constantly amaze us with the depth of their understanding of concepts. Behavior referrals to the principals' offices have been reduced significantly, and there is a calm, inviting feeling in our buildings that is contagious. There is a sense of community in our classrooms, and as a result, inclusion of special education students in regular classrooms is working. We are seeing more students achieve learning goals then ever before. Parents and the local press actively support the ITI concepts.

Recently, when one local elementary school had its introductory ITI meeting for parents, over 350 parents attended. What started out as a vision shared by two MAISD consultants has ended up being an exciting and promising program which has continued to flourish. Never under estimate what one person can do when he/she has a vision and collaborates with other very skilled and talented people.

Working Effectively With Special Interest Groups

by Susan Brash and Jane Rasp McGeehan

Introduction

Many a plan for substantive educational change is in response to the activity of well-organized special interest groups. Such groups vary widely: backers of one school board candidate over another, proponents of environmental issues, advocates for anti-drug curriculum, opponents of sex education, parent-teacher groups, local business people, alliances of ministers, members of the Christian Coalition, and employees devoted to the status quo or to changing it, just to name a few. Some groups are formal, some informal, but all seek to influence the decisions at the school. Their letter-writing campaigns, newsletters, and other grass-roots approaches typify democracy in action but the best interests of children may not be a group's driving force.

The long and strong tradition of local control of schools in this country rests on the assumption that the public schools ought to be responsive to the needs and interests of the community they serve. This thinking, grounded in the tenets of democracy, is part of the rationale for having schools governed by lay boards. Schools must teach well all of the children of all of the people if a democracy is to become and remain strong.

We believe that the best vehicle for doing so is the ITI model with its base in the biology of learning. However, since such information is usually new to parents and the general community, becoming a successful ITI school means becoming successful at working with the community, including its various special interest groups, in the on-going process of school improvement.

This chapter takes a closer look at working with special interest groups so that change efforts may be enhanced rather than aborted. The discussion is organized around the following three strategies: 1) Be politically aware, 2) Practice prevention, 3) Respond to concerns based on your commitment to providing brain-compatible learning.) We intend to raise questions to promote constructive dialogue in this highly controversial and potentially divisive area of ITI implementation.

Be Politically Aware

School administrators have chosen their careers for many reasons. Love of politics is seldom among them. Be that as it may, school administration IS a highly political field. Just as the elected official who wishes to remain in office seeks to discover the common ground among constituents, so the school administrator seeks to discover and articulate a shared education mission and marshal the human and financial resources of the community to benefit students in every possible way.

It is often easier to agree on the general mission of the schools than on the specific actions to pursue it. For example, people coming from varied backgrounds will agree that schools should prepare students to function as responsible citizens of the society. These same individuals can easily disagree about whether community service projects focused on environmental preservation, to take but one example, are a worthwhile and effective way to act on the stated mission.

Such points of disagreement call for the skills of the politician who has integrity. The starting point is to identify the school's constituents. Who are those served directly and indirectly by the schools and what services do they receive?

This kind of analysis must be done within the school's neighborhoods by those who know the territory best. The list of constituents obviously includes students but whose children are they? Are their parents from a professional community accustomed to influencing decisions by having the direct ear of the superintendent? Is there a solid group of middle class parents organized to make sure that the schools continue to serve their children well and prepare them for post-secondary training? How do working class parents make their voices heard? Are formal groups such as the band boosters and the athletic boosters actively involved? What about parents, grandparents, and other citizens who have no direct link to the schools? And within the school or school district, who are the informal opinion leaders? How extensive is each one's sphere of influence?

Each group of constituents has expectations of the school, but what is the source of those expectations? The school leader needs to know. Do expectations arise from the perception that graduates can't make change or measure using a ruler, or from experiences where graduates are prized employees? What are the positions of the service organizations in the community with respect to the schools? Are people forming opinions based on "That's how it was done when I was in school" or on a current understanding of brain research? None of the answers to these and related questions can be left to chance or guess work. The challenge for the educational leader/politician is not merely to discover and deliver what people think they want, but to paint a vivid picture of what schools can be that is based on best knowledge and best practice. The leader helps to translate new understandings into the best possible learning environments for students.

The process of developing a deep understanding of the school's constituents happens best when school and community leaders cooperate. For example, the administrator schedules breakfast and lunch meetings with people who know the community best. Brainstorming sessions generate the best thinking of the staff and uncover the range of views they hold. Groups such as School Improvement Planning Teams or School Site Councils pool their expertise and collect additional information from a series of community coffees. The more inclusive and informed the information-gathering is, the more effective the subsequent planning to build support will be. Don't forget to consult school employees such as bus drivers, secretaries, custodians, teachers, food services staff, and instructional assistants.

As hard as it is to make the time for gaining a thorough understanding of the school community, it is the necessary beginning. Certainly those who omit or abbreviate this step find that new programs are stalled by lack of support, lack of understanding, or unanticipated opposition. Based on a thorough understanding of the community, the administrator and planning team can then thoughtfully analyze the local power structure.

- Who is charged with making decisions that affect the school directly and indirectly?

- Who is influencing those who are making the decisions?

- What sources of information about the school have the greatest credibility with each group identified?

- Who are the key communicators in each part of the community, including those inside the school system?

- Who can be trusted to listen with open minds and clearly relay information to others?

- What groups have established a strong agenda for action that could enhance or undermine the mission of the school?

- Which groups are likely to be school detractors?

The answers to these and other questions lead to knowledge of how things get done in the local community and prepare the leadership team to work from a politically informed foundation.

Practice Prevention

Excellence often invites sabotage. Consider the "A" student who is labeled a nerd by peers, or the Fortune 500 company targeted by detractors in advertising campaigns. When excellence and change threaten the status quo, negative responses born of fear are common. Peer influence and the desire to be accepted among colleagues can work together to bolster the status quo. Several personal experiences illustrate this point.

It was an exciting day in the middle school earth science classes. We used air pressure to crush empty ditto fluid cans—relics that they are—to gain a better understanding of the force that air exerts. My students, typical adolescents, had many priorities above earth science. Therefore, I was particularly pleased to see them come alive with interest and questions. Feeling pleased with the way things had gone, I was putting equipment away when the teacher from across the hall stopped by to chat. Following the usual small talk, he said, "What were you trying to do with all of this activity today, make the rest of us look bad?"

It was a powerful reminder that at least some of my colleagues wanted me to tone it down and return to "read the chapter and answer the questions."

An experienced principal, newly trained in use of the ITI model, moved to a different part of the country. Working with other administrators in the district, she received a grant to bring ITI training to the school. Susan Kovalik and an associate introduced the model to the teachers in the pilot project. During the next three years, success with ITI involved many students and teachers beyond that original pilot team; however, barriers to success arose. They included embarrassing public attacks on the principal by the superintendent, last-minute questions from the superintendent's office that required the staff to drop present work and assemble data, and other strategies seemingly designed to undermine the principal's authority and judgment. In combination, the barriers drained time and energy away from ITI implementation.

In another situation, a principal chosen to open a new middle school achieved significant changes against the odds working with the children of migrant workers in a neighborhood rife with gang activity. The principal energetically used the ITI model to increase faculty collaboration, build student pride, raise test scores, reduce discipline referrals, and instill a respectful school climate. Learning became the primary focus. However, the principal ultimately lost his job over seemingly minor mistakes. Behind-the-scenes investigation revealed a superintendent responding to community pressure. Leaders with power and influence did not want to see Hispanic students become potential competitors for college admission with students from more influential families.

Given the frequency of negative responses to proposed change, we advocate the sports slogan, "The best defense is a strong offense." Three vital strategies can help prevent sabotage or abandonment of ITI:

1. Examine your heart to understand your own motivations.

2. Be proactive and invite potential detractors inside the circle of influence as part of the decision-making team.

3. Teach people what you are doing at each step of ITI implementation, emphasizing the impact on children.

We'll examine each strategy in the context of our experiences with ITI implementation.

Examine Your Motivations

Assume that you've decided to become a brain-compatible school or school district. Before launching the marketing to marshal a broad base of support, examine your own motivations. As you develop the plan to methodically contact key opinion leaders in the community and within the groups served by the school, is your goal to manipulate them into a supportive posture? Is your goal genuine service to the community and the desire to do the right things for children and families? Do you intend to listen honestly and openly to community views that may not match those of the school? If you (and the organization) are motivated by the school's mission and service to others, then making direct contact with both supporters and detractors is more likely to advance the school's mission.

Invite Potential Detractors Inside

Building community trust requires both hard work and patience. Based on your in-depth community analysis, invite the leaders of each group of potential supporters and detractors to meet with you personally and tell them about the ideas you have for improving the school. You do not need to meet with them one at a time for the information gained to have value. Ask them to identify concerns; they may have heard from families who have not expressed their views at the school. At this early point, listen without passing judgment. Don't expect agreement and trust to spring forth from one meeting or discussion, but work to lay the groundwork for a working relationship that can benefit the students. Focus on an exchange of information, as opposed to personal philosophies.

Here's an example. Susan Brash contacted the friends of a man who regarded her and the school with skepticism. Having established trust with the friends, she asked their help in recommending her as a trustworthy individual to the skeptic. It worked. Combined with subsequent school visits and conversations, the skeptic finally began to trust her and to share important information from a part of the community whose views were out of the mainstream. He was invited to the school for lunch with a group of parents and community people who shared views similar to his own. They toured the school, looked at curriculum materials, and participated in an honest dialogue with the principal. Because the principal truly wanted to know the views of the group, the session was productive.

Remember, from the school's perspective it is much better to have an early understanding of differing views and to bring potential detractors inside the circle.

In another instance at Amy Beverland Elementary, a complaint led to a new resource for expanding the students' learning. Jewish parents complained to the principal that artifacts of Christianity were displayed during school holidays. Working through the immediate situation, the principal asked what these parents thought students needed to know in order to approach Jewish people with understanding, appreciation, and respect. The parents provided the names of two outstanding speakers who then addressed the faculty about Jewish culture. These parents moved from outside to inside the circle of influence as they acted to improve the school's program.

As you form key groups to plan for change and monitor results in the school or the school district, find a way to include diverse points of view among the membership. People who are a part of the decision-making process as it relates to proposed changes are much less likely to engage in sabotage later.

Another key point: If your decision-making group does represent differing constituencies, take the time to provide practical training in how to function as an effective group. One helpful resource is the book, *How to Make Meetings Work* (Doyle and Straus 1976). Use it and your group's prior experiences to establish agreements in advance guiding how you will do business together.

Teach People About ITI Along the Way

Keep the focus on sharing information rather than arguing educational philosophies. The more people understand about the biology of learning and it's power to transform schools, the more support ITI implementation will enjoy. Identify an effective team of people to take the message to the community—all parts of it. Create a plan for regular communication that includes the usual newsletters and the less common coffees at the neighborhood center, with child care provided. Make it easy for people to find out about ITI through orientation meetings, open houses, a speakers' bureau for community programs—whatever it takes!

Carefully train your representatives so that the information is absolutely accurate, and people can learn more if they wish. Teach strategies for avoiding controversy, defensive postures, and drifts into personal philosophies. Keep the focus on implementing the biology of learning through documented best practice. Make it clear that ITI is not a philosophy of education; it is a means of implementing what we know about how the human brain learns.

Whether your audience is a parent group, service club, or the school board, showcase what children are experiencing in ITI classrooms. When ITI is new for your school, you can share stories and visual images from staff visits to other schools already using ITI. Until your teachers are ready for such visits, invite parents and community members to join you in visiting neighboring ITI classrooms where feasible. In a short time you'll have your own stories and pictures to illustrate student learning success in brain-compatible classrooms. Invite guests to student demonstrations and celebrations of learning. Invite representatives of the media to talk with students about how they use the Lifelong Guidelines and LIFESKILLS. Take a delegation of your students to help make the report to the school board about their ITI learning experiences. Provide an ITI workshop for your secretaries and bus drivers. Be creative and show some of the ways in which learning is meaningful and fun.

A small but vocal group can give school board members an impression of size and influence that is out of proportion to their numbers. When the views of ITI nay-sayers are balanced by opposing, informed views of other constituents, the impact on the school board is even more powerful. Furthermore, in the neighbor-to-neighbor talks over fences and at groceries, ITI wins even more supporters.

Respond to Concerns

It would be naive to assume that political awareness and prevention strategies will take care of all problems. Leaders must be ready to respond in constructive ways in the face of controversy. We suggest the following four strategies to frame such responses:

1. Be clear about the goals.

2. Do research, listen, and follow up.

3. Be ready to change strategies and the projected schedule for reaching the goals.

4. Know what you stand for and when to take a stand.

Leaders must plan their responses in these four areas. When things are going smoothly, it is easy to put off such work for lack of time. However, being prepared is part of the key to working effectively with detractors. Make the time!

First, **be clear about ends**. Know and be ready to share what you plan to accomplish for students as you work with the ITI model. Describe the way classrooms and schools will look, sound, and feel. Explain the impact you expect on academic achievement and how you will measure that achievement. Prepare your audiences to understand the benefits and limits of standardized testing. Demonstrate alternative approaches that educators refer to as authentic assessment of student progress. Share stories about how ITI implementation has renewed the professional lives of teachers, and thus benefitted their students.

In addition to creating pictures of where ITI will lead, be clear about basic beliefs of the school and school system. Make the connection between basic beliefs and ITI as the vehicle for acting on them with conviction. Practice your presentations by sharing with the school board and the staff in the superintendent's office. School board members do not like surprises any more than do superintendents and their staff. Be sure that there is strong support for the goals you have in mind among people with authority over school programs.

Second, when an individual or a special interest group is concerned about ITI, discipline yourself to listen actively, thoroughly look into the person or group's point of view, and meet with them again. At each meeting, ask questions to be sure that you understand fully. Take notes about details you might easily forget. It is often a good idea to invite other school personnel to participate, to add their listening skills to yours. Avoid planning responses and defenses while you are listening—remember, undivided attention.

If the concern is something you can answer easily, then address it at the time. If it is more complex, explain that you need time to gather more information or to reflect thoughtfully before you respond. Then ask the opinions of others, observe in a classroom—whatever it takes to understand the concerns fully.

Establish a specific time by which the person or group will hear from you. Mark it on your calendar and, at all costs, honor that commitment. Building trust requires on-going effort by all involved.

At your follow-up meeting, you may now be able to resolve the issue. If not, be sure to report what you have done and learned so far. Provide a new time frame and planned action, again using your calendar to ensure follow-through. If you anticipate that your next communication may be difficult, schedule a face-to-face meeting to take advantage of the powerful non-verbal aspects of human interactions and to make clear that the non-resolution is not the result of lack of caring or effort.

An example from our experience shows how effective these steps can be. An ITI school made extensive use of trade books, both fiction and non-fiction, to support the theme and teach the skills of reading for pleasure and for learning. A parent was concerned about a book with magic woven into the story. The principal listened and recorded the details of the parent's concerns. She explained that she wanted to do some research on the matter and would get back to the parent within the week. The principal then read the book in question and noted its inspiring theme. In her next meeting with the parent, she led the conversation to an agreement about the book's theme. The parent said it was indeed a theme she could support. She saw the magic event that had raised her initial concerns as secondary and withdrew her complaint.

Naturally, some issues will not be resolved in favor of the school's initial position or on the first try. So third, if the issue is one of how brain-compatible education in being translated into action, be ready to change or adjust strategy or the implementation schedule if the concern is thoughtful and appropriate. Ask yourself or the leadership team if the suggested adjustment is significant or if it is incidental. Would it directly affect the school's ability to act in accord with basic brain-compatible principles? If it would, there is no room to negotiate and you must focus on educating the individual or group about those principles. Search for commonly valued examples of how the principles are visible in the homes and work lives of individuals. On the other hand, if the change would not contradict brain-compatible principles, there is room to craft a compromise.

Finally, know what you stand for and when to take a stand. Part of knowing when to compromise is recognizing when to take a stand. In general, taking a stand is not a good idea from a political viewpoint if you are standing alone. It can happen, but usually doesn't serve to advance ITI implementation. Much stronger is the posture of school board, administrators, teachers, staff, and community representatives standing together. This solid collaboration can only occur when all parties know and understand what it means to be a brain-compatible organization, with agreed upon basic beliefs. Such knowledge and agreement are part of what the leaders must weave into the fabric of the culture and climate of the school and school district.

When prevention strategies fail, we recommend knowing who can convincingly articulate the majority view. Democracy is not well served when the vocal minority manipulates the system to have its ideas imposed regardless of the views of the many, the brain research findings, or the greater good of the community.

Conclusion

Leaders of significant change in education enjoy the sweet rewards of success—renewed teachers and staff, students eager to learn, and supportive community members. They do not sit and wait for special interest groups to sabotage their efforts. However, our experience shows that half-truths, misinformation, and politically unpopular successes can be the enemy of any program improvement effort.

We believe that many concerns of special interest groups can be addressed in constructive ways that enlarge support for the school's mission and for brain-compatible learning. Leaders must think and plan in advance and then take the time to let the plan unfold to its full potential. If it is to succeed, ITI implementation can't be rushed.

We have suggested a number of strategies for leaders' consideration in this chapter. Become politically aware by doing the requisite homework.

Take the initiative to prevent concerns from becoming problems that block forward progress with ITI implementation. Teach about ITI and what you are doing at the school. Finally, know in advance how you will respond if there are unresolved concerns.

Throughout, use concepts from the brain research and the ITI brain-compatible elements as your guide. Ask yourself and leader colleagues if you are collaborating in ways that capitalize on the diversity within your community? Are you planning specifically to build and then to nurture trust once it is born?"

Thinking about the Lifelong Guidelines and the LIFESKILLS can illuminate the search for increased trust. Do you make it your business to understand the views of detractors fully through active listening so that you can discuss ways in which the ITI model is meaningful from their perspective? Do you take the initiative to invite feedback from various perspectives to enlighten future planning? The answers to these and countless other questions are both simple and complex but they always begin by returning to basic beliefs translated into action. A final word of advice. Don't forget the LIFESKILLS of courage and integrity when meeting the challenges presented by your work as a school leader building support for ITI.

Systemic Change and Assessment: A Fresh Look

by Jane Rasp McGeehan

Introduction

It's time for formal evaluation by the new principal. Even the highly respected master teacher frets as her day to be observed arrives. She wonders if the principal will understand why the students in her high school biology class talk as they work together to reconstruct skeletons from bones retrieved from owl pellets. The classroom will not be a quiet place this day! Will the principal understand why the time for large group instruction (lecture, direct instruction) is limited to just ten minutes? Perhaps she will leave after that ten minutes believing that the "teaching" for the day has ended, and later request another day to observe when the teacher will "teach" for most of the period. And then there's that new checklist developed by the school district to guide teacher evaluation. Where did that come from? The master teacher doesn't doubt that her students are excited about biology and really learning, but she feels anxious about the evaluation process with its mysteries and uncertainty.

Assessment, whether focused on the learning of youth or of adults, can be a threatening process. What if, instead, it became a natural, welcomed part of the learning process full of vital information. In the ITI model, assessment strategies **are** teaching strategies, friendly to the brain, that provide immediate feedback to the learner about his/her mastery of the curriculum.

Recall from chapters one and two Leslie Hart's description of learning as a two-step process: 1) meaningful patterns to recognize and understand, and 2) useful mental programs to acquire (Hart 1983). This definition of learning forms the logical foundation for assessment within ITI. In this chapter, I will describe how it works for students and adults.

In ITI classrooms, schools, and school districts, individuals know clearly what they are expected to master. No surprises. Also, the tools, strategies, and interactions that comprise assessment of learning are consistent with the conditions that favor optimal performance of the human brain. In other words, finding out how things are going for students, teachers, and administrators in a brain-compatible school is done brain-compatibly!

Definitions and Focus

ITI assessment involves the processes and products that provide convincing evidence of how well the learner has mastered key points. The more closely assessment is tied to the learning process, the more powerful it is in achieving its goals: revealing how the learning is going, and suggesting the most productive steps to promote additional learning. The learner wants to know, "How am I doing and what can I do to be even more successful?" Remember that the term, "learner," here refers to students, teachers, and administrators.

Figure 12.1 ────────────────────────────────────

ITI Assessment Guide

BRAIN BASIC	CURRICULUM QUESTION	CURRICULUM TOOLS	ASSESSMENT QUESTION	ASSESSMENT TOOLS
Meaningful patterns	What do you want them to *recognize* and *understand* to become more responsible citizens?	Key Points: • Conceptual • Significant Knowledge • Skill	What DO they *recognize* and *understand*	Rubrics 3 "C's" *Correct* *Complete* *Comprehensive*
Useful mental programs	What do you want them to be able to *do* to become responsible citizens?	Inquiries: • choice • apply in practice or contrived situations	What CAN they *do*?	INQUIRIES • real audience/ situation • demonstration of mastery

By Jane Rasp McGeehan

The "ITI Assessment Guide" in Figure 12.1 shows the progression from learning through curriculum to assessment. Assessment is an integral part of the learning process; the learner must perceive all aspects of the assessment process as threat-free and meaningful. When the learner plays an **active and direct role** in that assessment, he/she feels a greater sense of control. Fear and apprehension are reduced.

For example, through dialogue with their teacher and peers, ITI students agree on the specific characteristics that qualify a product as "correct, complete, and comprehensive—Susan Kovalik's three "C's." Instead of a grade, a product is judged by the student himself and then his teacher against the specific definitions agreed upon for correct, complete, and comprehensive. It meets the criteria or it is not done. If not done, the student receives coaching and returns to work knowing what to do to reach completion of a quality product. Such rubrics along with examples of completed work that illustrate the characteristics of "a good one" set the stage for self-assessment as the learner compares his/her own performance or product with the rubric and example.

Additionally, learners who are clear about the learning goals as stated through key points are less fearful about assessment. They know what they are working to accomplish so the old "I wonder what will be on the test?" mentality is replaced by a desire to demonstrate mastery in the specified content or skill areas. Further, learners who then choose from several possible strategies for demonstrating their mastery feel they have more control and voice in the assessment process. When assessment is truly a brain-compatible part of the learning process, the activities are welcomed by the learner, and even seen as challenging and enjoyable. ITI assessment is significant, motivating for the learner, and meaningful as it documents achievement and points to the next learning goals.

Assessing Student Learning

Key Points and Inquiries

The key point is the heart of the connection between learning and assessment for students. Within ITI, the key point is a concept, a statement of significant knowledge, or a skill that students will master. Key points make clear which meaningful patterns are the target of teaching and learning activities.

Typically, one key point provides the focus for the teacher's direct instruction and student learning activities across traditional disciplines/subjects for a day, depending on the complexity of the material and the developmental level of the learners. Older students often work on the mastery of more than one key point during a day, while younger ones may use several days to master just one.

ITI teachers (and students) write multiple inquiries, activities which provide learners the opportunities to develop new mental programs related to the key points. Initially, inquiries are vehicles through which learners think about and use the key point information. They invite the learner to **do** something useful with the information, thus laying the neural groundwork in the wiring of the brain that can lead to a useful mental program and complete the desired learning.

In many cases, the best inquiries trigger an appropriate assessment activity. ITI teachers seek ways to view student mastery of the patterns and related mental programs for applying key point information. They look for meaningful use of the key point material in real world settings. They look for activities that clearly answer Kovalik's ITI assessment questions, "What do students recognize and understand?" and "What can they do with the information?" with unequivocal evidence of mastery.

In their discussion of evaluation, Geoffrey and Renate Caine offer useful guidelines to help teachers select the most appropriate assessment inquiries.

"We suggest that there are at least four relevant indicators that guide evaluation:

- the ability to use the language of the discipline or subject in complex situations and in social interaction

- the ability to perform appropriately in unanticipated situations

- the ability to solve real problems using the skills and concepts

- the ability to show, explain, or teach the idea or skill to another person who has a real need to know." (Caine and Caine 1994)

Assessment conducted within a real context, one that has meaning for learners, produces the most convincing demonstrations of mastery. Again referring to the "ITI Assessment Guide," consider an over-simplified example as an illustration. If the pattern to be learned is "cup," one possible inquiry could be as follows:

Illustrate in a poster or a mindmap prepared with a partner your plan for serving coffee, iced tea, and hot chocolate to a committee of eight parent volunteers at our school. Show the specific cup you will provide for each beverage and write a supporting rationale for your choice of the container.

An assessment version of the same inquiry could be:

> Serve coffee, iced tea, and hot chocolate to a committee of eight parent volunteers at our school using the plan you and your partner created. Invite several younger students to whom you can teach what you have learned as they observe you carrying out your plan. Record with your partner your observations about the event on a cassette tape to be shared with the teacher.

You can see the pattern of preparation and practice followed by doing the real thing.

Consider the high school geometry class in California who used mathematical principles to analyze ways to improve a freeway entrance ramp with a very high accident rate. While inquiries provided plenty of hypothetical practice, and study trips to the site provided the real world connection, the evidence of mastery came when students took their activity to the next level. They shared their ideas and proposals with the appropriate governing body. One proposal was chosen for action, and the ramp was reconstructed. By the time these students had graduated from high school, they had witnessed a reduced accident rate at the ramp as a direct result of their work.

Consider a more common example. If the pattern being learned is "paragraph," we can expect such inquiries as:

> Write a paragraph giving your personal opinion about one of the main characters in the novel you completed. Prepare a mindmap to organize your ideas. Exchange paragraphs with a partner, provide and receive suggestions for improvement using the rubric for effective paragraphs. Revise your paragraph.

An assessment inquiry might be:

> Design and produce a colorful poster with a symbol representing an outstanding characteristic of a main character of the novel you recently read. Include a paragraph about the character prepared on the computer in final draft form, and be prepared to share your poster with parent guests at the "Cast of Characters" classroom reception.

Note that in each example the assessment strategy was implied in the inquiry itself—testimony to the essential connection between learning and assessment. Picture yourself as the teacher working with students who completed the above inquiries and assessments. You would know how much each student understood and how each could apply the newly learned information and skills. From what I have witnessed in ITI classrooms as teachers use such assessment strategies, teachers and students know much more about the learning that has occurred than they know from more traditional paper/pencil tests of memorized facts. Furthermore, the assessments themselves enrich the learning process and nurture student interest in the topic at hand.

In addition, the more we understand Howard Gardner's theory of multiple intelligences, especially as articulated by Thomas Armstrong, (Armstrong 1994) the more we realize that assessing students' work by more than the traditional paper/pencil testing approaches is vital. Because ITI inquiries are written with consideration for Gardner's multiple intelligences, it naturally follows that assessment strategies also reflect Gardner's theory. If a teacher or administrator is limited to paper/pencil assessment tools alone may not reflect what the learner really knows and can do.

Patterns Over Time

As the student and teacher record key assessments, a dynamic picture of the student's learning accomplishments emerges over time. There are varied ways to do this. ITI students might place examples of visual or written work that reflects their personal best into portfolios— lively testimony to their mastery of concepts, knowledge, and skills. Such portfolios increasingly exist as computer files with growing access to more sophisticated technology. What if students prepared periodic video-taped statements assessing their achievements, including how they plan to use what they learned?

It can't be over-emphasized: more importance should be placed on what the student does over a block of time, such as a month or a six-weeks component of the yearlong theme is studied, than is placed on the work of a single day. If a student's work doesn't indicate mastery, then additional inquiries, coaching, or collaboration, will likely lead to mastery before re-assessment.

When students see how much they are learning and realize what they can do with it, both at school and in their communities and homes, they are even more motivated to try their personal best.

Computers are invaluable for recording what students have mastered. In fact, students from the intermediate elementary school grades through high school do much of their own record keeping to document achievement.

Reporting Results of Student Learning

Several audiences care about the results of assessments of student learning to varying degrees. At the top, we hope, is the student followed by his/her parents, teachers, school administration, school board and finally the larger community including the state and nation. We haven't discovered or created the most effective ways to reach each of these audiences with the news about student learning, but promising possibilities include teacher as coach, face-to-face conferences (including those led by students), and alternative report card formats.

Any student knows that it is much easier to learn something new than it is to re-learn something that was learned incorrectly the first time. Therefore, the most powerful assessment information in terms of its impact on pattern recognition and mental program creation is that which occurs promptly as the learning is just taking place. Realizing this, teachers circulate as students work on inquiries. They ask questions and provide immediate feedback to affirm correct learning or re-direct learning that is incorrect.

Self-assessment plays an important role in building student confidence and responsibility throughout the learning process. Using rubrics, a growing understanding of Kovalik's three "C's," and feedback from real audiences for their products, ITI students continually gain a realistic perspective of their own strengths and how to recognize a quality product or performance.

Dialogue with others is a natural form of assessment. A personal conference between teacher and student (even a brief and focused one) has particular power in assessing one's progress. Comments about a product or performance from one's learning peers are also invaluable. Often, teachers require that students share their completed inquiry with a student in their cooperative learning group (sometimes referred to as their "Learning Club") to gain another beneficial perspective before seeking the views of their teacher/mentor.

As mentioned before, rubrics generated collaboratively by the students and teacher help define worthy products and performances. Students are likely to give and get some great ideas for improving their work from classmates. In the dialogue that occurs as the work is examined, each student practices discussing the material at hand, thereby strengthening his/her own related mental program.

Naturally, parents expect a regular report about their children's achievements. Most parents believe in the more prevalent system of grades and various other marks, although even a cursory review of student report cards makes it painfully obvious that most contain little valuable information about student learning. What does an "A" in American literature tell parents about what students understand and can use? What knowledge, concepts, or skills were mastered, and to what degree? The recent books of Alfie Kohn, such as *Punished by Rewards* (Kohn 1993), present a convincing case for the distinct damage to student motivation done by the current grading system. Increased cheating is one apparent result of overemphasis on grades as rewards for achievement. In a recent article (Levine 1995), Daniel R. Levine cites enough examples of cheating to leave the reader quite concerned about this issue.

Typically, parents are very resistant to any suggestion that schools do away with grades, yet grades are surely **not** an example of brain-compatible reporting. A number of ITI schools have discovered that student-led conferences involving student, parent, and teacher are both brain-compatible and revealing in terms of student learning. A practical book to consult about such conferences is *Portfolios and Student-Led Conferencing* by Shelly A. Potter. (Available from The Potter Press, P. O. Box 1803, Birmingham, MI 48012.)

To replace traditional grade report cards, consider a periodic written summary about each student's content and skill mastery. Combined with student-led conferences, such reports give parents a clear picture of their child's learning so that they can see how best to offer support. While each school district must create its own format for such a report, it must yield meaningful information and align with that district's learning goals.

Assessing Teacher Learning and Performance

Like their students, teachers need assessment feedback along their ITI journeys. Journeys are punctuated by signposts and destinations. Refer to Figure 12.2. Just as signs along the Interstate let the traveler know how many miles remain before arrival at the next town, the signposts in the teacher's growth mark steady progress toward professional growth goals. Such information comes through self-assessment and feedback from knowledgeable ITI coaches.

Destinations, on the other hand, are more like the summary information gleaned from formal evaluations by the responsible administrator to document goals that have been reached during a specific period of time. ITI teachers thrive when both layers of assessment are readily available and handled in a brain-compatible way.

For teachers who seek to create brain-compatible classrooms, the assessment process provides answers to two key questions—answers that provide insights into professional growth goals:

1. What am I doing now that supports ITI/brain-compatible learning?

2. What are my next steps to become even more effective?

    a. What do I need to recognize and understand? (pattern)

    b. What do I need to be able to do with that understanding? (mental program)

The best answers to these questions are generally known to the teacher herself, but the administrator/coach/mentor provides the invaluable "outside eyes" to give focus and affirmation.

Coaching by someone who has achieved a greater competence in ITI implementation than the teacher being reviewed is a critical element of brain-compatible teacher assessment. But successful coaching also requires a trusting and respectful relationship between the teacher and the coach. Teaching is all about relationships. This is especially true for the teacher as learner as she works with the coach/mentor. Trust between the individuals is an important prerequisite to a fruitful outcome—the teacher's continuous growth. However, the coach should not be the one to implement the formal assessment/evaluation process required by the school board.

The coach helps the teacher to craft what we might think of as key points and inquiries for the teacher's mastery of the ITI model. Looking again at the "ITI Assessment Guide," if the **pattern** the teacher wants to understand is ITI key points, the coach can suggest a number of **inquiries** (activities) to build the teacher's pattern recognition and later the mental programs for producing effective key points. What better assessment, therefore, than an "assessment inquiry." Here, the teacher shares key points with the coach and invites the coach to observe as she provides direct instruction for her students based on one of the key points. You can see how the Assessment Guide works for teachers, too.

The formal evaluation of teacher effectiveness remains separate from the on-going self-assessment and coaching. Who should have input into that process? Ask, "Who knows about the teacher's competence in addition to the teacher and coach/mentor/supervisor?" Consider several interesting responses that may have also occurred to you—both students and their parents/guardians have valuable insights as well.

When I was a classroom teacher, I provided formal ways to collect feedback from my students and their parents about my effectiveness and about perceptions of student learning—all part of my effort to know how I could improve. **When parents and students trust that there will be no reprisals,** the information is truthful and extremely worthwhile. Leaders must help to create the culture in which it is safe for teachers to collect and use feedback from students and parents without fear of unfortunate comparisons or other misuses of the information.

One suburban ITI elementary school using the ITI model is developing a brain-compatible approach to formal teacher evaluation. At the beginning of the school year each teacher receives an evaluation folder from the principal. It contains the district's contract language regarding evaluation, and the district's teacher evaluation checklist. In addition, it contains a self-evaluation guide based on the ITI model that the teacher may choose to use. Teachers choosing the self-evaluation route may request released time to accomplish the task. The teacher completes the district's form and then documents his/her own growing competence in applying the ITI model. Some teachers have created a portfolio complete including such items as work samples, curriculum documents, photographs. Finally, the teacher creates a Personal Goal Action Plan (GAP) stating improvement strategies that support his/her competence as an ITI teacher and contribute to the school-wide improvement targets.

The principal receives the completed folder at least twenty-four hours before making a formal classroom visit. (This principal is in each classroom informally at least once each week.) During the post-observation conference, the contents of the folder become the centerpiece for dialogue. If the principal has specific concerns about the teacher's performance, he/she shares them, and the cycle may repeat itself after the teacher has had adequate time to improve. When the process is completed, the summary form required by the district is submitted to the central office; all other documentation remains in the teacher's school personnel file.

Is this process a lot of work for the teacher and the administrator? Yes. Is it meaningful and less threatening than a more standard approach to teacher evaluation? Undoubtedly. However, the principal reports that a large majority of teachers do select this alternative to the principal's usual completion of the district's evaluation checklist. Teachers are using the formal evaluation process, with input from administrator/coach/mentor, to determine their own road map for continuous professional growth.

Figure 12.2

Key Elements of Brain-Compatible Teacher Assessment

Signposts:

- Use ITI Rubric for classrooms for self-assessment and to derive professional growth goals (key points and inquiries)
- Obtain specific feedback from coach/mentor based on direct classroom observations targeting goal activity
- Arrange for classroom observations and informal feedback from several perspectives, e.g., colleague, parent, school board member, etc.
- Gather student and parent input through interview and/or survey
- Provide released time for meaningful self-assessment
- Emphasize formative strategies and immediate feedback, such as the items listed above

Destinations:

- Share mutual expectations of teacher and administrator, including general agreement about what constitutes effective practice for each in a brain-compatible school
- Provide released time for the teacher to reflect on self-assessment and coaching experiences
- Provide a document for the principal's use to summarize the teacher's progress toward meeting professional growth goals
- Ensure the opportunity for direct teacher input into the summarizing document to be placed in his/her personnel file
- Base all formal evaluation documents on ITI brain basics and the brain-compatible district mission
- Conduct formal evaluation annually
- Provide the administrator with assistance for routine management tasks to free adequate time for observing and conferencing with teachers about their professional growth

But what if the teacher isn't growing and doesn't see the need to do so? An often unavoidable part of the administrator's job is determining if a teacher's professional goals, skills, talents, and temperament are a good match for the demands of the teaching profession. Unfortunately, the process of choosing a profession can be a bit like making a commitment to marry. One really doesn't know fully just what is involved until **after** you are in the situation! Some teachers may be suited for more traditional schools, but have no desire to move toward ITI implementation.

Whatever the reason for the lack of match, the administrator must have the courage to remove the teacher from the present setting. If teaching turns out to be the wrong career choice, help the person to make an appropriate change. If the school is committed to becoming brain-compatible, individuals who don't support that goal and who have something to offer in another learning environment must be encouraged to move to that environment. The time frame for such determinations always depends on the situation and requires the collaboration of the administrator and the teacher.

Naturally, removal or transfer will not be the starting point in working with a teacher about whom there are concerns. Gary Phillips, education consultant, shares one effective way to avoid placing blame and to open the way for genuine dialogue with a teacher whose performance is in question. Early in the school year, he suggests, open the conversation with, "What are three things I would need to do this year to be the best principal you ever had" (Phillips 1991)? What follows may give birth to a collaboration that results in significant teacher growth. If it doesn't, however, the responsibility for action lies with the administrator as described.

Assessing Support Staff Performance

There is no more influential teacher than the model that adults provide for the children who observe them closely. That is why it is so important for **all** of the adults in a school to provide consistent examples. If the Lifelong Guidelines and LIFESKILLS are good for children, then they are good for the adults who must incorporate them into their daily behavior if they want children to take them seriously.

That is another way to say that all staff who provide services for children and adults at the school must learn about the ITI model and consider what the brain-compatible elements look like, sound like, and feel like for them in their various roles. Performance evaluation documents will reflect the brain-compatible elements in addition to specific aspects of each person's job description. While the administrator can and should have input on many of the evaluations of support staff, it should be the person(s) with whom individuals work most closely who have primary responsibility to evaluate.

The key elements that apply to teacher evaluation generally apply to support staff assessment as well. Especially important are involving the staff member in self-assessment and ensuring ways to provide feedback of a formative nature throughout the year. It is much easier and more effective to discuss one small issue shortly after it arises than it is to keep a list to be dragged out at the end-of-year conference when behaviors have been allowed to continue, and addressing them constructively can be overwhelming at best.

Assessing Administrator Performance

If brain-compatible assessment is good for the teachers and the support staff, it is good for the principal. If it is good for the principal, it is good for the superintendent and his central office administrators. Begin with mutual expectations of one another, gather views of effectiveness from representatives of all who have a strong interest in the school's work, incorporate reflections of the brain-compatible elements into documents and forms, emphasize the formative feedback, target mutually created improvement goals, and incorporate other activities discussed under suggestions for teacher assessment.

Also, ask new questions. What if principals, teachers, parents, and students helped to assess the performance of superintendents and their staff? What if teachers, support staff, parents, and students helped to evaluate the performance of principals? Such strategies point once again to the importance of relationships, building community, and building trust. In a positive climate where the culture strongly values the goal of continuous improvement, getting many involved in helping to assess their own and others' effectiveness will translate into more brain-compatible learning for students.

Conclusion

Seasoned veterans who are still reading without rolling their eyes are optimists! The traditional evaluation procedures used in most school districts take less time to implement than the locally-created form of the brain-compatible assessment outlined in this chapter. **Administrators already have a serious lack of time in which to carry out the existing**

procedures, so why would they embrace something requiring even more time?

There is much to be said for the familiar adage, "less is more." As part of the systemic change demanded by thorough ITI implementation, the ways in which administrators at all levels currently spend time must be reviewed. Is what they are doing helping to create a school district that places learning at the top of the organization's priorities, along with a commitment to act on the brain research findings? For many, the answer is "no." Leaders in ITI implementation must work to reduce some of the demands on administrators. They must free more time for often slighted but critically important work, such as the assessment procedures suggested in this chapter. All district personnel need adequate time to take an active role in self-assessment.

Finally, as schools and school districts create assessment processes and documents that reflect their commitment to becoming brain-compatible organizations, they must constantly test their work against the template of the ITI brain basics and elements. The key questions must be asked repeatedly to insure that the effort remains aligned with the district's stated mission. Examples include:

- Does the culture reflect absence of threat?

- Are we allowing adequate time for mastery of new strategies?

- Is there adequate time for meaningful assessment?

- Is collaboration a regular feature of district culture?

You see the pattern. Each part of ITI implementation finally must show its merit when tested against what we know about the brain and learning.

How else can organizations in the business of learning establish and retain credibility?

XIII

The Beginning

by Jane Rasp McGeehan

Introduction

The end of this book is the beginning for leaders seeking to transform traditional schools and school districts to brain-compatible ones. For the first time in history, existing and emerging research about the biology of learning have created the basis for defining best knowledge and best practice within education. As Robert Sylwester so aptly stated at a Kovalik summer institute in 1996, "The brain research became available on our watch. What will we tell our grandchildren we did as a result?"

Transformation: So Much Work— Why Bother?

We are witnessing some of the most perplexing and complicated dilemmas ever faced by humans. At polar extremes we have the knowledge and capability to destroy the earth as a habitat and also to create new life, even to clone genetic copies. Now more than ever, caring humans must act to release and energize the tremendous creative capacity of our species to identify, understand, prioritize, and act responsibly to resolve the interrelated problems and challenges that threaten our very survival.

A keystone of democracy is the belief that all citizens must be prepared to be contributing, responsible citizens. Today, when the action or inaction of one country affects the rest of the world, this citizenship ethic extends to a global level. The stakes are high and education is a critical element in citizenship preparation.

If we care about our children and their children, we will initiate and participate in dialogues to define the elements of responsible citizenship. As we examine expenditures of precious time, effort, and money on education, we must ask the question posed by Susan Kovalik, "How will this contribute to making a responsible citizen?"

Transformation: Relationship, Beliefs, and Changing Bias

Two of Margaret Wheatley's books, *Leadership and the New Science* and *A Simpler Way*, present inspiring, brain-compatible perspectives on the challenges, limitations, and rewards of leadership.

"To those in a world of change and chaos we need to accept chaos as an essential process by which natural systems including organizations renew and revitalize themselves, share information as the primary organizing force in any organization, develop the rich diversity of relationships that are all around us to energize our teams, and embrace vision as an invisible field that enables us to recreate our workplace and ourselves" (Wheatley 1992).

Change is the friend of renewal and transformation, but it scares us. It is messy and unpredictable; it requires us to venture into uncharted, uncomfortable waters. We may experience failure before we experience success.

However, rich, diverse relationships are the enemy of such fears. We humans are social beings who find the sense of personal risk diminishes when we venture forth with others at our sides—others whom we trust. Wheatley describes the benefits of building trust among people in an organization.

"But in systems of trust, people are free to create the relationships they need. Trust enables the system to open. The system expands to include those it had excluded. More conversations— more diverse and diverging views—become important. People decide to work with those from whom they had been separate" (Wheatley and Kellner-Rogers 1996, 83).

Trusting relationships flourish among people who use the Lifelong Guidelines and LIFESKILLS and who intentionally build community among everyone involved. In the absence of trusting relationships, most transformations fall short of the goal.

As members of a community characterized by trusting relationships, we can take the risk to examine the deep beliefs—our own and those of others in the community—that govern and explain daily behavior. What are the highest goals of education in a democracy? What are the characteristics of successful learners and teachers, and can we teach those to more people? What curriculum is the most valuable? What is the proper role of a principal or superintendent? What is the school's role when youth lack caring parents? What is the school's role in "sorting and labeling" students? Who are the gifted students?

Very often such critical questions lie unexamined and certainly undiscussed within the community, and yet the answers comprise our deepest beliefs, biases, mental models, or paradigms—our personal pictures of reality. It takes courage even in a caring community to reveal them, and it takes even more courage to consider changing them.

In his ground-breaking book, *Human Brain and Human Learning*, Leslie Hart provides insights into changing bias. Defining behaviors as mental programs in action he states,

> "Biasing involves all that is stored in the brain, relevant to a program decision, from plans, aims, fears, and older brain influences and from the current, situational input...If the biases remain unchanged, the program selection will remain unchanged. To affect a change of behavior, or 'open a door' to learning, we must try to change biases, not behavior directly" (Hart 1983, 97).

Behavior choices arise from deepest beliefs—or biases—placed within the context of the moment at hand.

Ed Oakley and Doug Krug concur in *Enlightened Leadership: Getting to the Heart of Change:* "In every stage of life, we bring our attitudes and our personal collection of paradigms, which form the basis for our actions and our opinions" (Oakley and Krug 1991, 122).

But changing biases isn't easy. In fact, you must create a new one that is more powerful. Paraphrasing Hart, it requires a new set of experiences, plans, aims, fears, and situational input that result in new patterns of communication among the brain's neurons leading to different behavior choices. Borrowing William Calvin's (Calvin 1996, 96) metaphor of competing choirs, the "new choir" of neurons bolstered by recent experiences finally recruits more members and takes over, replacing the old choir that sang the old bias.

How do such ideas translate into leadership practice?

Here are a few actions to consider:

- Take a year to read and discuss with colleagues a brain research book focused on applications to education such as those by Robert Sylwester or Geoffrey and Renata Caine.

- Arrange for teams to visit ITI schools and districts and then report, share pictures, and lead discussions upon their return.

- Involve students in honest discussions about what works for them.

- Take one aspect of brain-compatible practice, learn how to use it, and agree to try it with coaching and feedback. Cooperative learning strategies and application of Gardner's theory of multiple intelligences are two fruitful examples. (Yes, even if you are an administrator.)

- Completely redesign and decorate a part of the school for which you are responsible and see how it feels. For example, create a school cafeteria that looks like a "restaurant" with a theme and soothing colors.

- Take students into the community and focus your lessons for a week on understanding the place(s) you visited.

It takes experiences, time, effort, and plenty of honest discussion to change a bias. "When enough people within an organization become change-friendly, renewal is naturally continuous" (Oakley and Krug 1991, 122).

Transformation: The Tools and Resources Exist

Starting from the research, theory, and experiences of others, you and those with whom you provide leadership can craft the unique journey to brain-compatibility that best fits your school and district. This book points to the brain research base, summarizes the ITI model for applying it, and shares practical strategies that have worked for others as they met common challenges along the way. Use it to your advantage.

The appendix provides the ITI Rubrics for classroom and schoolwide implementation. As described in the chapter on assessment, they are rich sources for self-assessment and for professional goal-setting. You'll also find examples of instruments, such as the various climate audit tools, that you can use or revise to understand and work with factors unique in your situation.

In addition to the leadership books mentioned above, consult *The Fifth Discipline Field Book* (Senge 1994) for clear descriptions of how to build a learning organization. Especially helpful are the sections on mental models and shared vision and the practical strategies offered. Try the strategies with a small group who share your vision and want to help provide leadership. Build your confidence and then be bold enough to try those strategies with the entire faculty of a school or the district office leadership team.

Will transformation cost money? Obviously, yes. Taxpayers are already investing huge amounts of money in education with much to show for it. However, we can't expect to lead people toward creating new biases, adapting new behaviors, and transforming schools into brain-compatible learning organizations unless we invest in people. **Staff development must be a priority in the budgets of educational organizations.** A meer two days in August followed by three more days interspersed throughout the year will not change biases. Where do you find the money to fund quality staff development, especially when money is tight?

Here's one idea. You may already have money that could be reallocated. For example, look at the budget for copy machine paper. Ask whether or not the amount spent translates into brain-compatible student learning. In other words, uncover the ways in which the money you have can be spent to meet brain-compatible goals as you pursue dollars beyond the general fund as described in chapter eight.

Transformation: Courage, Heart, and Faith

As a leader, you can read the books, attend the workshops, visit the schools, raise the money—and still fail to mobilize others. While transformation starts with your personal preparation, it must extend to ever-widening circles of influence if the goals are to be achieved. That extended involvement and motivation to act take large measures of courage, heart, and faith.

It takes courage to stand up for what you believe is right for students when the teachers have become accustomed to what makes the job more manageable. It takes courage to seek employment elsewhere when your vision is not supported by the school board. It takes courage to try something new and feel awkward in front of those whom you lead. It takes courage to admit you don't have all the answers in a school culture, where leaders are supposed to know. It takes courage to relinquish control and involve others in making key decisions.

It also takes heart—heart to convey your message with enthusiasm, sincerity, and conviction. It takes heart to be playful and have fun trying something in a different way. It takes heart to reveal the child inside and to communicate with the child in others as you discover renewed delight in the learning process. It takes heart to listen with empathy as a veteran teacher cries over a failed lesson after trying a new approach. It takes heart to orchestrate the right celebrations for victories small and large along the journey to brain-compatibility. It takes heart to witness a child's misbehavior, pain, or anger and respond from a new bias.

Above all, it takes faith to persist. Faith in yourself. Faith in the human spirit. Faith in the basic goodness of people working in and with schools. Faith that people can make dramatic changes, given good reasons to do so and the support they need.

Now is the time to take the first step.

Appendixes

ITI Classroom Rubric

Assessing Implementation of Brain-Compatible Learning

By Karen Olsen and Susan Kovalik

Introduction

In a time of inflamed rhetoric about the shortcomings of public education and its reform efforts, of fundamental disagreement about the purpose and goal of our public schools, and of authentic assessment procedures and tools applied to the learning of unauthentic curriculum, it is important that we state clearly the desired results of our current efforts so that all may see what is intended, so that all may measure, in concrete ways, whether we are reaching our mark or not. This is particularly true for those engaged in the degree of significant, systemic change—classroom and schoolwide—inherent in the ITI model.

The purpose of the ITI rubric is to provide clear pictures of what ITI looks like, sounds like, and feels like from the perspective of students and teachers—before staff, parents, students, district office personnel, and school boards consider implementing the ITI model. This allows for informed decision-making and solidification of personal as well as institutional commitment to a shared, and clear, set of pictures. In simple terms, the rubric is designed to allow individuals, schools, and districts to answer these four questions:

- Do we want what the ITI model, when fully implemented, will deliver?

- Do we want these results enough to make the necessary changes in policies and school/district culture ("the way we do things here")?

- How will we know if we are on track or merely caught up in change for the sake of change?

- How can we measure our progress?

Why a Rubric?

The ITI rubric grew out of a need to assess the progress and results of ITI implementation over long-term, intensive efforts of large groups of schools and districts implementing ITI, particularly those funded by the David and Lucile Packard Foundation to improve science education in grades K-6. The questions were obvious enough:

- To what degree are teachers implementing what we know from recent brain research about how the human brain learns? How would we know and what happens when they do?

- Are there common patterns in implementation stages, results for students,

We invite you to join us on a journey into ITI, a journey that will transform your world both professionally and personally.

Acknowledgments:

Frank Paul School, Alisal Elementary School District in Salinas, California, initiated the quest to answer these questions. Our thanks to the pioneering work of Vickie Hogan (ITI Coach), and Jackie Muñoz (Restructuring Coordinator) from Frank Paul School, and Dr. Victoria Bernhardt, (Education for the Future, a project of Pacific Telesis at Frank Paul School), and Jeanne Herrick, (Coordinator of Bilingual Education and Restructuring for the Alisal Elementary School District). Their first draft of a rubric for Frank Paul School provided a springboard for discussions by the coaches and mentor teachers from other districts participating in the Mid-California Science Improvement Program (MCSIP): Diane DellaMaggiore, Julita Galleguillos, Vickie Hogan, and Cheryl Larison of Alisal School District, and Ginger Anderson, Marsha Isaacson, Kris Kennedy, and Olga O'Brien from Santa Cruz Elementary School Districts. Special thanks also to Jeanne Herrick for sharing her perspective of what's important for children and to associates of Susan Kovalik & Associates for their national perspective of the issues of implementing the ITI model: Pattie Mills, Ann Ross, and Karen Olsen. The final version of this rubric, however, is written by Susan Kovalik and Karen Olsen.

Using the Rubric

The rubric is a blueprint for action from which to start through step-by-step descriptions of how to achieve full implementation of the ITI model, from its brain-compatible roots to full integration of all basic skills and content areas. The rubric is without time frames and deadlines—speed and quality of implementation are a function of levels of commitment of district and school policies to support brain-compatible education.

While the items in the "Expectations" column may seem unduly optimistic, they are the very real outcomes experienced in dozens of schools across the country where brain-compatible learning/ITI are implemented schoolwide and at the level of quality described at each of the stages of implementation.

Significant improvement of America's public education system and quantum jumps in student outcomes are possible and very doable. The necessary tools are within our grasp.

and responses from staff and parents that can be predicted? If so, support could be better designed at all stages of implementation.

- Do the outcomes vary when implementation is schoolwide vs. limited to a few individuals or teams?

Because the degree of change and restructuring inherent in the ITI model is so great, single-dimensional views of a classroom and school are not adequate. Many issues must be examined simultaneously with full understanding of the rich webbing of one aspect to another. Thus, curriculum and instruction cannot be examined profitably in an isolated sense. What is needed is a simultaneous view of the interaction of curriculum, instruction, and brain research. And the assessment tools to do so must speak of practicalities as well as theory, tools that are cast in down-to-earth language reflecting a common, shared vocabulary. The rubric can be used to assess program implementation on an individual, team, and/or schoolwide basis.

Stage 0 *Traditional means and ends*

Curriculum	Instructional Strategies	Expectations	Indicators
• Subject areas and specific skills are taught in isolation. • Curriculum is textbook-driven and teacher-centered. • Social development and interaction is based on external rewards and consequences.	• The classroom is textbook- and lecture-driven. • Students sit in rows; there is little collaboration; students are unfocused and mental fibrillation is apparent. • Environments are sterile and/or cluttered with competing colors/patterns and old materials.	• Students are teacher-dependent. • Students do not understand the interrelationships among concepts common to various subject areas. • Students do not see connections between school and real life.	Standardized tests and other paper and pencil tests graded on the bell curve are the primary means of assessment.

Stage 1 *Entry level for making the learning environment brain-compatible*

Stage 1 of ITI implementation begins not with themes or integration but with the brain research basis for learning.

Implementors are advised to go slowly with curriculum development until significant strides toward maintaining a brain-compatible learning environment are achieved. While a brain-compatible learning environment cannot be fully realized until curriculum becomes brain-compatible, curricular changes have little impact if the learning environment is not consistent with how the brain learns.

Stage 1 of the rubric, entry level into a brain-compatible environment, is to be applied to the classroom 100 percent of the time.

Curriculum	Instructional Strategies	Expectations	Indicators
• The elements of absence of threat are taught as an important and	• The teacher's classroom leadership and management is based upon modeling the Lifelong Guidelines and LIFESKILLS. "Discipline" is based upon helping students develop personal skills and behaviors needed to successfully practice the Lifelong Guidelines rather than upon a	• Absence of threat has been established in the classroom. • Students are beginning to take responsibility for their own behavior through the use of LIFESKILLS.	• Post-lesson processing about academic or collaborative

- system of externally imposed rewards and punishments.

- The calmness of the teacher's voice contributes to a settled classroom environment.

- The classroom is healthful (clean, well lighted, and pleasant smelling), aesthetically pleasing (calming colors and music, living plants, well laid out for multiple uses), and uncluttered yet reflects what is being learned.

- Written procedures and agendas provide consistency and security for students.

- Students sit in clusters with easy access to work tools; collaborative learning is a frequently used learning strategy.

- Limited choices are introduced through student selection of supplies, time allocations, materials and processes used for completing projects, etc.

- Teacher includes real life experiences—being there, immersion, and hands-on experiences—to supplement classroom instruction; resource people are invited to the classroom.

- Teacher is developing a variety of instructional strategies to supplement direct instruction.

- Teacher meets frequently with a professional or peer coach who supports the implementation of a brain-compatible learning environment for students.

- on-going part of the curriculum: Lifelong Guidelines, including the LIFESKILLS, the triune brain, problem-solving and product-producing using the seven intelligences, and collaboration.

- Time frames for activities and areas of study are no longer rigid and students are given adequate time to complete their work.

- An atmosphere of mutual respect and genuine caring is obvious among and between students and adults. Students do not put each other down; their behaviors with each other support absence of threat.

- Students demonstrate collaborative skills, e.g., active listening, taking turns, and respect for others' opinions.

- Students focus their attention on learning as soon as they enter the classroom.

- Lack of self-directedness and responsibility for learning has been replaced by a student focus on school as a safe and pleasant place to learn and grow; there is a growing sense of calm and openness.

- Parents understand the purpose and research behind brain-compatible education and are supportive of the teacher's efforts.

- Parents notice evidence of LIFESKILLS at home.

- Teacher confidence and enjoyment in teaching increases.

- experiences occurs daily.

- Decline in classroom and schoolwide discipline problems.

- Differences in student engagement when real life experiences are provided are obvious to teacher and parents.

- Teacher includes student input when selecting work for the student's portfolio folder.

Stage 2 *Entry level for making curriculum brain-compatible*

The beginning steps in making curriculum brain-compatible assume that significant progress has been made implementing Stage 1, making the learning environment brain-compatible.

Whereas rubric Stage 1 is applied to the classroom 100 percent of the time, rubric Stage 2 is applied only to that portion of the day, week, or year for which teachers have developed brain-compatible curriculum using the ITI model. The time frames and content that teachers may select to begin implementation of their brain-compatible curriculum vary widely. Typically teachers begin where they feel they will be most successful and stretch from there. Whatever the starting point, however modest or bold, the rubric at this stage applies only during the time when a teacher is implementing his/her brain-compatible curriculum.

Curriculum

- Teacher provides for real-life experiences by basing the integrated curriculum upon a physical location, event, or situation that students can and do frequently experience through "being there." Science is either the core for or a prominent part of the curriculum integration.

- Teacher has identified the concepts and skills that will be taught to the levels of mastery and application. Key points focus on critical concepts

Instructional Strategies

- Immersion and hands-on-of-the-real-thing are the primary input used to supplement and extend there experiences.

- Instructional strategies are varied and provide the most effective methods for the particular content at hand: direct instruction, ITI discovery process; collaboration; personal study time; mindmapping; organizing materials; cross-age/multi-age interaction, etc.

Expectations

- Students participate actively, initiating ideas, responding to teacher's questions, staying on task with minimal guidance from the teacher.

- Students see the connections between the classroom and real life.

- Mental fibrillation has been replaced by a sense of calm, relaxed alertness, confidence in success in learning, and purposefulness.

Indicators

- Post-lesson processing about academic and social experiences.

- Use of selected inquiries to assess mastery of key point, e.g., projects, presentations, and some traditional tests.

rather than isolated facts.

- Inquiries for each key point provide students choices, multiple opportunities for real world application, and allow for multiple ways of problem-solving and product-producing.

- The curriculum includes most of the elements that appear as a natural part or extension of the being there focus, e.g., science, math, technology, history/social studies, fine arts, as well as reading, writing, and oral expression. Integration of content is natural, not contrived.

- Content is age-appropriate.

- Resources to support the theme are multiple, varied, and rich. Resource people and experts are regular visitors to the classroom and off-campus learning sites.

- Choices are regularly provided through inquiries and other means.

- Adequate time is allowed to let students complete their work.

- There are sufficient inquiries for students to complete to ensure mastery and development of mental programs for using the knowledge/skills of the key points.

- Collaboration is effectively used and enhances learning for academic and social growth.

- School as a place to learn and exercise one's personal best is the accepted norm.

- Absentee rates are dropping, library checkout rates are increasing.

- Students engage in problem-solving in a collaborative manner at least once a day.

- Teacher and student select work for the student's portfolio folder.

- Assessment of mastery is based upon the 3 C's of Assessment.

Stage 3

Stage 3 assumes that a brain-compatible learning environment has been established and is consistently nurtured and maintained throughout the day (Stage 1) and that the tools for developing brain-compatible curriculum are consistently and effectively used during the time targeted for ITI curriculum (Stage 2). Stage 3 represents a refinement of implementing a brain-compatible environment and curriculum for students. Targeted time for ITI curriculum increases to approximately 25 percent of the year in Stage 3.

If either Stage 1 or 2 is not fully in place at this time, do not attempt to apply this rubric stage regardless of the amount of teacher-developed curriculum being implemented. It is the quality, not the quantity, of ITI curriculum that is key. The power of the ITI model lies with its brain-   compatible underpinnings.

Curriculum

- A yearlong theme, prominently displayed on the wall for both students and teacher, serves as the framework for content development. On average, more than 25 percent of instruction during the school year is based upon brain-compatible curriculum developed for this theme.

- Curriculum content, as expressed in the key points, enhances pattern-seeking, making it easy for students to perceive and understand the most important ideas and concepts in the curriculum; inquiries are designed to help students make connections to

Instructional Strategies

- Immersion and hands-on-of-the-real-thing are the primary input used to supplement and extend being there experiences.

- All instructional time during the theme and for a growing portion of time during traditional instruction is based upon the progression of "being there > concept > language > application to the real world" rather than the traditional "language > concept . . . application."

- Collaboration is used daily whenever it will enhance pattern seeking and program building.

Expectations

- Students demonstrate LIFESKILLS throughout the day (in and out of the classroom); students are self-directed.

- Students as well as the teacher use the 3 C's of Assessment as a means of assessing learning.

- Students exercise more shared leadership while doing collaborative activities and actively seek connections to and applications in

Indicators

- Celebrations of learning and social/political action are key assessment tools for each component; they are designed to allow students to demonstrate mastery and application of the key points in the curriculum.

the real world and to develop mental programs for long-term memory.

- Most of the time, the curriculum includes almost all of the elements that appear as a natural part or extension of the being there focus, e.g., science, math, technology, history/social studies, and fine arts, as well as reading, writing, and oral expression, including second language acquisition.

- The content of the theme is consistently used as a high interest area for applying the skills/knowledge currently being taught in at least one basic skill area (e.g., math, reading, writing).

- Curriculum for collaborative assignments is specifically designed for group work.

- Time is allocated in accordance with the nature of the tasks and student and teacher need for adequate time; such time allocations are made in recognition of the need to develop mental programs for using knowledge and skills in real world contexts.

- Peers and cross-age tutors substantially increase teaching and practice time for students in areas of individual need.

the real world.

- Student absentee rates drop to less than 3 percent; visits to the school nurse due to emotional, upset-based problems drop significantly. Library circulation rates increase by 50 percent.

- Parents report student levels of interest in school and learning as being higher than ever before. Parents' support levels are higher than ever before; volunteerism has doubled.

- Selections, for the portfolio folder, of work completed as part of the theme are made primarily by the student.

Stage 4

Stage 4 assumes that a brain-compatible learning environment has been established (Stage 1) and that the tools for developing brain-compatible curriculum as described in Stages 2 and 3 are fully in place. Stage 4 represents a further refinement and extension of those tools and a consistent implementation of brain-compatible curriculum for students, i.e., at least 50 percent of the time during the school year. If Stages 1, 2, and 3 are not fully in place, do not attempt to apply this rubric stage regardless of the amount of time one implements teacher-developed curriculum. Again, the power of the ITI model lies with its brain-compatible underpinnings.

Curriculum	*Instructional Strategies*	*Expectations*	*Indicators*
• Curriculum is based predominantly on visitable locations that provide being there experiences and connections with the real world.	• Learning experiences are predominantly based on real life, immersion, and hands-on of the real thing; the teacher regularly utilizes explorations and discovery processes to make learning real for students.	• All students master the key points in all content and basic skill areas.	• Except for district-required assessments, grading on the bell curve has been replaced with assessment of mastery and program-building demonstrated by culminating performances chosen by the teacher (using selected inquiries and the 3 C's of assessment).
• The yearlong theme includes a rationale statement and conceptual idea that provide an unforgettable pattern-shaper. On average, more than 50 percent of instruction during the school year is based upon brain-compatible	• All instructional time during the theme and for a growing portion of time during traditional instruction is based upon the progression of "being there > concept > language > application to the real world" rather than the traditional "language > concept . . . application."	• Students demonstrate responsibility for their learning and act in a self-directed, self-initiating manner throughout the day; they have internalized the Lifelong Guidelines, including LIFESKILLS, and use them as the basis for interacting with others off campus as well as in the classroom and school.	• Students' yearlong research projects reflect high interest and understanding.
			• Guest resource people acknowledge the high degree of student understanding.

curriculum developed for this yearlong theme.

- The content of the theme is used daily as meaningful content for teaching *at least one* area of basic skills (e.g., math, reading, writing, oral expression, second and primary language acquisition) and is used for applying *all* the basic skills.

- Basic skills taught within the theme are taught as a means to an end, not as an end in themselves. Thus, while the teacher utilizes specific techniques for teaching the basic skills on a daily basis, such as Early Effective Teaching, the primary focus of students is on meaningful content which the basic skills help the student unlock.

- The teacher takes advantage of the power of "incidental learning" (as defined by Frank Smith) to build mental programs applying the basic skills.

- Choices, to allow for individual students' ways of learning, interests, and needs, are consistently provided for.

- Students use technology as a natural extension of their senses to explore and learn.

- Students use what they learn in school to creatively solve real-life problems.

- Student absentee rates drop to less than 1.5 percent; visits to the school nurse are for serious physical illness, none for emotional upset.

- Library circulation rates are double those before the implementation of brain-compatible/ITI learning.

- *All* students who have experienced a consistent brain-compatible program for three years or more perform at least at grade level. The *average* for the classroom is one grade level or more above national norms.

- The class newspaper or magazine, published at least twice a year, reflects writing skills at least one year above grade level.

- Students, having learned to assess their own learning, participate in parent-teacher conferences, describing how selections of their work demonstrate their progress (academic, personal, and social) and their goals for learning during the next component/quarter.

Stage 5

Like Stages 3 and 4, Stage 5 assumes that a brain-compatible learning environment has been established (Stage 1), and is being maintained, and that the tools for developing brain-compatible curriculum are in place and are highly refined as described in Stages 3 and 4. Stage 5 represents an extension of those tools and a consistent implementation of brain-compatible curriculum for students 100 percent of the time during the school year. If either Stage 1 or 2 is not fully in place and consistently nurtured and maintained or Stages 3 and 4 are not in place, do not attempt to apply this rubric stage. Again, the power of the ITI model lies with its brain-compatible underpinnings.

Curriculum

- The yearlong theme serves as the framework for content development and implementation for all basic skills and content 95 percent of the day/year. Key points and inquiries effectively enhance pattern seeking and program building.

- The curriculum of the district, upon which there is both school- and district-wide agreement, provides each teacher with pattern-enhancing tools for curriculum planning.

Instructional Strategies

- All instructional strategies identified in Levels 1 through 4 are in place 95 percent of the day/year.

- Students have the same teacher two or more years (either due to multi-aging or the teacher moving with the students).

- Teacher utilizes the power of incidental learning during both planned instructional strategies and the unplanned teachable moments.

- Technology in the classroom allows teacher and students full access to databases and communications

Expectations

- Self-responsibility for and self-initiated engagement in learning are valued schoolwide and clearly evident. Students display a love of learning and keen curiosity; they are mastering the skills and attitudes for lifelong learning.

- Students direct their own learning by assisting in the development of inquiries, refinement of key points. They can identify and know how to pursue lifelong interests and career options, and in focusing their efforts, they can apply what they know to real world situations.

Indicators

- Parent-teacher conferences have become student-parent-teacher conferences that, in the upper grades, are led by the student.

- Students initiate and engage in a wide range of community volunteer tasks, social and political action projects, and other

- Brain-compatible curriculum is implemented schoolwide, providing consistency for students as they move through the school.

systems throughout the country. Being there experiences near the school are used as a starting point from which to examine similar, age-appropriate situations around the world.

- Students have learned the personal and social skills for solving problems. They recognize the need for everyone's participation when making decisions that affect all.

means of contributing to society.

ITI Schoolwide Rubric*

Planning and Assessing Schoolwide Implementation of Brain-Compatible Education

By Karen Olsen and Susan Kovalik

Like the *ITI Classroom Rubric*, the *ITI Schoolwide Rubric* is designed to provide both a roadmap of the journey ahead and a means of assessing the progress made. However, as its name implies, this rubric examines the schoolwide elements needed to support and nurture teachers' efforts to create brain-compatible learning for students in the classroom as they become responsible citizens. Thus, this rubric examines the learning and working environment for adults and the governance structures and processes through which all staff and involved parents and community members can learn and work together to best support student learning and citizenship. As used here, "schoolwide leadership" means the combined efforts of the principal, certificated and classified staff, and involved parents and community members.

This rubric parallels the *ITI Classroom Rubric* and assumes that implementation of ITI, under ideal conditions, would begin first on a school-wide basis and then continue one stage ahead of implementation of ITI in the classroom. In other words, under ideal circumstances, the work of teachers at the classroom level would be preceded by schoolwide work to commit to the use of best knowledge and best practice. Implicit in this assumption is the belief that teachers working within their individual classrooms need support from the schoolwide environment to succeed. Experience has clearly shown that working alone is painfully slow and laborious. Implementing ITI is a team affair; to succeed it must begin with and be continuously supported by a schoolwide environment that is brain-compatible for adults as well as students.

As you read through this rubric, key concepts and resources for further reading about them are explained at the end of each stage in "Toward a Common Vocabulary."

Thank you for your willingness to engage in school improvement efforts at a deep and fundamental level.

*Stages 1 and 2 only. Contact Books for Educators at 1-888-777-9827 or www.books4educ.com to obtain entire document.

Stage 1 *Committing to use of best knowledge and best practice*

Learning and Working Environment

Training and Implementing	Expectations	Indicators
All certificated and classified staff have a solid working knowledge of the role of emotions in the learning process. Each staff member can explain the concept of emotions as gatekeeper to learning and the implications for everyday life on the job and at home. Each has made significant progress toward learning to apply this knowledge to his/her role at school.	Knowledge of the concept of the emotions as gatekeeper is consistently used on a daily basis as the foundation for adult-adult interactions. Adults provide an emotionally consistent environment for themselves and students. The physical environment is less institutional and more conducive to learning and working together.	Sharing stories about "upshifting" and "emotional override" in home and neighborhood as well as at school is a daily occurrence. The physical environment of the school—entry area, cafeteria, hallways, student restrooms, playground, and staff lounge—has been transformed based on knowledge of how color, lighting, cleanliness, order, and music affect the brain's readiness and capacity to learn.
All staff, certificated and classified, have also received training in the brain research concepts of intelligence as a function of experience (physiology of learning), multiple intelligences, and personality preferences.	Staff have applied this information to an analysis of instructional practices and curriculum tools for their school program including policies and practices. They have begun the process of prioritizing areas of improvement critical to achieving an atmosphere of absence of threat in the classroom.	Teachers can describe behavior issues they have had with students that are a result of elements of curriculum, instructional practices, and classroom management/"discipline" approaches that are inconsistent with brain research findings.
All staff (certificated and classified) have had extensive training (workshop presentations and follow-up coaching) in using the Lifelong Guidelines and LIFESKILLS and in	The Lifelong Guidelines and LIFESKILLS are used consistently throughout the school in adult-adult interactions including informal interactions in the staff lounge and team	Brain-antagonistic "discipline" approaches in the office and during schoolwide funcions have been replaced by consistent use of target talk focused on the Lifelong Guidelines

and LIFESKILLS. Similarly, target talk is used when changes in adult behavior are needed to remain consistent with Lifelong Guidelines and LIFESKILLS; staff are beginning to consciously model the Lifelong Guidelines and LIFESKILLS with fellow adults and with students. Written procedures communicate clear expectations. The school is becoming a multi-age learning community characterized by inclusion, influence, and affection—the inner engines for achievement of the school mission.

Indicators

Staff uses a common vocabulary based on a shared core of best knowledge and best practice. This vocabulary and the shared understandings it represents are used daily in informal and formal settings. They are shaping the emerging culture of the school. Staff have made a formal commitment to align behavior with, and base decision-making on, what is best for students in accordance with best knowledge and best practice; disagreements based on differing educational "philosophies"

---

planning sessions as well as more formal meetings such as staff meetings and community events. Doing one's personal best is the norm, a daily expectation of self and others.

Expectations

Key books have been read by all staff and involved parents and community members; the books have been thoroughly discussed and processed during large and small group meetings. (For example, for elementary schools—*Endangered Minds: Why Our Children Don't Think, Human Brain and Human Learning, Smart Moves: Why Learning Is Not All in Your Head,* and *ITI: The Model* or *Kid's Eye View of Science;* for middle schools—*Endangered Minds,*

---

community-building strategies for working together as a cohesive schoolwide community. Participation in school life, for staff and students, is viewed as a beginning step in building citizenship.

Governance

Training and Implementing

The source of the culture of the school, "the way we do things here," is changing from an historical perspective ("we've always done this and done it this way") to a commitment to using best knowledge (most recent brain research) and best practices (curricular and instructional approaches that would best implement brain research). The emerging sense of community that embodies these professional commitments is based on the Lifelong Guidelines and LIFESKILLS.

Human Brain and Human Learning, and The Way We Were, The Way We Can Be: A Vision For Middle Schools; for high schools—Inside the Brain: Revolutionary Discoveries of How the Mind Works, Human Brain and Human Learning, Making Connections: Teaching and the Brain, and Synergy: Transformation of America's High Schools Through ITI).	are rare and sharing of new brain research findings and discussion of how best to implement them are daily occurrences; next steps in training have been planned.
Members of work groups serve willingly and with enthusiasm. Committee membership and leadership roles change frequently enough to maximize opportunities for participation and personal and professional growth while also balancing the need for continuity of perspective. Staff are empowered to participate in important decisions and to implement them using common sense and personal best.	Groups use direct democratic processes for decision-making (all effected by a decision have a say in it). By exploring alternative courses of action, and their short- and long-term consequences, crisis management has been significantly reduced. Addressing underlying causes, rather than symptoms of problems, is giving participants hope that the changes in their governance processes will make a difference.
Each staff member annually writes a description of his/her part to play to help achieve the school's mission. Included are the specific actions needed to carry out those roles and the professional/personal growth needed to best carry out his/her part to play.	Daily behaviors of all are consistent with the mission and the school improvement plan and are sufficient for achieving the mission within a reasonable period of time.

Governance structures and procedures are shifting from hierarchical power to widespread shared decision-making including leadership groups such as school site council, grade level teams, study groups, the committee-as-a-whole, quality circle groups, and involved parent and community groups.

The written mission of the school reflects the central and pivotal purpose of creating responsible citizens and providing a brain-compatible learning environment for students and adults. The mission also commits the school to supporting lifelong learning of all staff and parents.

Before beginning Stage 2, the staff, parents, and community members meet to discuss, and celebrate, their progress to date and to formally recommit to becoming a brain-compatible school using best knowledge and best practice. This analysis and recommitment process includes a thorough brain-compatibility audit as well as a review of relevant data about student growth and achievement. The school mission statement is revisited and revised as appropriate as is each individual's personal mission statement; the school's improvement plan is also revised as needed.

Stage 1

Toward a Common Vocabulary

Because education is such an old field of endeavor, most of the terms used within it have become freighted with special and often highly personalized meanings. As the saying goes, there are as many definitions for an educational term as there are people in the room. Thus, one of the earliest and most important tasks of any group is to come to terms with its vocabulary so that members can feel confident that what they said is what gets heard. To assist in the task of common vocabulary-building, important terms from Stage 1 of this rubric are defined here in alphabetical order. Many definitions are accompanied by recommended books for further reading.

Absence of threat — the first of eight brain-compatible elements of the ITI model. For more information, see the ITI book appropriate for your grade level(s): *ITI: The Model* or *Kid's Eye View of Science* (for elementary grades), *The Way We Were … The Way We CAN Be: A Vision for the Middle School* (for middle school grades) or *Synergy: Transformation of America's High Schools* (for high school). (S1-2)

Best knowledge and best practice — a term coined by John Champlin to describe a mindset dedicated to acquiring the best available knowledge about how learning takes place (brain research and its implications for curriculum and instructional practices) and commitment to full and rigorous use of such information in design and execution of curriculum and instructional practice. Also implies a commitment to root out all   current practice that does not align with best knowledge. (S1-1 through 4)

Brain-antagonistic "discipline" approaches — refers to discipline approaches that are behaviorist (based on Skinner's stimulus-response, reward and punishment) and tend to maintain an external locus of control rather than developing an internal locus of control; the opposite of "brain-compatible" disciplinary approaches. For more information, see the ITI book appropriate for your grade level(s): *ITI: The Model* or

Kid's Eye View of Science (for elementary grades), *The Way We Were ... The Way We CAN Be: A Vision for the Middle School* (for middle school grades) or *Synergy: Transformation of America's High Schools* (for high school). (S1-2)

Citizenship — the ultimate goal of the ITI model, to produce adults who are ready (skill and knowledge) and willing (have a sense of commitment to the success of the community, not just their own) to undertake their responsibilities to nurture and support our democratic way of government and life. Citizenship to maintain and nurture our democratic society should be the core goal of education.

In Carl Glickman's view, "Democracy as a core belief transcends empirical argument. Rational analysis can proceed, data can accumulate, and thoughtful logic can apply. In the end, however, there is no universal proof that democratic societies produce better mathematicians, less crime, or fewer people in hunger than undemocratic societies, do. What the belief in democracy does it to ensure that the issues of our society are issues that citizens care about, participate in resolving, and take responsibility for. Many democracies are democracies in name only; they do not engender the participation, involvement, and responsibility of their citizens. That is why the role of public education and school renewal is so crucial to the rejuvenation of a more caring, a more enlightened, and a wiser citizenship.

The belief in, rather than the empirical truth about, democracy is the foundation of a society that millions of people throughout the world have given their lives to create, protect, and maintain. We must do the same in our schools. To return to their central mission of preparing democratic citizens, schools must be founded on the same bedrock of belief. We need to strive for the same micro-community in our schools that we as a people would wish to have as a macro-community in our society." (*Renewing America's Schools: A Guide to School-Based Action*, pp. 155-156) (S1-2)

Committee-as-a-whole — refers to the entire school community—certificated, classified, and involved parents and community members—all who will be affected by the implementation of a decision to be made. (S1-4)

Common vocabulary — a shared vocabulary with agreed upon meanings is the basis for relating to others, whether it is among family or friends. Without a shared vocabulary with agreed-upon meanings, school improvement efforts always fail. (S1-5)

Community — a quality of interaction with others (adult-adult, adult-student, and student-student) that enhances achievement. Defined by Jeanne Gibbs as having three stages: inclusion, influence, and affection. For more information, see *TRIBES: A New Way of Learning* (S-2)

Culture of the school— defined by Terrence Deal as "the way we do things here," socially and personally, in the classroom and schoolwide. (S1-3)

Educational "philosophies" — "Tell me your philosophy of education" used to be a standard interview prompt for educators. In an era of exploding brain research, this question is now outdated because philosophies of education have been based on changing models of instruction such as behaviorist, Dewian, etc. The question today should be, "What do you believe to be the most significant brain research findings and how do you apply them in your classroom?" (S1-3)

"Emotional override" and "upshifting" — terms used in the ITI model with students to describe mental states related to the learning process. Emotional override occurs when the emotions hold primacy (most frequently as the result of perceived threat) and academic learning gets put on hold; upshifting describes the quality of emotional calm or "relaxed alertness" during which the cerebral cortex reengages in academic learning. For more information, see the ITI book appropriate to your grade level(s). (S1-1)

Emotions as gatekeeper to learning — since postulation of the triune brain theory by Dr. Paul MacLean in the 1950s, scientists have made discovery after discovery about the role of emotions in overall mental processing. Recent research, particularly that by Candace Pert, into the role of peptides and steroids significantly expands our understanding of "informational substances" that are produced, and received, throughout the body and brain. These, in addition to the familiar neurotransmitters in the brain, make up a complex and compelling view of emotions and their primacy in the learning environment. For more information, please read *Molecules of Emotion* by Dr. Candace Pert and *Human Brain and Human Learning, Revised 1998*, Chapter 5, by Leslie Hart. (S1-1)

Emotionally consistent environment — a calm environment maintained by staff who "leave their own problems at the door," whether they be personal or caused by an upset within the school, who are calm and consistent in their classroom leadership/management, and who are even-handed in their discipline of students, giving consequences appropriate to the infraction. (S1-1)

Governance — as used here, a term denoting decision-making in its broadest sense and means of affecting compliance with those decisions. In the ITI model, governance is primarily based on consensus-building among all interested staff and involved parents in all issues, including school budgeting. In advanced stages of implementation of this rubric, governance operates under a contract with the district office, thus allowing school-level control of all issues within the scope of the contract. (S1-3)

Intelligence as a function of experience — one of six concepts from brain research upon which the ITI model is based. Because of the recent extraordinary advances in technology, the biology of learning is now observable, e.g., what kinds of input most activate the brain and result in building long-term memory. For more information, see the ITI book appropriate for your grade level(s): *ITI: The Model* or *Kid's Eye View of Science* (for elementary grades), *The Way We Were . . . The Way We CAN Be: A Vision for the Middle School* (for middle school grades) or *Synergy: Transformation of America's High Schools* (for high school). (S1-2)

Lifelong Guidelines and LIFESKILLS — the Lifelong Guidelines, truthfulness, trustworthiness, active listening, no put-downs, and personal best (as defined by the LIFESKILLS), are key ITI structures for classroom leadership/management, for creating a sense of community, and for teaching the social and personal skills for citizenship. (S1-2)

Mission — a written statement of what the school community intends to make happen for students. It emerges from the written statement of best knowledge/practice the school has committed itself to and directly addresses the real work of the school, not platitudes. It is updated yearly to ensure it remains a working document that guides people's on-going planning and discussion. (S1-4)

Multi-age learning community — this term builds on two definitions: Learning community as put forth by Peter Senge in *Fifth Discipline Fieldbook* and multi-age referring to the span between beginning and veteran teachers and teachers from all grade levels; also includes a willingness to also learn from students, their parents, and involved community members. (S1-2)

Multiple intelligences — one of six concepts from brain research upon which the ITI model is based. The eight intelligences identified by Howard Gardner are: logical-mathematical, linguistic, spatial, musical, bodily-kinesthetic, naturalist, intra-personal, and interpersonal. For more information, see Gardner's original work, *Frames of Mind: Theory of Multiple Intelligences*. More user-friendly books include *Seven Kinds of Smarts* by Thomas Armstrong (good for parents as well as teachers) and *Multiple Intelligences in the Classroom*, also by Thomas Armstrong. (S1-2)

Part to play— one of four stages of planning for transition outlined by William Bridges. The four stages are: agreeing on purpose, painting a picture of what the purpose would look like, developing a plan for how to implement the picture, and a description by each person specifying their individual part to play. For more information, see *Managing Transitions: Making the Most of Change*. (S1-4)

Personal best — one of the Lifelong Guidelines of the ITI model, personal best is defined by the 17 LIFESKILLS: integrity, initiative, flexibility, perseverance, organization, sense of humor, effort, common sense, problem-solving, responsibility, patience, friendship, curiosity, cooperation, caring, courage, and pride. (S1-2)

Personality preferences or temperament — an area of psychological research and application beginning with the work of Karl Jung through Briggs and Myers and, more recently, Keirsey and Bates. For a user-friendly version, see *Please Understand Me: Character and Temperament Types* by Keirsey and Bates which provides a quick, self-administered "test" with explanations of each of the 16 types. Areas covered are: orientation to others and the world (introvert-extrovert); how people take in information (sensor-intuitor); decision-making (thinker-feeler), and lifestyle or how one organizes one's life (judger-perceiver). Provides invaluable information for staff to have about self and others; helps explain what "irritates" us about others and helps each person "slide along" the four scales to better communicate with another. Recommended as a group-building and group-maintenance activity. For a description of how to use the four temperament scales in designing staff development trainings, see *Mentor Teacher Role: Owners' Manual*, Chapter 4, pp. 91-97 (S1-2)

Physical environment of the school — because so many "informational substances" (see *Emotions as gatekeeper* above) monitor and respond to elements in the physical environment, issues of relationship (teacher-student and student-student), cleanliness, smell, lighting, color, sound, order, and beauty are far more important to academic learning than previously surmised. (S1-1)

School improvement plan — the up-to-date, annual statement of what is to be accomplished and how; also reflects why the areas of work for the year were chosen. (S1-1 through 4)

Target talk — a term coined by Pat Belvel. As used in the ITI model, target talk is the judgement-free use of descriptions of behavior that, over time, define for students what a Lifelong Guideline or LIFESKILL does, and does not, look like, sound like, and feel like in real world terms. Target talk is used during the teachable moment on an on-going basis. (S1-2)

Written procedures — a key classroom leadership/management structure in the ITI model. Written procedures are the social and personal behaviors that provide the context for doing an assignment or task (as distinguished from the directions for doing the task). Written procedures should be established for frequently-performed tasks such as entering and leaving the room, using classroom resources, what do to with spare time when an assignment is completed, and what to do when a substitute teacher comes to the classroom, etc. (S1-2)

Stage 2 *Creating a brain-compatible environment in which to learn and work*

Stage 2 of the *ITI Schoolwide Rubric* assumes that significant progress has been made implementing Stage 1. If not, it is inappropriate to apply this stage of the rubric. One cannot begin at the end or middle of a task. First things must come first.

Learning and Working Environment

Training and Implementing	*Expectations*	*Indicators*
Lifelong Guidelines and LIFESKILLS are continually retaught and their application extended and deepened as all staff and involved parents consistently model their use both inside the classrooms and school-wide (in the school office, hallways, outdoors, and during schoolwide events). Lifelong Guidelines form the basis for staff interactions, formal and informal.	The principal, during staff meetings, models Lifelong Guidelines and LIFESKILLS and the use of written procedures and agendas. Staff participation during meetings also models Lifelong Guidelines and LIFESKILLS and the behaviors each would like to see in their students. Likewise, leaders and team members of committees, sub-committees, and grade level/subject specialist teams operate with these norms.	An atmosphere of absence of threat for all is a noticeable and prominent quality of school environment. A sense of community—inclusion, influence, and affection—exists throughout the school community. Put-downs are rare in all aspects of school life. When they do occur, they are politely countered with a reminder of the schoolwide agreement to eliminate put-downs. Unkind and hurtful comments are not left to fester but are resolved promptly. Isolationism and congeniality have been replaced by a strong sense of collegiality and full practice of the Lifelong Guidelines and LIFESKILLS. There is a lively sense of challenge balanced with confidence in succeeding at the tasks at hand.
All staff, certificated and classified, and involved parents and community members have continued their exploration of the brain research concepts of intelligence as a function of experience (physiology of learning),	As a result of training in brain research, staff members assist each other to learn new job skills and knowledge using the multiple intelligences, to appreciate temperament differences as strengths for achieving	There is greater maximization of skills and talents (utilization and coordination) which

benefits the organization and engenders greater job satisfaction for each individual. Each person is learning to ask for the kind of input he/she needs to achieve high level mastery of new job skills and to extinguish old behaviors related to brain-antagonistic practices. Staff members volunteer for tasks and request reassignment to a different position based upon their knowledge of the match between their strengths and the demands of the job to be done.

Indicators

The entry hall is welcoming and accurately reflects the important work of the school currently in progress. The hallways are attractive and part of the learning process. Student restrooms are clean, pleasant smelling, and cheerful. The cafeteria looks and sounds more like a restaurant rather than a school cafeteria. Soft music, mostly 60 beats a minute, classical as well as popular, can be heard throughout the school.

overall success of the mission and the school improvement plan, and to "slide along" the temperament scales when required by the task at hand. Each staff member understands how he/she learns and the importance of "being there" experiences for children. Each recognizes, appreciates, and validates his/her own strengths and those of others.

Expectations

The environment is welcoming, less institutional, and more reflective of real life outside of the school.

multiple intelligences, and personality preferences. In addition to stressing how these concepts apply to how students learn, the training also focused on how to apply the knowledge to learning and working together on the job.

Governance

Training and Implementing

Transformation of the school environment—based upon knowledge of the impact of color, lighting, cleanliness, order, and music on emotions as the gatekeeper to learning of—has been completed.

Staff and parents new to the school each year receive training in the brain research concepts so that they can become full, contributing members of the community within a year of their arrival. Newcomers are invited into the school's mission/plan and develop a plan for their part to play.

Staff and community share a common vocabulary for best knowledge and best practice. All staff, new and continuing, are knowledgeable about and committed to the school mission and school improvement plan.

There are no cliques among staff. All consider themselves members of the same team dedicated to a common mission. Staff and involved parents and community members see themselves as lifelong learners.

Each person responsible for implementing the school improvement plan's strategies and procedures needed to achieve the school's mission has been involved in the planning of such roles and tasks. The planning has been extensive, in-depth, and thorough.

The school's mission and subsequent planning to implement brain-compatible education as described in the school improvement plan are important to the staff and community and guide daily planning and implementation efforts.

Implementation of the school improvement plan is on target and all see evidence that significant progress is being made toward achieving the school's mission. Individual staff members report that they are implementing the plan they developed for carrying out their part to play, including plans for professional/personal growth.

In working to plan and implement the mission, there is strong and universal commitment to the use of best knowledge and best practice rather than arguing educational philosophy or accepting a favored position of those holding the most formal or informal power. Initial planning and ongoing planning for implementation centers on commitment to best knowledge and best practice, not upon personal philosophies or the opinions of those holding formal or informal power.

All are fully committed to the use of best knowledge and best practice to achieve the mission/school improvement plan and frequently voice their personal commitment to do so.

Staff and parents use best knowledge and best practice to examine powerful, underlying belief systems. Such analyses are viewed by staff as a valuable way to clarify the goals to be attained and to paint a more detailed picture of the job ahead. Conflicting beliefs are examined respectfully but thoroughly. While opinions about how to best implement brain-compatible learning may vary, commitment to implement best knowledge and practice is unanimous.

Governance

Training and Implementing

Governance structures are changing to align with the new mission/plan and ways of interacting. In addition to the Committee-as-a-whole and an on-going School Improvement Committee, various committees, short- and long-term, are in place, with authority to analyze problems, generate alternatives, choose among alternatives, and help determine resource allocation. The work of the committees addresses the real work of the school, not symptoms of problems or programmatic issues limited to a particular source(s) of supplemental funding or sub-population of students.

Expectations

Hierarchy, institutional and social, has been replaced with a commitment to use all available talents and abilities to the fullest extent possible for the benefit of students and the implementation of a brain-compatible environment. A spirit of collaboration, based on the Lifelong Guidelines and LIFESKILLS, has replaced the brain stem behaviors of inflexibility, territoriality, maintaining social hierarchies, tribal clustering, and preening and other ritualistic displays.

Indicators

There is a unity of vision, a congruence in understanding of how to carry out the school mission/plan, a commitment to operating in ways that enhance the sense of community and an insistence that decisions be consistent with best knowledge and best practice. Staff readily volunteer for standing and ad hoc committees. All serve on at least one committee each year; leadership and membership rotate. As there is greater focus in the classroom on creating responsible citizens, there is also a shift for staff from working in a bureaucracy to participating fully in a self-governing workplace.

Before beginning Stage 3, the staff, parents, and community members meet to discuss, and celebrate, their progress to date and to formally recommit to becoming a brain-compatible school using best knowledge and best practice. This analysis and recommitment process includes a thorough brain-compatibility audit as well as a review of relevant data about student growth and achievement. The school mission statement is revisited and revised as appropriate as is each individual's personal mission statement; the school's improvement plan is also revised as needed.

Stage 2

Toward a Common Vocabulary

Because education is such an old field of endeavor, most of the terms used within it have become freighted with special and often highly personalized meanings. As the saying goes, there are as many definitions for an educational term as there are people in the room. Thus, one of the earliest and most important tasks of any group is to come to terms with its vocabulary so that members can feel confident that what they said is what gets heard. To assist in the task of common vocabulary-building, important terms from Stage 2 of this rubric are defined here in alphabetical order. Many definitions are accompanied by recommended books for further reading.

Absence of threat — the first of eight brain-compatible elements of the ITI model. For more information, see the ITI book appropriate for your grade level(s): *ITI: The Model* or *Kid's Eye View of Science* (for elementary grades), *The Way We Were . . . The Way We CAN Be: A Vision for the Middle School* (for middle school grades) or *Synergy: Transformation of America's High Schools* (for high school). (S2-1)

"Being there" — an ITI term for a learning situation at a real life location which provides full sensory input from the 19 senses. More than just a field trip site, "being there" locations are the basis for curriculum planning and integration. (S2-2)

Best knowledge and best practice — a term coined by John Champlin to describe a mindset dedicated to acquiring the best available knowledge about how learning takes place (brain research and its implications for curriculum and instructional practices) and commitment to full and rigorous use of such information in design and execution of curriculum and instructional practice (also implies a commitment to root out all current practice that does not align with best knowledge). (S2-3 and 4)

Brain-Compatibility Audit — an analysis, conducted annually, of the curriculum, instructional strategies, and administrative policies and procedures of the school using the ITI Decision-Making Template. The purpose of the audit is to determine what elements of the current program are inconsistent with the school's written statement of best knowledge and best practice in order to identify what resource allocations (time, effort, money) should be eliminated or altered thus creating time and money for implementing the school's improvement plan. For more information, see Appendix A.

Brain stem behaviors — although the triune brain as a conceptual construct for understanding the functions of the brain has largely been replaced by an expanded view obtained in the past decade, information about the role of the brain stem continues to be serviceable. The behaviors are innate to human behavior; they cannot be "fixed" or eliminated. They are part of "human nature" and continue to complicate classroom and school life. (S2-5)

Brain-antagonistic practices — curricular, instructional, and governance practices that are inconsistent with best knowledge and best practice. (S2-2)

Brain-compatible education — a term first coined by Leslie A. Hart, author of *Human Brain and Human Learning.* Hart took a layman's view of complex brain research findings coming from a number of fields and synthesized the information into understandable and useable descriptions of how the brain functions. His work from the late 1970s and early 1980s, particularly his description of learning as a two-step process, i.e., making meaning of patterns and developing mental programs for using what is understood, still stands today, further confirmed by research through the 1980s and 1990s. The ITI model is indebted to Mr. Hart, a pioneer in applying brain research to classrooms and schools. (S2-4)

Bureaucracy — bureaucracy is never neutral in its messages to those who work within it. Common messages are "Consistency of rules applied are more important than the quality of the idea or the goals of the people involve." "One size fits all, be it rules and expectations (often of mediocre level) or consequence/punishment." "If you want to succeed, following the rules is the name of the game; achieving the stated goals of the organization are not what is really valued." "Don't rock the boat even if it deserves to be." Etcetera, etcetera. A school truly interested in systemic improvement must uncover the messages within its fundamental structures and take proactive steps to silence the change-killing messages. (S2-5)

Committee-as-a-whole — refers to the entire school community—certificated, classified, and involved parents and community members—all who will be affected by the implementation of a decision to be made. (S2-5)

Common vocabulary — a shared vocabulary with agreed upon meanings is the basis for relating to others, whether it is among family or friends. Without a shared vocabulary with agreed upon meanings, school improvement efforts always fail. (S2-3)

Community — a quality of interaction with others (adult-adult, adult-student, and student-student) that enhances achievement. Defined by Jeanne Gibbs as having three stages: inclusion, influence, and affection. For more information, see TRIBES: A New Way of Learning (available through Books for Educators). (S2-1)

Congeniality versus collegiality — a distinction drawn by Carl Glickman in *Renewing America's Schools: A Guide for School-Based Action*. According to Glickman, "congenial schools are characterized by an open, social climate for adults. Communications are friendly, [people] socialize easily with one another. Faculty meetings are pleasant, holiday parties are great, refreshments at meetings are plentiful, and faculty members spend time together away from school. Members describe their school as a nice place where everyone gets along well. Collegial schools are characterized by purposeful, adult-level interactions focused on the teaching and learning of students. People do not necessarily socialize with one another but they respect their differences of opinion about education. Mutual respect comes from the belief that everyone has the students' interest in mind. The result of such responses is seen in school meetings, where the school community members debate, disagree, and argue before educational decisions are made. Even in the hottest of debates, people's professional respect for others supersedes personal discomfort. People believe that differences will be resolved and that students will benefit. Social satisfaction is a by-product of professional engagement and resolution, of seeing how students benefit, and of the personal regard in which adults hold one another. They become colleagues in the deep sense of being able to work and play together, and each side of the relationship strengthens the other. Being collegial means being willing to move beyond the social facade of communication, to discuss conflicting ideas and issues with candor, sensitivity, and responses. For many schools, the first job is to move from being conventional to being congenial, but the big job for public education is to become collegial, so that social satisfaction is derived mainly from the benefits derived from efforts on behalf of students." (*Renewing America's Schools: A Guide to School-Based Action*, pp 22). (S2-1)

Educational "philosophies" — "Tell me your philosophy of education" used to be a standard interview prompt for educators. In an era of exploding brain research, this question is now outdated because philosophies of education have been based on changing models of instruction such as behaviorist, Dewian, etc. The question today should be "What do you believe to be the most significant brain research findings and how do you apply them in your classroom?" (S2-4)

Emotions as gatekeeper to learning — Since postulation of the triune brain theory by Dr. Paul MacLean in the 1950s, scientists have made discovery after discovery about the role of emotions in overall mental processing. Recent research, particularly that by Candace Pert, into the role of peptides and steroids, significantly expands our understanding of "informational substances" that are produced, and received, throughout the body and brain. These, in addition to the familiar neurotransmitters in the brain, make up a complex and compelling view of emotions and their primacy in the learning environment. For more information, please read Molecules of Emotion by Dr. Candance Pert and Human Brain and Human Learning, Revised 1998, Chapter 5, by Leslie Hart. (S2-3)

Environment of the school — because so many "informational substances" (see emotions as gatekeeper above) monitor and respond to elements in the physical environment, issues of relationship (teacher-student and student-student), cleanliness, smell, lighting, color, sound, order, and beauty are far more important to academic learning than previously surmised. (S2-3)

Governance — as used here, a term denoting decision-making in its broadest sense and means of affecting compliance with those decisions. In the ITI model, governance is primarily based on consensus-building among all interested staff and involved parents in all issues, including school budgeting. In advanced stages of implementation of this rubric, governance operates under a contract with the district office, thus allowing school-level control of all issues within the scope of the contract. (S2-3)

Governance structures — the structures and processes by which a school goes about its decision-making and affecting compliance with those decisions are not, and should not be, stamped out in cookie cutter fashion. Although there may be similarities from school to school, people should be free to make their way forward as they see fit, responding to problems to be solved and to opportunities to be maximized. (S2-5)

Intelligence as a function of experience — one of six concepts from brain research upon which the ITI model is based. Because of the recent extraordinary advances in technology, the biology of learning is now observable, e.g., what kinds of input most activate the brain and result in building long-term memory. There are six concepts critical for the content of the school's best knowledge/best practices agreements. For more information, see the ITI book appropriate for your grade level(s). *ITI: The Model* or *Kid's Eye View of Science* (for elementary grades), *The Way We Were ... The Way We CAN Be: A Vision for the Middle School* (for middle school grades) or *Synergy: Transformation of America's High Schools* (for high school). (S2-2)

Lifelong Guidelines and LIFESKILLS — the Lifelong Guidelines, truthfulness, trustworthiness, active listening, no put downs, and personal best (as defined by the LIFESKILLS), are key ITI structures for classroom leadership/management, for creating a sense of community, and for teaching the social and personal skills for citizenship. (S2-1 and 5)

Mission — a written statement of what the school community intends to have happen for students. It emerges from the written statement of best knowledge and best practice that the school has committed itself to and directly addresses the real work of the school, not platitudes. It is updated yearly to ensure it remains a working document that guides people's on-going planning and discussion. (S2-2-5)

Multiple intelligences — one of six concepts from brain research upon which the ITI model is based. The eight intelligences identified by Howard Gardner are: logical-mathematical, linguistic, spatial, musical, bodily-kinesthic, naturalist, intra-personal, and interpersonal. For more information, see Gardner's original work *Frames of Mind: Theory of Multiple Intelligences*. More user-friendly books include *Seven Kinds of Smarts* by Thomas Armstrong (good for parents as well as teachers) and *Multiple Intelligences in the Classroom*, also by Thomas Armstrong (S2-2)

Part to play — one of four stages of planning for transition outlined by William Bridges. The four stages are: agreeing on purpose, painting a picture of what the purpose would look like, developing a plan for how to implement the picture, and a description by each person specifying their individual part to play. For more information, see *Managing Transitions: Making the Most of Change*. (S2-3)

Personality preferences or temperament — an area of psychological research and application beginning with the work of Karl Jung through Briggs and Myers and, more recently, Keirsey and Bates. For a user-friendly version, see *Please Understand Me: Character and Temperament Types* by Keirsey and Bates which provides a quick survey "test" with explanations of each of the 16 types. Areas covered are: orientation to others and the world (introvert-extrovert); how people take in information (sensor-intuitor); decision-making (thinker-feeler), and lifestyle or how one organizes one's life (judger-perceiver). Provides invaluable information for staff to have about self and others; helps explain "what irritates" us about others and helps each person "slide along" the four scales to better communicate with another. Recommended as a group-building and group-maintenance activity. For a description of how to use the four temperament scales in designing staff development trainings, see *Mentor Teacher Role: Owners' Manual*, Chapter 4, pages 91-97. (S2-2)

Put-downs — "No Put-Downs" is one of the five Lifelong Guidelines. Put-downs can be verbal (as in the back-handed compliment), tone of voice, gestures (rolling one's eyes), or deeds (tapping forehead and lolling tongue from the mouth). The goal of a put-down is to elevate the speaker to a position of being in the spotlight, of controlling the behavior of those around them, undermining the relationship between people, sidetracking the real issues, promoting him/herself by creating a laugh at someone else's expenses, and the like. A put-down is a way of saying, "I'm better than you, richer than you, smarter than you, have more power and options than you." (S2-1)

The real work of the school — a term used here to signify decision-making in traditional areas of power, e.g., budget, policy-setting, important issues of the work place, etc. All too often, school improvement committees have limited power and authority. In worst case scenarios, they are mere rubber stamps; even in forward-thinking schools their role is often limited to issues and budgeting for special funding only (e.g., state and federally funded programs that require school improvement committees. (S2-5)

Self-governing workplace — refers to a community ethic characterized by a sense of purpose, commitment to that purpose, and individual and group accountability to uphold and carry out the agreed-upon ways to implement that purpose. (S2-5)

School improvement plan — the up-to-date, annual statement of what is to be accomplished and how; also reflects why the areas of work for the year were chosen. (S2-1-5)

Temperament scales — the four areas of personality preference or temperament are represented on a sliding scale (*see Personality preferences above*). (S2-2)

Written procedures and daily agendas — two key classroom leadership/management structures in the ITI model. Written procedures are the social and personal behaviors that provide the context for doing an assignment or task (as distinguished from the directions for doing the task). Written procedures should be established for frequently-performed tasks such as entering and leaving the room, using classroom resources, what do to with spare time when an assignment is completed, and what to do when a substitute teacher comes to the classroom, etc. The agenda, usually in mindmap form, is a means of sharing with students the game plan for the day so that they, rather than being passive receivers, can take responsibility for their own learning, directing their attention and learning to manage their time. (S2-1)

ITI Resources

Books

Anchor Math

Integrated Thematic Instruction: The Model

It's Not About Math, It's About Life

ITI Classroom Rubric: Assessing Implementation of Brain-Compatible Learning

ITI Planning Guide

ITI Schoolwide Rubric: Assessing Schoolwide Implementation of Brain-Compatible Education

Kid's Eye View of Science: A Teacher's Handbook for Implementing an Integrated Thematic Approach to Science, K-6

Science Continuum of Concepts, K-6

Study of Reality: A Supradisciplinary Approach, Teacher Edition

Study of Reality: A Supradisciplinary Approach, Workbook

Synergy: The Transformation of America's High School Through Integrated Thematic Instruction

The Way We Were . . . The Way We Can Be: A Vision for the Middle School

What's Worth Teaching: Selecting, Organizing, and Integrating Knowledge

Videos

Classroom of the 21st Century (video/book)

I Can Divide and Conquer (video/book)

Integrated Thematic Instruction: The Model (9-video set)

Jacobsonville: An ITI Micro Society

Let's Get Moving: Movement in the Classroom (video/manual)

Spread Your Wings: The Lifelong Guidelines

Getting Started Video Set:
> Stage 1 of the ITI Rubric: First Things First
> LIFESKILLS: Creating a Class Family

Stage 2 of the ITI Rubric: Creating Conceptual Curriculum

Stage 2 of the ITI Rubric: Intelligence is a Function of Experience

Audio Tapes

Keynote: It's All In Your Head

Spread Your Wings: The Lifelong Guidelines (audio)

The Why and How of Integrated Thematic Instruction—Volumes 1,2, & 3 (audio)

Poster Set

Lifelong Guidelines/LIFESKILLS (19-poster set)

Lifelong Guidelines

Trustworthiness

Truthfulness

Active Listening

No Put-Downs

Personal Best

LIFESKILLS

Integrity—to act according to a sense of what's right and wrong

Initiative—to do something because it needs to be done

Flexibility—to be willing to alter plans when necessary

Perseverance—to keep at it

Organization—to plan, arrange, and implement in an orderly, readily useable way

Sense of Humor—to laugh and be playful without harming others

Effort—to do your best

Common Sense—to use good judgment

Problem-Solving—to create solutions to difficult situations and everyday problems

Responsibility—to respond when appropriate, to be accountable for your actions

Patience—to wait calmly for someone or something

Friendship—to make and keep a friend through mutual trust and caring

Curiosity—a desire to investigate and seek understanding of one's world

Cooperation—to work together toward a common goal or purpose

Caring—to feel and show concern for others

Courage—to act according to one's beliefs

Pride—satisfaction from doing your personal best

Fifth Grade Team Meeting Procedure

- Agenda items are submitted prior to meeting with approximate time needed.
- Detailed agenda is distributed before meeting.
- Anything that can be handled in "survey form" is made into a written survey and routed.
- Strict time allotments on each agenda item are adhered to.
- The meeting end time is posted on the agenda.
- Begin promptly at 3:00 regardless of attendance.
- Items to be "shared with team" are routed immediately in a bright yellow folder (not shared at meeting).
- Routed items are stored in a binder for future reference. This facilitates timely routing.

Student Assistant Team Meetings Procedure

- Have an agenda/schedule for each meeting.
- Keep a checklist during SAT meetings of steps to follow, including time limits for each step.
- Appoint one team member as procedural person to move team from one step to next and keep team within time limits.
- Have team members rotate roles—recorder, team leader, timekeeper.
- Team leader makes copies of teacher request for all team member prior to meeting.
- After team meeting, recorder makes copies of all suggestions for requesting teacher.
- Appoint team member to assist teacher in filling out request form completely. (Especially important for a teacher using the SAT for the first time.)

—Created by teams at Amy Beverland Elementary

AMY BEVERLAND FAMILY ASSOCIATION
VOLUNTEER SIGN-UP SHEET 1995-1996

As we begin our seventh year at Amy Beverland, here we go again with many opportunities for volunteer involvement and support!! The Amy Beverland Family Association (ABFA), through its dedicated and committed volunteers, has done a tremendous job in enhancing our children's education and our school facility. It is due to these volunteers that ABFA has been such a success. Nearly all the committee chairperson positions were filled over the summer and we are now looking for help to serve on these committees. Please circle the committees that you are interested in and return the form to school as soon as possible. You will be contacted by the person as the event nears.

If you have any questions or suggestions, please call either Volunteer Coordinator, _____ _____ or ABFA president _____. Approximately three weeks after the start of school, there will be a volunteer coffee to further explain the jobs available. Room mothers will be solicited by the class teachers.

ADAPT—help with Red Ribbon Week in October
BUTTERFLY GARDEN—help to plant and maintain our outdoor atriums
CAMPBELL SOUP LABELS—help in cutting, sorting and counting labels
CARNIVAL—help with organization and planning winter carnival
COMPUTER LAB—assist students in the computer lab
DIRECTORY—proofread sheets for accuracy
FALL FUNDRAISER—assist in collecting orders and distributing merchandise and prizes
HOLIDAY GIFT SHOP—help on sale days to aid students in gift selection & collect money
HOSPITALITY—prepare or donate food and paper products or help set up, serve & clean
            up for various school functions
LUNCHROOM ASSISTANT—assist in lunchroom to keep order
MATH ENRICHMENT—work with Math teacher and students who need assistance
MATH PENTATHLON—help to coach students in practice
MEDIA CENTER—assist in filing books and student check-in and check-out of books
MUSIC ASSISTANT—help pick props and costumes for musical programs during the year
OPERATION STARSHINE—assist in food or clothing drives and the Giving Tree
PARTNER ROAST—Spring, 1996. Set up, serve and clean up for Celebrity Roast dinner
PHYSICAL EDUCATION ASSISTANT—assist teacher with clerical duties, special func-
            tions and/or field day
PUBLIC RELATIONS—help to take pictures; write articles for local publications
READING INCENTIVE PROGRAM—tabulate students' reading progress and help with
            final Spring celebration
RECESS DUTY—help during recess in Fall and Spring
SCIENCE FAIR—open to 4th and 5th grade students. Help in set up & judging of event
SKATING PARTIES—help monitor skating areas and sell tickets at lunch time at school
SPECIAL EVENTS—whenever and wherever needed
STAR BOOSTERS—collect donations & write receipts at Evening with the Stars
VOLUNTEER SUBSTITUTE TEACHER
YEARBOOK—help alphabetize student pictures

NAME _____ PHONE_____

CHILD'S NAME _____ TEACHER_____ GRADE_____

CAN HELP DAYS_____ EVENINGS_____ ANYTIME _____

GREAT NEWS FROM **YOSHIKAI ELEMENTARY SCHOOL**

Name_____

Date_____ Home Room _____

_____ used the LIFESKILL of:

_____ Integrity	_____ Organization
_____ Initiative	_____ Sense of Humor
_____ Flexibility	_____ Common Sense
_____ Perseverance	_____ Problem-Solving
_____ Effort	_____ Responsibility
_____ Patience	_____ Friendship
_____ Curiosity	_____ Cooperation
_____ Caring	_____ Courage
	_____ Pride

By: _____

_____

_____

_____

Teacher's Signature _____

Comments:

_____

Principal

Pittsburg Unified School District
K-5 Positive Student Referral
Los Medanos Elementary School
610 Crowley Ave. Pittsburg, CA 94565 (510)473-4330   Referred to: Principal

Student: _____ Date: _____ Time: _____

Campus Area/Class: _____ Referred By: _____

    Our policy is to recognize those students who demonstrate behaviors which exemplify the qualities we are working to instill in all children. We refer to these behaviors as the LIFESKILLS, and the Lifelong Guidelines. We are using this form to inform parents of incidents which are worthy of recognition and appreciation.

I.   Reasons:
        A. This student followed the Lifelong Guideline(s):
1.___Trustworthiness 4.___No Put-Downs
2.___Truthfulness   5.___Personal Best
3.___Active Listening

        Comment: _____

_____

_____

A. This student followed the LIFESKILL(s):
1.___ Integrity   7.___ Problem-Solving 13.___Effort
2.___ Initiative   8.___ Responsibility 14.___Caring
3.___ Flexibility   9.___ Patience   15.___Common Sense
4.___ Perseverance 10.___ Friendship   16.___Courage
5.___ Organizations 11.___Curiosity
6.___ Sense of Humor 12.___Cooperation

        Comment: _____

_____

_____

II.   Administrative Action Taken:
    A.___ Student Conference   C.___ Parent contacted by phone
    B.___ Sent back to class   D.___ Letter home to parent
        Parent/Student Response: _____

Principal's Signature: _____ Date: _____

Conducting a Climate Audit

Prepared by the Indiana Principal Leadership Academy
(Reprinted with permission of IPLA)

Introduction

A school's climate is its atmosphere for learning. It includes the feelings people have about the school. It reflects how people perceive they are being treated, rewarded, and acknowledged as individuals. In order for people to feel satisfaction and to produce at their optimum level, having a positive climate is important.

When people visit a school for the first time, hearing remarks about the school's climate is common: "This is a good school; This school has a good feeling; This school has a pleasant atmosphere." These are typical of first impressions. What criteria do people use when making a judgment about a school's climate? What factors do they have in mind describing the quality of the school in terms of feelings?

The purpose of the climate audit is to reduce these vague impressions into more concrete criteria. Specific criteria can be used to actually assess a school climate in a systematic manner. Once data have been gathered through group interviews and, perhaps, a paper and pencil audit, they can be analyzed to suggest the positive and/or less positive aspects of the school's atmosphere for learning. From these data, we can establish priorities for improvement. Task force groups of teachers, students, parents, administrators, and non-certified staff may be brought together to decide ways in which the existing climate can be improved. The overarching goal is to enhance both personal satisfaction and productivity of those who come to school to work and learn together.

> *All champions have coaches who assist them to get better. Therefore, no one need be offended by the suggestion that there is room for improvement.*

Six Sequential Steps: Conducting a School Climate Audit

1.)Set the date and announce to staff.
2.)Prepare materials—introduction comments and interview questions.
3.)Select a cadre to conduct the audit/assessment.
4.)Develop a schedule for the audit/assessment.
5.)Carry out the audit/assessment.

- The audit team debrief and submit reports to the audit team leader.
- The team leader analyzes data/information to identify patterns, common themes.
- The team leader prepares a narrative report of findings and general recommendations, if any.
- The audit team submits a narrative report to the building principal for distribution.

6.) Principal will prepare a brief report for IPLA and/or other audiences including:
   a. members of audit team
   b. date of audit/assessment
   c. number interviewed by group (i.e., parents, certified staff, etc.)
   d. reflective writing on perceived value of the audit in developing a school improvement project.

Helpful Tips for the Audit Team

1.) It is best to interview more than one individual at a time. This puts the participants more at ease. Additionally, it helps to balance the validity of individual perceptions and opinions. We recommend the following:

WHO?	HOW MANY?
Professional staff	2 or 3 per interview
Support staff	3 or 4 per interview
Maintenance/Food Services staff	4 or 5 per interview
Parents	3 or 4 per interview
Students	4-8 per interview (depending on age)

2.) It is best if interviewers can work in teams. This allows one to ask questions, while the other records responses. Often this is not possible.

3.) Build a master schedule for the interview team, allowing for breaks and lunch. It would be good to allow time for team members to visit classrooms, the cafeteria, and other areas of the school.

4.) Always assign a team leader, whose responsibility it is to keep things going on the interview day, lead the debriefing meeting, and prepare the final narrative report. Ideally, this responsibility should be assigned to a different person at each building if the team is doing multiple audits.

5.) Be sure to allow at least 45-60 minutes to debrief among team members at the end of the day. Although all will be tired, notes and ideas will still be fresh.

6.) The team leader should complete the narrative report as quickly as possible. Delaying will result in greater frustration, as team comments and conclusions will be forgotten over time.

7.) Balance the type(s) of students interviewed. Avoid selecting all student council representatives and high achievers.

8.) REMEMBER: This packet is just a guide! Determine your own priorities. Be willing to be flexible when the situation dictates.

Scheduling by the Principal

Master Schedule
Have copies of the master schedule for all members of the interview team.

Interview Schedule
Determine the approximate numbers of students, staff, and parents to be interviewed and prepare an interview schedule. We recommend 15-20 minutes maximum per interview.

It is best to have the interview room(s) located in an easily accessible, yet quiet area. Provide sufficient space for interview teams to spread out, avoiding noise interference.

A good schedule will address the following:
- a break time every 1 1/2 to 2 hours.
- a lunch time.
- time to visit classrooms and tour the building
- debriefing time at the end of the day

When determining the appropriate numbers, we suggest the following:

- minimum of two professional/support staff interviewed together (support staff numbers could be higher.all grade level or building aides, all custodial staff, etc.)
- minimum of three parents interviewed together.
- minimum of four students interviewed together

Sample School

GROUP	# PER SESSION	# SESSIONS	TOTAL
Staff (all)	3	17	51
Parents	3	4	12
Students	4	6	24
Totals		27	87

—Twenty-seven sessions of 15 minutes each = approximately 7 hours interview time

—Three teams of interviewers:

- 9 interview sessions per team—2 1/2 hours
- 30 minutes A.M. break(s)
- 30 minutes P.M. lunch
- 30 minutes A.M. break(s)
- 45 minutes casual observations, visitations
- 45 minutes P.M. debriefing

Total: 5 hours and 30 minutes

Opening Statements by Audit Team

Below are merely some suggested statements. Remember the purpose of the opening statement is to:

- clarify the purpose of the interview
- put the group at ease
- set a positive tone for the interview process

Opening Statement for Staff

Thank you for taking time for this interview. Improving schools requires planning and information for decision-making. We believe that individuals affected by decisions should be included in the decision-making process. You certainly have an investment in helping this school to continue to improve.

While you are being asked to make some judgments, it would be helpful if you support your statements with an example, or illustrative vignette. Rest assured that no individual names will be used in the final report.

Opening Statement for Parents

Thank you for taking time for this interview. The purpose of this interview is to improve our school. You as parents, are important participants in making good schools even better.

We ask that you answer the questions based upon your own experiences and source(s) of information. The very fact that you are not informed about some questions will be useful for us to know.

We are also interviewing staff and students. A school improvement committee will be making some important decisions based upon this process. Rest assured that no individual names will be used in this report.

Opening Statement for Students

Thank you for taking time for this interview. You were selected to be interviewed because we are talking to representatives of our student population to find ways to make our school even better. Certainly, students are the main reason we are here, and we believe that students should have an opportunity to make suggestions about ways to improve their school.

We ask that you answer the questions based upon your own experiences. Please give examples whenever possible. Rest assured that no individual names will be used in this report.

Note: Sample questions provided in the IPLA document are replaced here by questions that focus on aspects of brain-compatible learning.

Indiana Principal Leadership Academy
Room 229, State House
Indianapolis, IN 46204
(317) 232-9007

Personal Audit
Brain-Compatibility Check

Name: _____ Date: _____

Directions: Consider each item below and select responses that best match your behavior. Write notes of explanation as needed. Discuss your responses with a trusted colleague to see how closely his/her perceptions match your own. Establish personal growth goals. Repeat the audit periodically to compare with your first, or baseline, responses and chart your continual growth in brain-compatible behaviors.

ITI BRAIN BASIC	*RELATED BEHAVIORS*	*RESPONSES*		
EMOTIONS AS THE GATEKEEPER TO LEARNING		**Y**	**N**	**Sometimes**

Notes: 1. I am trustworthy when I:
- do what I say I will do or, if not, offer an explanation.
- maintain an even emotional temperament.
- recognize stress factors and respond constructively.
- make fair decisions based on stated criteria.
- keep a confidence unless health and safety are involved.
- prepare thoroughly for my role in group tasks.
- Other: _____
  _____

2. I am truthful when I:
- state both what I know and what I don't know
- ask a question about something that I don't understand
- recognize my own strengths and weaknesses
- describe for others their behaviors that appear to violate group agreements
- admit to my mistakes

ITI BRAIN BASIC	*RELATED BEHAVIORS*	*RESPONSES*		
		Y	**N**	**Sometimes**

- express my opinion even when others may disagree
- Other: _____

3. I am an active listener when I:
- stop other activities and give undivided attention.
- look toward the speaker.
- give non-verbal signs that I understand what is said.
- ask for clarification when I don't hear or understand.
- notice another's body language during dialogue.
- think about what another is saying rather than planning my response.
- wait for the speaker to finish before I respond.
- Other: _____

4. I avoid put-downs when I:
- refrain from telling or laughing at jokes that target others' weaknesses.
- eliminate demeaning comments about myself and treat myself with respect.
- support others in eliminating put-downs by using an agreed-upon word or phrase, such as "cancel," when I hear one.
- Other: _____

5. I achieve my personal best when I:
- apply best knowledge and best practice to produce quality results.
- use the appropriate LIFESKILLS for the situation and task.

ITI BRAIN BASIC	RELATED BEHAVIORS	RESPONSES

		Y	N	Sometimes
	—Integrity			
	—Initiative			
	—Flexibility			
	—Perseverance			
	—Organization			
	—Sense of Humor			
	—Effort			
	—Common Sense			
	—Problem-Solving			
	—Responsibility			
	—Patience			
	—Friendship			
	—Curiosity			
	—Cooperation			
	—Caring			
	—Pride			
	6. I make it a priority to arrange and decorate classrooms, offices, and common areas according to brain-compatible principles.			
	7. My work and the work I assign to others is challenging, satisfying, and a valued part of the school's mission.			
	8. The overall work atmosphere for which I am responsible communicates high expectations and provides the support necessary to succeed.			
	9. I feel joyful as I work.			
INTELLIGENCE AS A FUNCTION OF EXPERIENCE *Notes:*	1. When I want to acquire new knowledge or skills, I begin by going to a location where I can have a related first-hand experience.			
	2. When responsible for teaching others new information or skills, I start by providing a first-hand, "being there" experience.			

ITI BRAIN BASIC   _RELATED BEHAVIORS_   _RESPONSES_

Y | N | Sometimes

3. Before learning or teaching something new, I identify my own and others' prior related experiences. (This includes awareness of cultural and ethnic diversity.)

4. Other: _____

MEANING THROUGH PATTERN RECOGNITION

Notes:

1. Most of my work is meaningful and interesting to me.

2. In assigning work to others, I consider their interests and special knowledge.

3. When I need to learn new information, I use a variety of resources and allow adequate time to recognize and understand the key patterns.

4. I allow others adequate time to recognize and understand key patterns in new information.

5. I use my knowledge of patterns and programs to identify the important elements within a new experience.

6. Other: _____

MULTIPLE INTELLIGENCES

Notes:

1. I know my strongest product-producing and problem-solving skills and actively work to develop my weaker areas to achieve a richer range of possibilities.

2. Reports and other products I create represent more than one of my intelligences, increasing variety and appeal to others.

3. I seek alternate approaches for my own learning and sharing.

4. I provide options for others (including students) for the learning and sharing I ask them to do.

ITI BRAIN BASIC	RELATED BEHAVIORS	RESPONSES

ITI BRAIN BASIC *RELATED BEHAVIORS* *RESPONSES*

Y | N | Sometimes

5. Meetings I plan include a variety of strategies and opportunities for physical movement, or at e.g., stretch breaks or energizers.

6. Other: _____

_____

**USEFUL
MENTAL
PROGRAMS**
Notes:

1. I welcome feedback from mentor-coaches as I apply new skills.

2. I freely share feedback with others who seek it.

3. Understanding that I may feel awkward when I first apply a new skill, I expect to practice until I become proficient.

4. I focus time and energy on developing the capabilities that are most likely to increase my effectiveness.

5. I provide adequate time for skill acquisition before judging my own performance or the performance of others.

6. Other: _____

_____

**IMPACT OF
PERSONALITY**
Notes:

1. I understand my personality preferences and am aware of their impact on my behavior.

2. I recognize and respect the personality preferences of adults and students with whom I work.

3. I am able to select behaviors outside my personality preferences in order to communicate and work collaboratively with others.

4. Other: _____

_____

School or District Office Climate Audit
Brain-Compatibility Survey

Name (optional): _____ Role In District: _____ Date: _____

Directions: Please consider each item below and respond to reflect your personal observations and experiences at your primary work location. Return your completed survey to
the designated location for use by the climate audit team. All information will be kept in
strictest confidence. Thank you for taking time to share your views about the ways in
which the climate where you work does or does not reflect our district's goal to provide
brain-compatible work and learning experiences.

ITI BRAIN BASIC	*RELATED BEHAVIORS*	*RESPONSES*		
		Y	N	Sometimes
EMOTIONS AS THE GATE- KEEPER TO LEARNING				
Comments:	1. People trust each other			
	2. We are truthful with each other even when it isn't easy			
	3. We are active listeners who truly want to understand each others' views			
	4. Put-downs are not a part of the work place			
	5. Personal best is expected and is the norm			
	6. The Lifelong Guidelines and LIFESKILLS are a regular part of our language as we work together			
	7. When conflicts occur, we use agreed upon procedures for resolving them			
	8. The physical environment is inviting and helps to generate positive emotions			
	9. Communications are clear so that we know what is expected and can feel secure			
	10. People laugh a lot and enjoy coming here to learn and to work together			

ITI BRAIN BASIC	*RELATED BEHAVIORS*	*RESPONSES*		
		Y	**N**	**Sometimes**

EMOTIONS AS

11. Collaboration with others is a major approach to create new things and to solve problems

12. People here do not gossip

13. Other: _____

_____

_____

INTELLIGENCE AS A FUNCTION OF EXPERIENCE

Comments:

1. People recognize and value the experiences others bring from their personal backgrounds

2. New learning starts with related first-hand experiences

3. New learning takes place in an enriched environment that provides a variety of input from the senses

4. When someone lacks the necessary prior experience to succeed on a new talk, leaders provide access to such experience

5. Community locations are resources play an important role here

6. Other: _____

_____

MEANING THROUGH PATTERN RECOGNITION

Comments:

1. The assignments given are meaningful and important

2. When learning something new, we have many kinds of resources to use

ITI BRAIN BASIC	RELATED BEHAVIORS	RESPONSES

		Y	N	Sometimes
	3. Our leaders provide adequate time to recognize and understand the key patterns in something new			
	4. Our leaders provide examples of new things they want us to understand so we can identify common patterns			
	5. Other: _____ _____ _____			
MULTIPLE INTELLIGENCES *Comments:*	1. People here understand that individuals have different ways of expressing their intelligence			
	2. We can choose from among several strategies for learning something new or creating a product			
	3. Meetings and workshops present material using more than one intelligence			
	4. Quality results are measured and documented using more than one intelligence			
	5. We assume that groups whose members have different strengths and value those differences are more effective			
	6. Other: _____ _____ _____			
USEFUL MENTAL PROGRAMS *Comments:*	1. Our leaders provide specific feedback through internal and external coaching so that we know how things are going and can make continuous improvement			

ITI BRAIN BASIC	RELATED BEHAVIORS	RESPONSES		
		Y	**N**	**Sometimes**

RELATED BEHAVIORS

2. Leaders provide adequate time to practice doing something new before holding us accountable for demonstrating proficiency

3. We have many opportunities to develop new capacities to increase the quality and variety of each person's contributions

4. The mental programs each person has mastered are acknowledged and put to use to accomplish the work of the school/district

5. Other: _____

_____

_____

IMPACT OF PERSONALITY

Comments:

1. People are aware of their own and work associates' temperament differences and the related behaviors.

2. We understand that our personality preferences are strongest when we are in a new situation or feeling fearful

3. Work teams reflect different personality preferences so that the strengths of such diversity are tapped

4. People here use flexibility to behave beyond their own first preferences in order to meet group goals and be effective in collaboration

5. Other: _____

_____

_____

School or District Office Climate Audit
Examples of Questions for Small Group Interviews

Note: The climate audit team of interviewers should consult with people at the work location to determine which questions are most important and appropriate to reveal the climate. New questions may be needed to collect information about suspected concerns and strengths.

Emotions as the Gatekeeper to Learning
1. When and how are you supported in your work?
2. When you get better, who notices and how do they let you know?
3. What things do you look forward to at work?
4. To whom at work can you confide that you have made an error and need advice about next steps?
5. Do you believe that your present job is secure? Why or why not?
6. Is there a procedure here for sharing complaints?
7. When workers have a conflict, how is that handled?
8. Are put-downs generally considered to be "friendly joking?" If so, what is your view of this type of joking? If not, how are put-downs generally viewed? How does the usual joking in the work place affect your work?
9. Please comment about the quality of both the written and oral communication here. Specifically, does it meet your needs for access to relevant and timely information?
10. In general, do you have a clear idea of what is expected of you at work?
11. If you could change one thing at work to increase positive feelings about the time you spend here, what would it be and why? Does anything at work make you angry or upset? If yes, please describe your strategies for handling those feelings.
12. In what ways is your work challenging and stimulating to you?
13. What do you like about the physical environment here, e.g., colors, decoration, arrangement of space, and the like.
14. What else affects the way you feel about working here?

Intelligence as a Function of Experience
1. What works best for you when you want to learn something new? Does that work for you here?
2. When leaders here want you to try something new, how do they approach it?
3. What role do community organizations and businesses play in your learning and work?
4. When discussion here turns to a topic about which you have little or no experience that appears to be important to your future success, what do you do?

Meaning Through Pattern Recognition

1. Assume that you are expected to use a new strategy in your work.
    - What approaches are used to help you understand the new idea?
    - How much lead time are you usually given?
2. What kinds of resources do you have available to help you understand a new idea?

Multiple Intelligences

1. In what ways is Howard Gardner's theory of multiple intelligences important here?
2. Do you believe that understanding multiple intelligences is useful when people work in groups here? Why or why not?
3. Do people here have choices about the ways in which information about results are reported, e.g., video vs. a written report? Please describe.
4. Do workshops or classes sponsored by the school reflect more than one intelligence? Would you please describe an example?

Useful Mental Programs

1. How do you know if your work is meeting expectations?
2. Describe opportunities you have to expand your capabilities. Please include details about any learning you've done such as how much time you had to learn the new thing.
3. Do you have adequate time to master a new thing before being asked to demonstrate your proficiency?
4. Do you believe that your abilities are being fully used and developed here? Why or why not?

Impact of Personality

1. Do people here understand and use knowledge of different personality types? If yes, please describe.
2. How are people chosen to serve on committees or task forces here?
3. How are different personality types respected here?

Workshops Offered by the MAISD ITI
Facilitator to Support ITI
(See chapter ten for more information)

Movement in the Classroom: A classroom teacher who uses lots of movement provides others with practical ideas and suggestions for incorporating movement into the classroom.

A Celebration of Success: A big dinner celebration where newly trained ITI teachers get together to share success stories and plan for their professional development needs.

Review of Key Concepts: Our SK&A associate from the summer returns to review key concepts of the summer training and answer teachers' questions and concerns.

Multiple Intelligences: Lots and lots of practical ideas for implementing the multiple intelligences in the classroom.

Exploring the Multiple Intelligences: An introductory course on identifying students' intelligences along with practical ideas for using those multiple intelligences in the classroom.

How Do We Honor The Way Kids Are Wired? A parent program to help parents identify and understand the many ways that their children are intelligent.

TRIBES: A cooperative learning model that emphasizes building inclusion in the classroom and processing learning and group experiences.

Dittos Don't Grow Dendrites: A review of the brain research and its connections to learning in the classroom.

Games and Ideas to Support the LIFESKILLS: Classroom teachers share their ideas for games, activities, and literature.

Carousel of Choice: A mini-session workshop (choose four of eight different, forty-five minute sessions) in which teachers share their ideas for talking to parents about ITI, rubrics, multiple intelligences, teaching LIFESKILLS, and reviewing the brain research.

Links for Learning: A review of the key concepts of ITI for para-professionals working in ITI schools.

Teaching Reading with the Multiple Intelligences: Ideas for using the multiple intelligences to match the processing styles of struggling readers.

Reading and the Musical-Rhythmic Connection: Ideas for using music and rhythmic activity to teach reading to struggling readers who are strong in musical and/or bodily-kinesthetic intelligence.

Understanding the Many Ways That Children Can be Gifted: A program to help parents see the multiple intelligence strengths of their children.

Patterns and Programs for Learning: Practical ideas for using patterns and programs, as defined in the ITI model, to teach concepts.

Staff Retreats for Team Building: Activity-based workshops to assist staffs in communication, problem-solving, and building a sense of community.

References

Armstrong, T. 1994. *Multiple Intelligences in the Classroom.* Alexandria, VA.: ASCD.

Barker, J. 1992. *Future Edge.* New York: William Morrow and Company, Inc.

Baumgartner, J., Ed. 1995. *National Guide to Funding for Elementary and Secondary Education.* New York: The Foundation Center.

Bloom, B. and Others. 1956. *Taxonomy of Educational Objectives. Handbook I: Cognitive Domain.* New York: David McKay.

Bolman, L. and Deal, T. 1991. *Reframing Organizations.* San Francisco: Jossey-Bass, Inc.

Bridges, W. 1991. *Managing Transitions: Making the Most of Change.* Reading, MA.: Addison-Wesley.

Bridges, W. 1994. *JobShift: How to Prosper in a Workplace Without Jobs.* Reading, MA.: Addison-Wesley.

Caine, R. and Caine, G. 1991. *Making Connections: Teaching and the Human Brain.* Alexandria, VA.: ASCD.

California Department of Education. 1987. *Caught in the Middle.* Sacramento, CA.: Department of Education.

Calvin, W. 1996. *How Brains Think.* New York: Basic Books.

Carlson, M. 1995. *Winning Grants Step-By-Step.* San Francisco: Jossey-Bass Publishers.

Champlin, J. 1993. Comments at a Susan Kovalik Summer Institute. Lake Tahoe, CA.

Cuban, L. 1996. Comments for the Superintendents' Symposium 1996, Association for California School Administrators.

Diamond, M. and Hopson, J. 1998. *Magic Trees of the Mind.* New York: Dutton.

DeBono, E. 1985. *Six Thinking Hats.* Boston: Little, Brown and Company.

Deming, W.E. 1986. *Out of the Crisis.* Cambridge, MA.: Center for Advanced Engineering Study, Massachusetts Institute of Technology.

Doyle, M. and Straus, D. 1976. *How to Make Meetings Work.* New York: The Berkley Publishing Group.

Fullan, M. 1993. *Change Forces.* Bristol, PA.: The Falmer Press, Taylor & Francis Inc.

Gardner, H. 1983. *Frames of Mind: Theory of Multiple Intelligences.* New York: Basic Books.

Geever, J. and McNeill, P. 1993. *Guide to Proposal Writing.* New York: The Foundation Center.

Gibbs, Jeanne. 1995. *TRIBES: A Process for Social Development and Cooperative Learning.* Sausalito, CA.: Center Source Systems, LLC.

Hart, L. 1983. *Human Brain and Human Learning.* Kent, WA.: Books for Educators.

Keirsey, D. and Bates, M. 1984. *Please Understand Me: Character and Temperament Types.* Del Mar, CA.: Prometheus Nemesis Book Company.

Kohn, A. 1993. *Punished by Rewards.* Boston: Houghton Mifflin Company.

Kouzes, J. and Poser, B. 1993. *Credibility.* San Francisco: Jossey-Bass Publishers.

Kovalik, S. and Olsen, K. 1994. *ITI: The Model, Third Edition.* Kent, WA.: Susan Kovalik & Associates.

Ledoux, J. 1996. *The Emotional Brain: The Mysterious Underpinnings of Emotional Life.* New York: Simon and Schuster.

LaMeres, C. 1990. *The Winner's Circle: Yes I Can!* Newport Beach, CA.: LaMeres Lifestyles Unlimited.

Leaven, D. 1995. *Cheating in Our Schools: A National Scandal.* Reader's Digest, October.

Miller, W. 1996. Personal conversation with author.

Oakley, E. and Krug, D. 1991. *Enlightened Leadership: Getting to the Heart of Change.* New York: Simon & Schuster.

Olsen, K. 1994. Personal conversation with author.

Olsen, K. and Kovalik, S. 1994. *ITI Rubric: Assessing Implementation of Brain-Compatible Learning.* Kent, WA.: Books For Educators.

Orlich, D. 1996. *Designing Successful Proposals.* Alexandria, VA.: ASCD.

Pert, C. 1997. *Molecules of Emotion.* New York: Scribner.

Phillips, G. 1995. Statement shared in personal conversation.

Riley, Pat. 1993. *The Winner Within.* New York: Berkley Books.

Ross, A. and Olsen, K. 1995. *The Way We Were...The Way We Can Be: A Vision for the Middle School.* Kent, WA.: Susan Kovalik & Associates.

Sarason, S. 1990. *The Predictable Failure of Educational Reform: Can We Change Course Before It's Too Late?* San Francisco: Jossey-Bass.

Scearce, C. 1992. *100 Ways to Build Teams.* Palatine, IL.: IRI/Skylight Publishing, Inc.

Senge, P. and Others. 1994. *The Fifth Discipline Fieldbook: Strategies and Tools for Building a Learning Organization.* New York: Doubleday.

Sergiovanni, T. 1994. *Building Community in Schools.* San Francisco: Jossey-Bass Publishers.

Sylwester, R. 1995. *A Celebration of Neurons.* Alexandria, VA.: ASCD.

Sylwester, R. 1996. Remarks at a Susan Kovalik & Associates Summer Institute.

Teacher comment on feedback form. 1997. Workshop by Susan Kovalik & Associates.

Von Oech, R. 1983. *A Whack on the Side of the Head: How to Unlock Your Mind for Innovation.* New York: Warner Books, Inc.

Wheatley, M. 1992. *Leadership and the New Science.* San Francisco: Berrett-Koehler.

Wheatley, M. and Kellner-Rogers, M. *A Simpler Way.* San Francisco: Berrett-Koehler.

Subject Index

About the Authors

Susan Brash is the Director of Elementary Education in the Metropolitan School District of Lawrence Township in Indianapolis, Indiana. She was formerly the principal of Amy Beverland Elementary School, and Indiana training academy for ITI and a National Blue Ribbon School of Excellence. She speaks to various business, civic, and education organizations on systems thinking and learning. Mrs. Brash has received many local, state, and national awards, including the 1994 Indiana Principal of the Year and the 1995 National Distinguished Principal award. Her passion for teaching and learning is best expressed through her servant leadership.

Ken Horn is the Curriculum Resource Consultant at the Muskegon Area Intermediate School District in Muskegon, Michigan. Ken has facilitated and coordinated the service agency's ITI training for the last seven years. He has 18 years of classroom experience, and has taught at the pre-school, elementary, and secondary levels, as well as serving as an itinerant professor at Grand Valley State University. Ken has worked with educators in over 100 Michigan school districts along with educators in Illinois, South Carolina, and Texas. Ken, his wife Barb, and his two sons live on the top of a sand dune overlooking Lake Michigan.

Marilyn P. Kelly, Ed.D., currently serves as the Superintendent of the Sonoma Valley Unified School District in Sonoma, California. She received her B.A. from the University of California, Santa Barbara, her M.A. from Stanford University, and her Ed.D. from the University of La Verne. As Superintendent, she has integrated the Lifelong Guidelines, LIFESKILLS, and brain-compatible elements throughout the district. In addition to serving as the foundation for school's culture, they are used as expected standards in all administrative evaluations.

Jane McGeehan, Ed.D., is a career public educator who has taught grades three-nine, served as elementary and high school principal, and as assistant superintendent for curriculum and instruction. She completed her doctoral work at Indiana University, Bloomington, in both school administration and curriculum and instruction. To support the work of children's museums, she served on the boards of the Children's Museum in Indianapolis and the Discovery Museum in Charlottesville. After working to implement the ITI model at the high school level, she became an Associate and provided workshops for educators across the country through Susan Kovalik & Associates. Presently she is Chief Executive Officer of Susan Kovalik & Associates and lives with her husband, Joseph, in suburban Seattle.

Barbara Pedersen was an Indiana classroom teacher for many years and in 1989 became the Indiana recipient of the federal Christa McAuliffe Fellowship Award for excellence in teaching. As a result of receiving that award she was asked by the Indiana State Department of Education to implement and become Director of a State program called C.L.A.S.S. (Connecting Learning Assures Successful Students). Barbara has continued with C.L.A.S.S. as its director and today over 300 schools and more than 6,000 teachers are involved in the program. Barbara supervises a staff of instructors and coaches besides her own active participation as an instructor and an associate of Susan Kovalik & Associates. Barbara is married and has three sons. Jeff, their oldest, has written songs for the Lifelong Guidelines and the Multiple Intelligences

Geraldine Rosemurgy has been a project manager in the Sonoma Valley Unified School District for the past nine years. Her projects have included the transition of the middle school from 7-8 to a brain-compatible 6-8 and the management of $55.26 million in school facilities construction. Gery has a B.A. in psychology and a Master's Degree in human resources and organizational development. She won the University of San Francisco Graduate Research Award for her thesis on the use of brain research in the private sector and its implications for training and development.